SOCIAL ENTREPRENEURSHIP

A MODERN APPROACH TO SOCIAL VALUE CREATION

Arthur C. Brooks

Maxwell School of Citizenship and Public Affairs
Whitman School of Management
Syracuse University

D1328774

PEARSON EDUCATION INTERNATIONAL

Editor-in-Chief: *David Parker*
Acquisitions Editor: *Jennifer M. Collins*
Product Development Manager: *Ashley Santora*
Editorial Assistant: *Elizabeth Davis*
Marketing Assistant: *Ian Gold*
Associate Managing Editor: *Suzanne DeWorken*
Project Manager, Production: *Ann Pulido*
Permissions Project Manager: *Charles Morris*
Senior Operations Supervisor: *Arnold Vila*
Operations Specialist: *Carol O'Rourke*
Senior Art Director: *Janet Slowik*
Composition: *ICC Macmillan Inc.*
Full-Service Project Management: *Teresa Christie/ICC Macmillan Inc.*
Printer/Binder: *STP/RR Donnelley/Harrisonburg*
Typeface: *10/12 Times Ten Roman*

Credits and acknowledgments borrowed from other sources and reproduced, with permission, in this textbook appear on appropriate page within text.

If you purchased this book within the United States or Canada you should be aware that it has been wrongfully imported without the approval of the Publisher or the Author.

Pearson Education Ltd., London
Pearson Education Singapore, Pte. Ltd
Pearson Education, Canada, Inc.
Pearson Education–Japan
Pearson Education Australia PTY, Limited
Pearson Education North Asia Ltd., Hong Kong
Pearson Educación de Mexico, S.A. de C.V.
Pearson Education Malaysia, Pte. Ltd.
Pearson Education, Upper Saddle River, New Jersey

10 9 8 7 6 5 4 3 2 1
ISBN-13: 978-0-13-606968-3
ISBN-10:   0-13-606968-1

Dedication

For the social entrepreneurs
who work each day
to make our world better

BRIEF CONTENTS

CONTENTS

PREFACE

The U.S. and world economies have become increasingly entrepreneurial, with greater percentages of wealth than ever before residing in new ventures. Economic growth depends less and less on older firms and more and more on the agile start-up companies that meet the economy's needs in real time. The same principle applies in the social sector, even if social opportunities are not reflected as clearly in countries' economic growth. Entrepreneurial skill and energy can be brought to bear on social problems and unmet needs, transforming them into authentic opportunities to create social value.

Unfortunately, professional training and development materials for social entrepreneurs have not kept pace with these opportunities. Most courses and textbooks on entrepreneurship offer little help for people who seek to establish and lead ventures outside the traditional commercial realm. Meanwhile, nonprofit and volunteer management materials are divorced from the growing scholarly field of entrepreneurship.

A new generation of social entrepreneurs needs to be able to avail itself of the latest thinking in entrepreneurship but in a way that expands beyond traditional commercial frontiers. Social entrepreneurs need to understand the similarities of what they do with the orientation and activities of for-profit entrepreneurs. However, they also face unique issues of measuring social benefit, acquiring donated resources, and knowing what "success" means in a nonprofit environment.

Social Entrepreneurship: A Modern Approach to Social Value Creation seeks to bring together the established pedagogy of entrepreneurship, as taught in today's best management schools, with cutting edge nonprofit and public management tools. This book is intended as a primary text for the growing list of courses offered in social entrepreneurship or as a secondary resource for courses in nonprofit management, nonprofit leadership, or commercial entrepreneurship.

ACKNOWLEDGMENTS

Many people helped me to develop, write, and refine this book, and I am deeply grateful for their assistance.

To begin with, my colleague at Syracuse University, Michael H. Morris, has his fingerprints all over this project. He built a top program in entrepreneurship at the Whitman School of Management and brought me into it, suggested I write this book, provided me with resources and materials to make the book better, and gave me critical feedback along the way. Mike is a model social entrepreneur, and I am lucky to have him as an intellectual collaborator.

The professionals who brought this book to fruition include the staff at Prentice Hall, Ashley Santora, and Jennifer M. Collins; the book series editors Michael Morris and Duane Ireland; and my literary agent at the Garamond Agency, Lisa Adams. I had exceptionally good research assistance on this book from two graduate students. Matthew Lenkowsky worked on the project with me from the beginning, digging up examples and editing my often-rough prose. Jessica Haynie did an outstanding job preparing cases that appear at the end of chapters, and editing the manuscript for publication.

I am grateful to Howard Husock at the Manhattan Institute for giving me access to the dossiers on the candidates and winners of the Institute's Social Entrepreneurship Award for the past several years. These dossiers gave a look behind the curtain at some of the most innovative social ventures operating today. Jon Van Wyk and (my brother) Jeff Brooks at the Merkle company generously shared fundraising data with me and also gave me valuable guidance on the fundraising chapter. Joe Iarocci at CARE and Martha Rollins at Boaz & Ruth graciously shared materials from their organizations for use in this book. Colleagues who advised along the way as I wrote this book include Leslie Lenkowsky at Indiana University, and my Maxwell colleagues David Van Slyke and John McPeak.

I received generous institutional support from Syracuse University's Maxwell School of Citizenship and Public Affairs, Campbell Public Affairs Institute, and Whitman School of Management. The American Enterprise Institute also supported this project while I was a visiting scholar in the summer of 2007.

Arthur C. Brooks
Maxwell School of Citizenship and Public Affairs
and *Whitman School of Management, Syracuse University*

ABOUT THE AUTHOR

Arthur C. Brooks is the Louis A. Bantle Professor of Business and Government Policy at Syracuse University's Maxwell School of Citizenship and Public Affairs and Martin J. Whitman School of Management. He is also a Visiting Scholar at the American Enterprise Institute. He earned his Ph.D. in Public Policy Analysis from the Rand Graduate School in 1998 and also holds an MA and BA in economics.

Dr. Brooks has published more than 60 scholarly articles and books on social entrepreneurship, nonprofit management, philanthropy, and cultural economics. He is a member of the editorial boards of the *Journal of Policy Analysis and Management, Strategic Entrepreneurship Journal, Nonprofit and Voluntary Sector Quarterly, Public Administration Review, Journal of Public Administration Research and Theory, Journal of Cultural Economics,* and *State and Local Government Review.* He is a frequent contributor to the *Wall Street Journal*'s editorial page and has also written for *Condé Nast Portfolio, The American, City Journal, The Chronicle of Philanthropy,* and *CBSnews.com.*

Dr. Brooks speaks frequently in the United States, Europe, and Asia on issues related to social entrepreneurship and nonprofit organizations. His 2006 book on American charitable giving is *Who Really Cares: the Surprising Truth About Compassionate Conservatism* (Basic Books), which the *Wall Street Journal* called "the text at the center of a constructive national debate," and on which he advised President George W. Bush in 2007. Each year, Dr. Brooks works extensively with social enterprises in the United States and other countries and regularly provides executive training on nonprofit management and philanthropy.

CHAPTER

AN INTRODUCTION TO SOCIAL ENTREPRENEURSHIP

INTRODUCTION

In 1974, a Bangladeshi economics professor named Muhammad Yunus visited a small rural village in Bangladesh in an effort to connect the economic theories he was teaching with the real-world poverty of his native country. What he found in the tragedy of rural poverty was a major social opportunity and the seeds of a social enterprise that has since transformed the way the world understands poverty relief.[1]

Professor Yunus saw that rural people were generally skilled and hardworking, but the returns to their skills were limited by their lack of access to credit to buy materials for their trades. For example, he found many women who made baskets for a living. Unable to obtain loans from any banks—because they had no collateral—the craftswomen were forced to borrow materials from middlemen in exchange for the right to sell the baskets at a punitively high commission. This left the women without a sufficient profit margin to buy any materials in the future—sending them back to the middlemen.

An opportunity Professor Yunus recognized in this problem was that the poverty of a village could be eased with access to just a few dollars in credit. According to Yunus, "Unleashing of energy and creativity in each human being is the answer to poverty," and unleashing this energy and creativity was a question of a relatively small amount of money.[2] He conceived of a new kind of bank, which made "micro-loans," loans that were so small that no collateral was necessary. Low interest rates meant that craftspeople could earn a fair profit on their work and slowly build up the capital to reinvest, grow their trades, and rise from poverty. The denomination of returns to this enterprise would be the rising incomes of rural poor borrowers and the falling poverty rates in their villages. To execute this enterprise at the beginning, the resources Professor Yunus needed were funds, expertise, and energy. Funds came from depositors and donors; expertise and energy came largely from Mr. Yunus himself.

The venture was launched in 1976, making a small number of loans to the inhabitants of one local village. Experiencing spectacular results, including a loan repayment rate of 99 percent, the enterprise grew quickly, spreading loans to neighboring areas. In 1983, the project was named *Grameen Bank* under a Bangladeshi government charter, which was necessary to make it a legal banking institution. It continued to grow and by 2005, the project had more than 1,500 branches in nearly 50,000 villages, covering about 70 percent of the country. It had approximately 5 million borrowers and annual revenues of about $80 million. The loans had grown beyond business development to include loans for housing, education, and basic subsistence for beggars.

Professor Yunus has attained many of his original goals over the past 30 years, with measurable evidence of high rewards, in terms of the rising incomes among the Bank's borrowers and the falling poverty rates in the villages the bank serves. The Grameen Bank has also spawned thousands of replicas around the developing world, which have helped millions of poor people to help themselves out of poverty by giving them recourse to the fruits of their own private enterprise.

In 2006, Professor Yunus was recognized for his and the Grameen Bank's work with the Nobel Peace Prize. Citing particularly Professor Yunus' efforts to "create economic and social development from below," the Nobel Committee recognized him as "a leader who has managed to translate visions into practical action for the benefit of millions of people" around the world. In particular, they commended the concept of micro-credit, used by the Grameen Bank, as an "important liberating force in societies . . . against repressive social and economic conditions."[3]

Muhammad Yunus' work has left more than a charitable legacy—it has created an intellectual one as well. The new field of *social entrepreneurship* often holds up Grameen Bank as a prime example of recognizing the opportunity to create social value and the development of that opportunity into a successful social venture.

WHAT IS SOCIAL ENTREPRENEURSHIP?

We often hear talk of *entrepreneurship* as if it were a modern concept. For example, we might hear that an organization needs to modernize by "thinking and acting more entrepreneurially." Or we read that value in the modern U.S. economy is increasingly driven by entrepreneurs.

However, the concept of entrepreneurship is not new. The word derives from the French *entreprendre,* or "to undertake," and its importance in the process of production was described by economists 200 years ago. These early economists noted that production processes required labor (mental and physical human effort), physical capital (plant and equipment), human capital (knowledge and expertise), and land (natural resources). But production also required something less tangible: managerial skill and the willingness to take risks for a venture. This was the human part of an endeavor that would be "left over" if you took away sheer manpower and technical know-how.

Over the years, in trying to pin down this magical element in venture creation, businesspeople and scholars have gone beyond management talent and risk to what is the real core of entrepreneurship: opportunity recognition, innovation, and a quest for results. The economist Joseph Schumpeter, often called the "Godfather" of our modern understanding of entrepreneurship, described the phenomenon as follows in 1934:

> First of all there is the dream and the will to found a private kingdom, usually, though not necessarily, also a dynasty. . . . Then there is the will to conquer: the impulse to fight, to prove oneself superior to others, to succeed for the sake, not of the fruits of success, but of success itself. From this aspect, economic action becomes akin to sport. . . . The financial result is a secondary consideration, or, at all events, mainly valued as an index of success and as a symptom of victory, the displaying of which very often is more important as a motive of large expenditure than the wish for the consumers' goods themselves. . . . Finally, there is the joy of creating, of getting things done, or simply of exercising one's energy and ingenuity. . . . Our type seeks out difficulties, changes in order to change, delights in ventures.[4]

A succinct definition of entrepreneurship that we often hear today is that it is the process of pursuing opportunities without limitation by resources currently in hand. The key here is the word *process*. Many authors about entrepreneurship in the commercial world describe this process as consisting of five parts.

1. *Opportunity recognition.* Entrepreneurship begins with the recognition that an opportunity exists to create value. For example, an entrepreneur may perceive an opportunity contained in a demographic shift, a change in consumer tastes, a new public policy, or an unmet need.

2. *Concept development.* An opportunity cannot yield a valuable venture without its translation into a business concept. For example, a change in consumer tastes may open the door to a new product geared to the change or the improvement of an existing technology. An opportunity and a business concept—for-profit or otherwise—are not the same thing. And as one entrepreneurship expert notes, confusion between the two is "one of the leading causes of product and business failure."[5]

3. *Resource determination and acquisition.* If an entrepreneur proceeds to develop a business concept, the next step involves the determination and acquisition of sufficient resources. These resources generally include money, of course, but they are not limited to the financial dimension. The entrepreneur also needs information and human resources as well. For example, the decision to start a business requires money to cover start-up costs, information about the market the entrepreneur is entering, and usually, some human assistance in executing the plan.

4. *Launch and venture growth.* After an opportunity is recognized and resources acquired, the venture can be launched. Then, an entrepreneur grows the venture in a way that will maximize its payoff. This frequently means continuing to invest, developing a larger business strategy, retaining (as opposed to acquiring) human resources, and dealing with inevitable conflict.

5. *Harvest the venture.* Ultimately, the entrepreneur exits from the venture, ideally in a way that maximizes his or her benefit. Exit may mean taking a company public, selling it to another company, liquidating assets, or passing the venture on to heirs.

The entrepreneurial process is arguably the most important creative force in the U.S. system of private enterprise. For example, we often hear that large corporations are cutting jobs, and it is true that more than 5 million jobs disappeared at Fortune 500 firms between 1980 and 2000. Over the same period, however, 34 million jobs were created, mostly in small businesses and fast-growing new firms.[6] Today, 9 percent of Americans are involved in entrepreneurial activity and are either providing jobs for others or are planning to do so within the next five years.[7]

Social entrepreneurship is a much newer concept than commercial entrepreneurship and has been defined in many ways over the past few years. The variance in definitions has been substantial enough that one standard definition has yet to emerge clearly. However, practically all of the definitions have contained one or more of the following concepts, articulated by major writers on the subject.

1. *Social entrepreneurship addresses social problems or needs that are unmet by private markets or governments.*
   - "Social entrepreneurship creates innovative solutions to immediate social problems and mobilizes the ideas, capacities, resources, and social arrangements required for sustainable social transformations."[8]
   - "Social entrepreneurs are people who realize where there is an opportunity to satisfy some unmet need that the welfare state will not or cannot meet."[9]
   - "Social enterprises are private organizations dedicated to solving social problems, serving the disadvantaged, and providing socially important goods that were not, in their judgment, adequately provided by public agencies or private markets."[10]

2. *Social entrepreneurship is motivated primarily by social benefit.*
   - "Social entrepreneurship is a multidimensional construct involving the expression of entrepreneurially virtuous behavior to achieve a social mission."[11]
   - "Social entrepreneurs are people with new ideas to address major problems who are relentless in the pursuit of their visions . . . who will not give up until they have spread their ideas as far as they possibly can."[12]

3. *Social entrepreneurship generally works with—not against—market forces.*
   - Social entrepreneurs "pay increasing attention to market signals *without* losing sight of their underlying missions, to somehow balance moral

imperatives and the profit motives—and that balancing act is the heart and soul of the movement."[13]

- Social entrepreneurs "combine innovation, entrepreneurship, and social purpose and seek to be financially sustainable by generating revenue from trading."[14]

A useful definition of social entrepreneurship employs these concepts and ties them to the way we understand the commercial entrepreneurial process. Considering social entrepreneurship to be related to commercial entrepreneurship in this way is not radical. In fact, one of the most common claims about social entrepreneurs is that they adopt a "business-like approach" to social innovation.[15] The primary difference, as we shall see throughout this book, is not the nature of the entrepreneurial process itself but rather the denomination of the rewards sought. In fact, social entrepreneurship maps into the traditional commercial entrepreneurship process neatly.

1. *A social entrepreneur recognizes an opportunity to create social value.* This might take the form of an obvious or not-so-obvious social problem or an unmet social need. Two aspects of social opportunity recognition are especially noteworthy. First, social entrepreneurs tend to see opportunities where others see only threats and tragedies. For example, where most people see a blighted industrial zone, a social entrepreneur might see an opportunity for cooperative gardening or a park. Second, an unmet social need might involve an actual unfilled demand, such as a group of inner-city parents who are unsatisfied with their local public school. Alternatively, however, it might involve a demand that is still "latent"; that is, the social beneficiaries might not know the benefit they could receive. For example, parents might not even know what kind of educational improvements their children could be experiencing or might not understand the importance of these improvements. Clearly, latent demand is a much more complicated type of opportunity for a social entrepreneur than actual demand because it involves selling the direct beneficiaries on the idea as well as the other steps in the entrepreneurial process. The process of identifying opportunities is the subject of Chapter 2.

2. *The opportunity leads to the development of an enterprise concept.* The enterprise concept has several basic parts. First, the social entrepreneur identifies specific new products or new markets to be served. For example, the opportunity to serve the homeless might involve the creation of a new soup kitchen or shelter where these people are concentrated or an expansion of other, existing homelessness relief operations to cover the people in this area. Second, the social entrepreneur identifies and defines the actual social rewards to be gained from the successful enterprise and sets enterprise goals in terms of these rewards. This second step has no clear corollary in the world of commercial entrepreneurship, where the metric is usually very clear: profits or something related (such as market share). Social entrepreneurs face the challenge of denominating the value of their enterprises in such a way that it is identifiable, defensible, and measurable. For example, a missionary organization might denominate value in terms of the number of converts that stay with their faith for a certain length of time, and set a

goal of reaching (if not converting) everyone in a specific area. The failure to identify and denominate social returns and set goals at this stage is a key reason that many social enterprises do not succeed.

Other parts of the enterprise concept development involve generating information about the market. Campbell (1998) lists these parts: Gauge the commitment to the enterprise; develop the infrastructure; generate and screen ideas for execution; conduct feasibility studies; and plan the venture.[16]

3. *Resource needs are determined, and the necessary resources are acquired.* Social enterprises rely on three main types of resources. First, there are financial needs. Financial resources come from earned revenues, philanthropy, and governments. The latter two are especially important at this early stage because typically, a social enterprise has nothing to sell (yet). Chapter 7 discusses the main avenues for philanthropy: individual, corporate, and from foundations, as well as the growing importance of venture philanthropy. Second, there are human resource needs in the form of donated and paid human resources. The volunteer resources are at the level of staff, or leadership—often the board of directors. The biggest human resource input usually comes from the social entrepreneur. Third, there are human capital resources. This refers to education, experience, knowledge, and expertise to make an enterprise operational and competent. For example, a social entrepreneur intent on starting a school voucher program must identify not just the money and labor needed to start the venture but also the necessary political and technical knowledge about this kind of cause.

4. *The social entrepreneur launches and grows the venture.* The venture's launch is followed by growth, which can be fast or slow, and often involves an expansion of the organization's size or scope of operations. In all cases, however, growth should follow a tangible business strategy, which includes a plan to meet growing human and financial resource needs, delegation of responsibilities from the social entrepreneur to others, a process for dealing with and negotiating inevitable conflicts, and a coherent plan to measure progress in terms of the social value metric defined in an earlier stage. For example, imagine a social entrepreneur intent on starting an arts and culture district (a zone in which the official or unofficial attraction is the arts) in a downtown area. A typical measure of social value for such an enterprise might be the number of arts patrons served per month in the designated area. The beginning of this project could involve the connection of the activities of two downtown arts groups in close proximity. However, there must also be strategy for growth, which most likely will involve expanding in budget, activities, and geography, such as more arts groups connected, geographic designation and signage sought from the city, a comprehensive arts Web site developed, and so forth. This expansion path should be explicit and include plans for staffing and financing and for removing obstacles to the project. It also must include progress measurement, meaning regular monitoring of the number of arts patrons in the district.

5. *Goal attainment and beyond.* One part of the social enterprise process that is often neglected is a plan for goal attainment. This does not mean simply planning to reach a venture goal but rather knowing what to do after this goal is reached.

There are at least four possibilities for a social enterprise that has measurably reached its goals: It can shut down, it can redefine itself to meet a new social mission, it can settle into a stable service equilibrium, or it can integrate into another venture. For example, imagine a social enterprise that seeks to vaccinate children in a certain region against a preventable disease. The performance metric is fairly obvious—the number or percentage of kids vaccinated—and the goal is to vaccinate enough kids that the disease can no longer spread within this community. After it meets this goal, the enterprise can shut down or turn its energies to other challenges, such as vaccinating in other communities, or fighting other diseases. Alternatively, it might seek to roll the venture, which has demonstrated its effectiveness, into a larger government public health program.

Figure 1-1 summarizes the process of social entrepreneurship.

FIGURE 1-1 The Process of Social Entrepreneurship

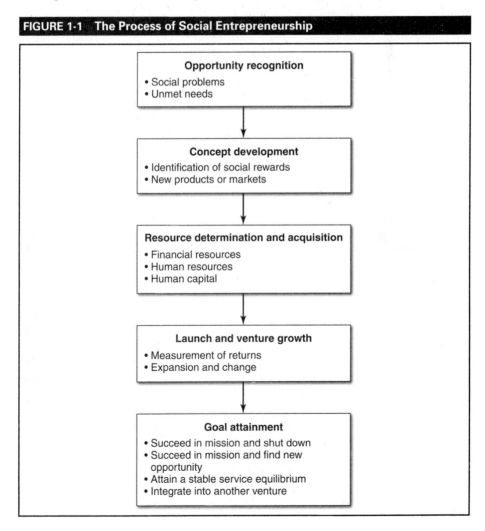

THE LANDSCAPE OF SOCIAL ENTREPRENEURSHIP

Similar to the for-profit sector, there is significant evidence of social entrepreneurship in the number of new organizations forming in the United States. Figure 1-2 illustrates the growth of all nonprofits with annual gross receipts above $25,000 from 1996 to 2004. It shows that nonprofits in general grew by 3 percent per year. Even more impressive growth occurred among public charities (hospitals, schools, arts groups, social welfare agencies, etc.) and private foundations. Keep in mind, however, that these data leave out two highly dynamic types of organizations: houses of worship and grassroots organizations. In other words, this probably significantly underestimates the levels of social entrepreneurial activity today in the U.S. economy.

Starting a venture is only one type of social entrepreneurship that is occurring in the United States. The enterprises "embedded" in established activities are harder to measure. For example, author Peter C. Brinckerhoff (2000) lists six categories of possible ventures for a social entrepreneur:[17]

1. Starting a new product or service
2. Expanding an existing product or service
3. Expanding an existing activity for a new group of people
4. Expanding an existing activity to a new geographic area
5. Acquiring an existing business
6. Partnership or merger with an existing business

The first category of social entrepreneurship is the one we most frequently think of, which is reflected in Figure 1-2. However, the best reaction to a social

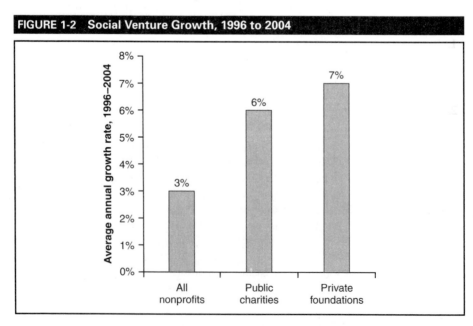

FIGURE 1-2 Social Venture Growth, 1996 to 2004

opportunity might be to leverage existing resources to create new services or serve new people and areas. For an existing organization that sees a new opportunity, it may be most appropriate to acquire or partner with another organization that is better positioned to meet the opportunity. The absence of a brand new venture does not necessarily make it any less socially entrepreneurial.

Although social entrepreneurship can occur in many ways, not every activity that falls in Brinckerhoff's categories should be classified as social entrepreneurship. On the contrary, it is easy to see how practically any of the categories can deviate from the process of social entrepreneurship. A new or expanded service is not necessarily based on a new opportunity, and a new opportunity may not be developed into any useful service. Acquiring or partnering with an existing business is frequently nonentrepreneurial, inasmuch as the opportunity and enterprise concept are not new. This is not to say that a nonentrepreneurial venture is worse or better than an entrepreneurial one, just that they differ in tangible ways.

THEORIES OF SOCIAL ENTREPRENEURSHIP

How do you explain social entrepreneurship? You might be tempted to answer this question by simply going back to the beginning of the social entrepreneurship process: Social entrepreneurship occurs because of a perceived opportunity. Yet this is circular reasoning, in that the opportunity *defines* the beginning of social entrepreneurship—it doesn't *cause* it. We need a theory of how and why the whole process of social entrepreneurship is stimulated, and for this, we turn once again to the well-developed literature on commercial entrepreneurship.

There are five basic theories of entrepreneurship, most of which are complementary to one another:

1. *Environment.* Under this view, entrepreneurship is a latent condition in the population that is stimulated when the environment is conducive to it. This environment can be inside a firm, in a person's social circle, or even in public policy and politics.[18]
2. *Resources.* The theory of entrepreneurship focuses on the availability of resources for new ventures. The idea here is that the availability of financial capital, human resources, and human capital are the key to understanding why entrepreneurs decide to try and exploit an opportunity.[19]
3. *Perturbation.* Also known as "displacement," this theory argues that entrepreneurship occurs when people are displaced from their regular business routines by political, cultural, or economic factors.[20]
4. *Personal traits.* This class of theories holds that there are identifiable traits of an "entrepreneurial personality." Entrepreneurship occurs because people with these traits are able to operationalize their tendencies.[21]
5. *Preparation.* Related to personality traits is the idea that entrepreneurship can be taught, and hence it depends on factors such as education and work experience.[22]

FIGURE 1-3 The Forces on Social Entrepreneurship

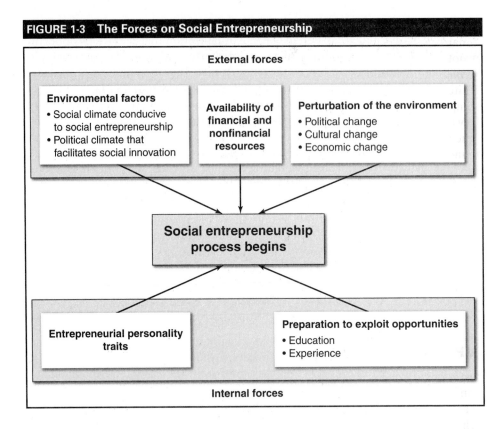

Social entrepreneurship can be understood with the same set of theories. Figure 1-3 illustrates how the forces represented in these theories can work together to trigger the social entrepreneurship process. The first three forces are external to social entrepreneurs, whereas the last two are internal. Together, they can reinforce or weaken the likelihood of the initiation of the social entrepreneurship process.

The aggregate model in Figure 1-3 is useful not just for combining and understanding the various strands of theory on entrepreneurship but also for predicting where we are likely to find social entrepreneurship, and even how we can best stimulate it. For example, we should predict a relatively high level of social entrepreneurship activity where the social and political climate is congenial to the idea of meeting social needs through private initiative, where resources are available to develop ventures, and where changes are occurring that make a social need perceptible. Furthermore, the people in this environment most likely to start social enterprises are those with sufficient background and an "entrepreneurial personality."

These predictions—especially those concerning the external forces—are consistent with what a number of commentators have identified as one of the key differences between the United States and the countries of Western Europe. Many authors have attributed the relatively high level of civic participation in the United States to the social and political environment, the ready availability of resources for good causes (including philanthropy and volunteer labor), and the fact that the dynamic culture and economy create constant change. In fact, this observation is not new. The French nobleman Alexis de Tocqueville wrote his classic book *Democracy in America* in 1835. This was a study of the civic peculiarities of the United States. What Tocqueville found most remarkable about the United States, compared with Europe at that time, was the number and variety of private, voluntary associations he found there, which were supported through voluntary gifts of time and money and dedicated to every sort of social purpose. In other words, he found evidence of dramatically different levels of social entrepreneurship.

> Americans of all ages, all conditions, and all dispositions constantly form associations. . . . The Americans make associations to give entertainments, to found seminaries, to build inns, to construct churches, to diffuse books, to send missionaries to the antipodes; in this manner they found hospitals, prisons, and schools. If it is proposed to inculcate some truth or to foster some feeling by the encouragement of a great example, they form a society. Wherever at the head of some new undertaking you see the government in France, or a man of rank in England, in the United States you will be sure to find an association.[23]

WHO ARE SOCIAL ENTREPRENEURS?

Just as there have been many early definitions of "social entrepreneurship," a number of attempts to define "social entrepreneur" have also emerged over the years. One definition comes from Dees (2001), who calls social entrepreneurs "change agents in the social sector" who do the following:

- Adopt a mission to create and sustain social value (not just private value).
- Recognize and relentlessly pursue new opportunities to serve that mission.
- Engage in a process of continuous innovation, adaptation, and learning.
- Act boldly without being limited by resources currently in hand.
- Exhibit a heightened sense of accountability to the constituencies served and for the outcomes created.[24]

This definition tells us more about what social entrepreneurs do than who they are. However, personal traits and preparation—the internal forces of commercial entrepreneurship and social entrepreneurship—are important to understand. We can reframe the question in this way: Who tends to become social entrepreneurs? There has been considerable demographic and psychological research on entrepreneurs that can help us describe social entrepreneurs with some precision.

To begin with, some scholars have studied entrepreneurs' innate characteristics— their demographic traits—for which they are not necessarily responsible. A number of provocative studies have found that there are, in fact, some groups with an elevated likelihood of engaging in entrepreneurial activity. For example, Saxenian (2000) describes a research finding that immigrants tend to be highly entrepreneurial.[25] Studies also show that first-born children are most likely to become entrepreneurs, and that entrepreneurship often occurs at milestone years (e.g., 30, 40, 50), when people feel restless.[26]

Some studies have looked at innate characteristics that specifically predict social entrepreneurship. There is evidence that gender matters, for example. Although most social entrepreneurs are men, the ratio of men to women is much lower than it is among commercial entrepreneurs.[27] Some scholars argue that social entrepreneurs are disproportionately likely to have suffered a personal trauma in their lives, such as depression, alcoholism, or drug addiction.[28]

Although interesting, these facts do not really get us much closer to understanding the true entrepreneurial identity. Demographics do not *determine* entrepreneurship; they simply correlate with the characteristics that do. For example, the fact of immigrating probably does not spur entrepreneurial behavior in and of itself. Rather, immigrants may be entrepreneurial because of their experiences overcoming adversity or perhaps because of an entrepreneurial self-selection toward becoming an immigrant in the first place.

More useful than innate characteristics, therefore, are the psychological attributes of social entrepreneurs. There are five that are most frequently identified in studies.[29]

1. *Innovativeness.* Given the fact that entrepreneurship typically involves innovation, it is not surprising that entrepreneurs tend to be innovative people. That is, they develop new ideas to meet specific challenges.

2. *Achievement orientation.* Entrepreneurs are nearly always exceptionally goal-oriented people. They set personal goals naturally and measure progress toward these goals.

3. *Independence.* Entrepreneurs are notoriously independent. Most are highly self-reliant, and many naturally prefer to work alone toward their goals.

4. *Sense of control over destiny.* Entrepreneurs rarely see themselves as victims of their environment but rather as in control of their own destiny. This may be due to the tendency to see negative circumstances as opportunities instead of threats.

5. *Low risk-aversion.* Although there is no evidence that any rational person— including entrepreneurs—seeks out risk for the sake of it, there is evidence that entrepreneurs are more tolerant of risk and more creative at finding ways to mitigate it.

6. *Tolerance for ambiguity.* Entrepreneurs are generally more comfortable than other people in situations that are dynamic and not particularly clear-cut.

   These are the psychological ingredients for an entrepreneurial orientation. Something else is necessary, however, for a *socially* entrepreneurial orientation. According to Bornstein (2005) a social entrepreneur is characterized by "initiative, creativity, energy, obsessive focus on results, capacity for self-correction, profound understanding of the market and, above all, a deep commitment to building a just and humane world."[30] To the preceding list, therefore, we might add one more characteristic.

7. *Community awareness and social concern.* Social entrepreneurs see the value of *social* rewards and are willing to devote their talents and energies to accumulate these rewards.

Figure 1-4 illustrates how psychological attributes work together to help create a social entrepreneur.

As useful as the model in Figure 1-4 is for describing and predicting who is a social entrepreneur, much research remains to be undertaken on the commercially entrepreneurial and socially entrepreneurial character. One important question is which of the characteristics in Figure 1-4 are necessary to stimulate entrepreneurship, and whether any combination is sufficient. In addition, little is known about the possible interactions between some of these characteristics. Morris (1998) explores one such interaction, with intriguing results. He asks how innovativeness and low risk aversion combine with each other, and then derives four possible outcomes, only one of which triggers entrepreneurship. These combinations are summarized in Table 1-1. Entrepreneurs have low risk aversion and are highly innovative. Noninnovative people who are open to risk are gamblers; innovative people who are not open to risk are dreamers; and noninnovative, risk-averse people are "stuck."

FIGURE 1-4   The Characteristics of a Social Entrepreneur

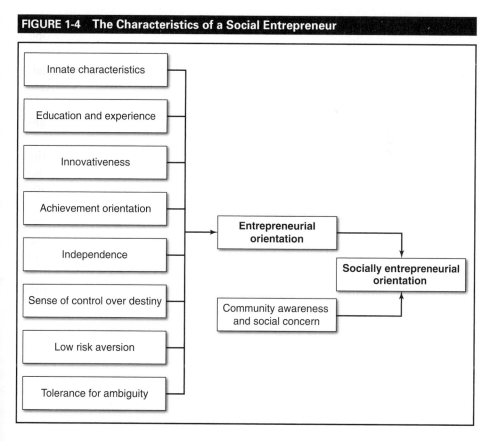

TABLE 1-1 The Combination of Risk Aversion and Innovativeness in Triggering Entrepreneurship		
	High Risk Aversion	*Low Risk Aversion*
Highly innovative	Dreamer	Entrepreneur
Not innovative	Stuck	Gambler

Another issue about the socially entrepreneurial character is how it relates to leadership. Clearly, in many cases, a social entrepreneur needs to lead as well as innovate. I have often heard that these competencies rarely occur in the same individual, although I have not seen evidence that this is necessarily so. Waddock and James (1991) constructed the following list of important leadership characteristics for social entrepreneurs.[31]

1. The social problem is characterized by extreme complexity, which the social entrepreneur is somehow able to bound into a vision that has the potential to reshape public attitudes when implemented.
2. Social entrepreneurs are individuals with significant personal credibility, which they use to tap critical resources and actually build the necessary network of participating organizations.
3. The social entrepreneur generates followers' commitment to the project by framing it in terms of important social values, rather than purely economic terms, which results in a sense of collective purpose among the social entrepreneur and those who join the effort.

The research shows that an entrepreneurial personality can manifest itself in many ways. For example, Miner (1996) has identified four distinct entrepreneurial "types."[32] The "personal achiever" innovates autonomously, the "super-salesman" innovates through service to others, the "real manager" is an entrepreneur from within an established organization, and the "expert idea generator" relies on expertise and creativity for innovations. These types have parallels in social entrepreneurship as well. Personal achievers look to start social ventures. Super-salesmen are usually found in fundraising and development, innovating in the way they identify and serve donors. Real managers take established social enterprises to new heights. Expert idea generators make it possible to meet social missions in new and innovative ways.

So far, this discussion of the entrepreneurial character has focused on the individual. However, this is not to imply that individuals must work alone for a social enterprise to succeed. Indeed, teams and networks are often necessary. For example, teams can provide synergy between people with complementary talents and diverse perspectives. Teams can mitigate enterprise risk by increasing the resources and sources of assistance for an enterprise. Wider interests and expertise can also mean greater potential for growth. There are potential costs from working in groups as well, however. For instance, as groups grow, an

---

BENJAMIN FRANKLIN
Social Entrepreneur

Benjamin Franklin (1706–1790) is one of the best-known of America's founding fathers. He was a scientist, statesman, businessman, and writer. One of the most famous men in colonial and revolutionary America, his career and writings are still held up as an excellent example of the American spirit.

Franklin was the quintessential entrepreneur, inventing and bringing to market dozens of products and services, from the Franklin stove, to bifocal eyeglasses, to the glass harmonica. Seeing and exploiting dozens of opportunities over his lifetime, he became a very rich and powerful man. Not surprisingly, there is ample evidence that he possessed all the characteristics of an entrepreneur. Consider the following famous quotations from his pithy writings.

Innovation: "When you're finished changing, you're finished."

Achievement orientation: "He that lives on hope will die fasting."

Independence: "Three may keep a secret, if two of them are dead."

Sense of control over destiny: "God helps them that help themselves."

Low risk aversion: "He that would fish, must venture his bait."

Tolerance of ambiguity: "The way to be safe is to never be secure."

But Franklin's genius also extended to social entrepreneurship. He created the first fire department and introduced the idea of fire insurance. He founded philosophical societies, hospitals, and colleges. He invented many devices out of community concern, such as the street lamp, flexible catheter, and the lightning rod.

In 1731, Franklin created the first public library in Philadelphia, doing so out of clear interest for the public good. He later wrote in his autobiography that this library "was the mother of all the North American subscription libraries, now so numerous. It is become a great thing itself, and continually increasing. These libraries have improved the general conversation of the Americans, made the common tradesmen and farmers as intelligent as most gentlemen from other countries, and perhaps have contributed in some degree to the stand so generally made throughout the colonies in defense of their privileges."[33]

---

enterprise can become more unwieldy and maneuverable. Enterprises can also be vulnerable if teams dissolve or become locked in uncreative "groupthink" (an unhelpful conformity in team members' perspectives).

MYTHS ABOUT SOCIAL ENTREPRENEURSHIP

Given the many definitions of social entrepreneurship floating around over the past decade, it is unsurprising that a number of myths have appeared as well. The last part of this chapter dispenses with the most common ones.

MYTH 1. SOCIAL ENTREPRENEURS ARE ANTIBUSINESS

One extremely common misperception about social rewards is that they are incompatible, or at odds with, financial rewards, and thus social entrepreneurs tend to be positioned opposite the commercial world. This is usually false. Many social entrepreneurs come out of the world of business, cutting their teeth in the commercial world before making social innovations. In his bestselling book *Begging for Change,* Robert Egger tells about the nightclub career, and the dream of starting his own club, that he had before ever thinking of starting the DC Central Kitchen, his innovative nonprofit to serve hungry and homeless people in Washington, DC.[34] Many other social entrepreneurs operate in the world of philanthropy, where there is a disproportionate number of wealthy individuals from the world of business. Furthermore, some of the most interesting social enterprises—discussed in a later chapter—involve collaborations between commercial and nonprofit organizations, in which the missions of the organizations are properly aligned for mutual benefit.

MYTH 2. THE DIFFERENCE BETWEEN COMMERCIAL ENTREPRENEURSHIP AND SOCIAL ENTREPRENEURSHIP IS GREED

Related to the first myth, there is a common misperception that, whereas commercial entrepreneurs are motivated by greed, social entrepreneurs are motivated by public good. This injects a moral dimension into social entrepreneurship that, although attractive, is not substantiated by the evidence. First, there is no evidence that commercial entrepreneurs are especially greedy. On the contrary, recall Joseph Schumpeter's famous claim that, for entrepreneurs, "The financial result is a secondary consideration, or, at all events, mainly valued as an index of success and as a symptom of victory. . . ." In other words, commercial entrepreneurs are more likely to be goal-obsessed than money-obsessed. Second, many social entrepreneurs are *also* commercial entrepreneurs. In fact, some of the most influential venture philanthropists—such as Andrew Carnegie and John D. Rockefeller 100 years ago or Bill Gates today—made their fortunes as commercial entrepreneurs. Acs and Phillips (2002) show that, in fact, social entrepreneurship is usually predicated on entrepreneurially derived wealth that is donated for social purposes.[35]

MYTH 3. SOCIAL ENTREPRENEURS RUN NONPROFITS

Most of the examples in this book are from the nonprofit sector, but nonprofit status is neither necessary nor sufficient to make social entrepreneurship. On the contrary, the social entrepreneurship process described previously can occur in any sector and with any legal status. Informal grassroots organizations can sometimes be ideally suited to exploit social opportunities quickly and effectively, particularly when the resource needs are rather modest. Governments can sometimes engage in social entrepreneurship, although as you will see in a later chapter, this is rarer because of the public-sector forces that frequently inhibit innovation and the willingness to take risk. Finally, commercial organizations can and do act in socially entrepreneurial ways, especially when commercial and social missions align.

MYTH 4. SOCIAL ENTREPRENEURS ARE BORN, NOT MADE

Among my graduate students in nonprofit management, I sometimes run into the belief that either they are social entrepreneurs, or they aren't. Recalling the discussion from the last section, this deterministic view of social entrepreneurship places too much weight on the idea that the typical characteristics of the entrepreneur are all about nature, rather than nurture. This is obviously not so for education and experience. However, it is also true that people can be taught to be more innovative, independent, and goal-oriented than they otherwise might be. Similarly, there is abundant evidence that people can gain a sense of control over their destiny, become more comfortable with risk and ambiguity than they otherwise might be, and have their level of community awareness raised. In short, although some people certainly naturally possess more socially entrepreneurial characteristics than others, there is evidence that these characteristics can be fostered as well.

MYTH 5. SOCIAL ENTREPRENEURS ARE MISFITS

The stereotypical social entrepreneur is someone who strikes out on his or her own because of an inability to work for others. Yet this has no empirical basis in reality. In fact, what the literature consistently demonstrates is that commercial entrepreneurs and social entrepreneurs come in many varieties, including people embedded inside organizations and working in teams. In one study of commercial entrepreneurs, for example, Vesper (1980) identified the solo, self-employed person as only one of nine entrepreneurial types.[36]

MYTH 6. SOCIAL ENTREPRENEURS USUALLY FAIL

Risk is a real component of social entrepreneurship, as a later chapter will show. However, it is commonly overstated in both commercial and social entrepreneurship. Kirchoff (1993) shows that, contrary to popular intuition, most for-profit businesses do not fail. For example, in 1993 he found that more than half of the U.S. businesses started in 1977 were still functioning, and that less than half of those that had closed had actually failed.[37] Similarly, Cordes, et al. (2001) show that, of the nonprofit health and human service organizations started in 1992 or later, more than 70 percent were still operating at the end of 1996.[38]

MYTH 7. SOCIAL ENTREPRENEURS LOVE RISK

It is one thing to assert that social entrepreneurs tolerate risk more readily than nonentrepreneurs or that they are better equipped to mitigate risk than others. It is another thing entirely to say they *like* risk, which is what people often imply. In fact, there is little evidence that anyone seeks risk *per se,* except perhaps people with a pathological gambling dependency. In fact, a later chapter will show that social entrepreneurship involves *calculated* risk-taking. This implies as much about the ability to *calculate* as it does about the willingness to take risks.

Summary

- Social entrepreneurship is a process that starts with a perceived social opportunity, translates it into an enterprise concept, ascertains and acquires the resources necessary to execute the enterprise, launches and grows the enterprise, and harvests the future upon attainment of the enterprise's goals.
- Social entrepreneurship can take many forms, from starting a business, to expanding an organization, to partnering with another firm.
- There are multiple stimuli for the social entrepreneurship process, including environmental factors, resource availability, a change in the social entrepreneur's environment, his or her preparation to see and exploit social opportunities, and personality traits.
- Research has identified several personality traits most closely linked to entrepreneurship. These include innovativeness, achievement orientation, independence, sense of control over one's destiny, relatively low risk aversion, and tolerance for ambiguity. Social entrepreneurship also requires a sense of community or social need.

Key Terms

- entrepreneurship
- social entrepreneurship
- social enterprise
- social venture
- social entrepreneur
- enterprise concept
- enterprise growth

End-of-Chapter Questions and Cases

THE PROGRAM FOR APPROPRIATE TECHNOLOGY IN HEALTH

The Program for Appropriate Technology in Health (PATH) is a socially entrepreneurial nonprofit based in Seattle Washington. It was founded in 1977 to adapt existing medical technologies in developed countries for use in the developing world.[39] The organization is active in more than 100 countries in Africa, Asia, South and Central America, and the former Soviet Union. According to the organization's mission statement,

> PATH is an international, nonprofit organization that creates sustainable, culturally relevant solutions, enabling communities worldwide to break longstanding cycles of poor health. By collaborating with diverse public- and private-sector partners, we help provide appropriate health technologies and vital strategies that change the way people think and act.[40]

One product PATH has developed is SoloShot, a cheap syringe which automatically disables after one use so that needle sharing is impossible—and thus accidental transmission of many communicable diseases such as AIDS and hepatitis are prevented.

1. The president of PATH, Christopher J. Elias, has been quoted as saying, "Success means we set clear goals and milestones for individual and company performance." How might you denominate the social rewards from the SoloShot program? How would you structure the "goals and milestones" toward success? What would constitute success?
2. Outline a plausible social entrepreneurship process for SoloShot, starting with a perceived social threat and ending with the attainment of social goals. Be specific about each step of the process.
3. What are the external forces most likely to have stimulated the social entrepreneurship process for SoloShot? Be specific.
4. What are the internal forces most likely to have stimulated the social entrepreneurship process for SoloShot? Be specific.
5. Which of Brinckerhoff's social entrepreneurship categories does PATH fall into?
6. In a case like SoloShot, where social entrepreneurship occurs within an organization already formed, which of the entrepreneurial personality characteristics do you think are probably most important?

DONORSCHOOSE.ORG

Charles Best demonstrates the social entrepreneurship process through his nonprofit organization, DonorsChoose.org.[41] At just the age of 24, Charles Best was a high school history teacher in an economically depressed area of the Bronx.[42] He experienced what most teachers deal with in these deprived districts: a lack of educational material in the classroom. Quickly noticing the direct impact it was having on students, as well as teachers like himself, he thought about ways in which he could solve this problem. Searching for a way to deal with the unmet needs of students and their teachers, he also thought about individual donors and their demand to choose where their money goes and how it is spent.

The opportunity to create a program that benefited students and teachers, as well as benefited frustrated donors, led Charles Best to develop an enterprise concept. He first established the mission:

> DonorsChoose.org is dedicated to addressing the scarcity and inequitable distribution of learning materials and experiences in our public schools. We believe this inequity is rooted in the following factors:
>
> 1. Shortages of learning materials prevent thorough, engaging instruction.
> 2. Top-down distribution of materials stifles our best teachers and discourages them from developing solutions for their students.

3. Small, directed contributions have gone untapped as a source of funding.

DonorsChoose.org will improve public education by engaging citizens in an online marketplace where teachers describe and individuals can fund specific student projects. We envision a nation where students in every community have the resources they need to learn.[43]

To accomplish this mission, a Web site was created as a way to provide students and teachers in need with educational material that otherwise would not be provided. Through this Web site, teachers can submit project proposals for materials or experiences their students need to learn and excel in the classroom. Potential donors can browse the Web site and choose a project of interest to fund. A feature of the Web site is that these donors can search for specific regions, schools, projects, or dollar amounts to fund. Additionally, after a project is funded, and the students receive and use their materials, donors receive letters and photographs from the students and teachers showing how their gift was used.

Charles Best determined that the initial resources he would need to get this enterprise started would be financial resources to establish a Web site and for administrative costs, as well as human resources, or teachers to submit proposals. Charles was determined to make a difference in the classroom, as well as create a new model for giving, so he sacrificed much of his own time and resources. Paying out of his own pocket, he financed the initial administrative costs and the funding of early proposals. He even gave up his apartment and moved back in with his parents to save expenses. Charles said, "My dad was an inspiration to me growing up because of his values and character. He was a corporate lawyer, but he encouraged me to do whatever it was that I'd most enjoy, not to care about money."[44] He soon got teachers in his school to submit proposals, and then one by one, additional schools began to join, and in 2000, DonorsChoose.org was born.

Over the past eight years, DonorsChoose.org has continued to grow in terms of the amount of funding received, as well as the amount of support given to classroom projects and the areas in which the funding is distributed. The impact has been measured in various ways. As of May 23, 2007, $12,646,212 has been given to 565,062 students from donors in 50 states. These donors include 27,438 individuals who have made 58,978 donations to the student projects. This generosity has encouraged 24,315 teachers in 6,880 public schools to submit 55,225 project proposals for their students. Of these proposed projects, 26,303 have been funded.

The venture has a goal "to be able to serve all schools in the United States."[45] After this goal is attained, DonorsChoose.org can attain stable service equilibrium, or it may integrate into another venue. According to Jonathan Alter of *Newsweek,* "The idea melds social justice, the Internet, and market principles. Right now, the mission is inner city education, but there is no reason it could not be extended to other areas of philanthropy."[46]

1. How does DonorsChoose.org measure success? How else might it do so?
2. Can you recommend any additional end goals for Mr. Best?

3. What are the limitations of having an Internet-based nonprofit organization? What are ways to overcome these obstacles?

End Notes

1. For further reading on Yunus and the Grameen Bank, see Yunus, Muhammad (2003). *Banker to the Poor: Micro-Lending and the Battle Against World Poverty*. New York: PublicAffairs; Bornstein, David (2005). *The Price of a Dream: The Story of the Grameen Bank*. New York: Oxford University Press.
2. See Sinclair, Paul (2006). "Grameen Micro-Credit & How to End Poverty from the Roots Up." www.oneworldonepeople.org/.
3. The Norwegian Nobel Committee (2006). The Nobel Peace Prize for 2006.
4. Schumpeter (1934: 93–94). Schumpeter, J. A. (1934). (trans. R. Opie). *The Theory of Economic Development,* Cambridge, MA: Harvard University Press.
5. Morris, Michael H. (1998). *Entrepreneurial Intensity: Sustainable Advantages for Individuals, Organizations, and Societies.* Westport, CT: Quorum Books, p. 29.
6. Reynolds, Paul D., Michael Hay, and S. Michael Camp (1999). *Global Entrepreneurship Monitor.* Kansas City, MO: Kauffman Foundation.
7. Minniti, Maria, and William D. Bygrave (2003). *National Entrepreneurship Assessment: United States of America.* Kansas City, MO: The Kauffman Foundation.
8. Alvord, Sarah H., L. David Brown, and Christine W. Letts (2004). "Social Entrepreneurship and Societal Transformation: An Exploratory Study." *Journal of Applied Behavioral Science* 40(3), 260–282.
9. Thompson, John, Geoff Alvy, and Ann Lees (2000). "Social Entrepreneurship — A New Look at the People and the Potential." *Management Decision* 38(5/6): 328–38.
10. Dees, J. Gregory (1994). "Social Enterprise: Private Initiatives for the Common Good." *Harvard Business Review* 76 (Jan.–Feb. 1998): 54–58.
11. Mort, Gillian Sullivan, Jay Weerawardena, and Kashonia Carnegie (2003). "Social Entrepreneurship: Towards Conceptualization." *International Journal of Nonprofit and Voluntary Sector Marketing* 8(1): 76–88.
12. Bornstein, David (2004). *How to Change the World: Social Entrepreneurs and the Power of New Ideas.* New York: Oxford University Press.
13. Boschee, Jerr (1998). *Merging Mission and Money: A Board Member's Guide to Social Entrepreneurship.* Washington, DC: The National Center for Nonprofit Boards.
14. Haugh, Helen. (2005) "The role of social enterprise in regional development." *International Journal of Entrepreneurship and Small Business* 2(4): 346–357.
15. See Pomerantz, Mark (2003). "The Business of Social Entrepreneurship in a 'Down Economy.'" *In Business,* pp. 25–28.
16. Campbell, Sandy (May, 1998). "Social Entrepreneurship: How to Develop New Social-Purpose Business Ventures." *Health Care Strategic Management,* pp. 17–18.
17. Brinckerhoff, Peter C. (2000). *Social Entrepreneurship: The Arts of Mission-Based Venture Development.* New York: Wiley, pp. 16–21.
18. Van de Hen, Andrew H. (1993). "The Development of an Infrastructure for Entrepreneurship." *Journal of Business Venturing* 8(3): 211–230.
19. Brophy, David J., and Joel M. Shulman (1992). "A Finance Perspective on Entrepreneurial Research." *Entrepreneurship Theory and Practice* 16(3): 61–71.
20. Kuratko, Donald F. and Richard M. Hodgetts (2001). *Entrepreneurship: A Contemporary Approach.* Fort Worth: Harcourt.

21. Shaver, Kelly G., and Linda R. Scott (1991). "Person, Process, Choice: The Psychology of New Venture Creation." *Entrepreneurship Theory and Practice* 16(2): 23–45.
22. Morris (1998), p. 77.
23. Alexis de Tocqueville, ed. J. P. Maier, trans. George Lawrence (1969). *Democracy in America.* Garden City, NY: Anchor Books.
24. Dees, J. Gregory (2001). "The Meaning of 'Social Entrepreneurship.'" Manuscript.
25. Saxenian, AnnaLee (2000). *Silicon Valley's New Immigrant Entrepreneurs.* Center for Comparative Immigration Studies, University of California, San Diego, Working Paper 15.
26. Bird, B. J. (1989). *Entrepreneurial Behavior.* London: Scott, Foresman; Ronstadt, R. C. (1984). *Entrepreneurship: Text, Cases, and Notes.* Dover, MA: Lord Publishing.
27. "Social Enterprise: The New Economic Engine?" *Business Strategy Review* (Winter 2004), pp. 40–43.
28. Barendsen, Lynn, and Howard Gardner (Fall 2004). "Is the Social Entrepreneur a New Type of Leader?" *Leader to Leader,* pp. 43–50.
29. See Morris (1998).
30. Bornstein, David (2005). "In My Opinion." *EBF* 20: 50–51.
31. Waddock, Sandra A., and James E. Post (1991). *Public Administration Review* 51(5): 393–401.
32. Miner, J. B. (1996). *The 4 Routes to Entrepreneurial Success.* San Francisco: Berrett-Kohler Publishers.
33. Franklin, Benjamin (1961). *The Autobiography of Benjamin Franklin.* New York: Signet Classics, p. 82.
34. Egger, Robert (2002). *Begging for Change.* New York: HarperBusiness.
35. Acs, Zoltan J., and Ronnie J. Phillips (2002). "Entrepreneurship and Philanthropy in American Capitalism." *Small Business Economics* 19: 189–204.
36. Vesper, Karl. 1980. *New Venture Strategies.* Englewood Cliffs, NJ: Prentice-Hall.
37. Kirchoff, Bruce A. (June 14, 1993). "A Surprising Finding on New-Business Mortality Rates." *BusinessWeek,* p. 22.
38. Cordes, Joseph J., C. Eugene Steuerle, and Eric C. Twombly (2001). "Dimensions of Nonprofit Entrepreneurship." Manuscript.
39. Overholt, Alison (January 2004). "Social Capitalists: The Top 20 Groups that Are Changing the World." *Fast Company,* p. 52.
40. See www.path.org.
41. This case comes from a dossier in the Manhattan Institute's Social Entrepreneurship Awards program and is used with the Institute's permission.
42. Ross, Dena (2006). "The Best Way to Give." www.beliefnet.com/story/149/story_14919_1.html.
43. www.donorschoose.org, retrieved on 5/23/2007.
44. Ross (2006).
45. Ross (2006).
46. Alter, Jonathan. "Social Entrepreneurship Award Nomination." Material from the Manhattan Institute.

CHAPTER 2

IDEAS AND OPPORTUNITIES

INTRODUCTION

In the previous chapter, you saw that the process of social entrepreneurship begins with the recognition of a social opportunity, and that the hallmark of social entrepreneurs is that they tend to see this opportunity when others only see a tragedy or threat. Consider the following example.

Martha Rollins was a successful entrepreneur in Richmond, Virginia, having started and operated Martha's Mixtures, Ltd., an antique and refinishing business. One of her great areas of personal concern was the incredible disparity in her city between rich and poor, a problem that is typical in many cities. A deeply religious woman, she found in the Bible an idea for how she could create positive change in a poor and crime-ridden section of Richmond called Highland Park. The book of Ruth is the story of a wealthy Israelite, Boaz, who shared his abundance — and ultimately married — Ruth, a poor Moabite woman. Her idea was to find a way that Richmond's "Boaz" communities could assist and be bonded to the "Ruth" that was Highland Park.

To most people in Richmond, Highland Park was a real tragedy from the outside — and a threat to walk through. It had one of the highest violent crime rates in the state, and exceptionally high unemployment levels and drug problems. Once a reasonably prosperous middle-class African American neighborhood, it was, by the late 1990s, an economic and social disaster area, by most estimations. One problem in particular was that the neighborhood had a very high number of unemployed people, who were largely unemployable because few jobs were to be had in the neighborhood, and many had problems with the criminal system in their backgrounds.

It was in this supposed problem that Mrs. Rollins saw an idea for a bold social enterprise. Where others saw a predatory population of potential criminals, she saw excess labor supply, a potential workforce of strong people, and the potential for revitalizing human resources for Highland Park. She conceived of an organization that used these people as apprentices in retail establishments, and in the skilled crafts necessary to revitalize properties in the neighborhood.

In the next chapter, you will learn more about the organization Mrs. Rollins founded in 2002, Boaz & Ruth, and its amazing social rewards. In the meantime, you need to understand better this process of ideas and turning them into opportunities.

THE CREATIVE PROCESS OF SOCIAL ENTREPRENEURSHIP

The process of social entrepreneurship laid out in the first chapter portrayed opportunity recognition as a fairly uncomplicated step: A potential social entrepreneur sees a social problem or unmet need as an opportunity for action. In reality, opportunity recognition is a bit more complicated. Opportunity recognition is worth understanding because it lies at the very beginning of the social entrepreneurship process and, as such, can mean the difference between a successful social enterprise and an unsuccessful one.

Opportunity recognition actually falls at the end of several steps, in which an *idea* becomes the core of social value creation.[1]

1. *Background.* Ideas are not generally immaculately conceived. People who conceive of new ways to create social value must first understand what the unmet needs of a population really are. For example, after the Taliban regime in Afghanistan was overthrown in 2002, it was not clear to average Americans what the needs of the Afghani population were simply from reading news reports. Those best suited to generating ideas on helping the victims of war and years of oppression were people who had first-hand knowledge of life in Afghanistan. People with this knowledge included U.S. aid workers, American military personnel, and journalists.

2. *Creativity.* The necessary background sets the stage for bright ideas, which depend on the creative process of generating ideas and converting them into opportunities. This has two parts.

   a. *Ideas.* The root of an opportunity is a bright idea for something new. For example, one idea for improving living conditions in Afghanistan, conceived at the U.S. Department of Health and Human Services (HHS), was to teach women about healthy childrearing habits. The way to do so, HHS concluded, was with educational materials that could be passed from household to household.

b. *Opportunities.* A useful idea is necessary for a social enterprise to start, but it is insufficient because there must be a willingness and ability of a target population to connect with the idea. That is, an opportunity occurs when there is both supply *and* demand for the idea. The problem with printing reading material about childrearing for Afghani women was that most women in Afghanistan are illiterate—they had been intentionally kept so by the Taliban regime. This meant that the bright idea and its conversion into a useful concept were inhibited by demand: Most Afghani women would be unable to use printed materials. Turning the idea into an opportunity meant thinking in terms of materials useful to women who could not read—in the form of pictures and sounds. (This opportunity later became an enterprise concept when the U.S. government asked toy manufacturers to produce such a device. Leapfrog Enterprises, Inc., produced Leap Pad talking books—a popular learning toy for American children—for Afghani women.)

Figure 2-1 illustrates the process of moving from background, through the creative process from ideas to opportunities.

The distinction between ideas and opportunities is far from academic—on the contrary, it can mean the difference between an idea that meets a demand and one that does not. For example, imagine that HHS had simply stopped with the (good) idea of educating poor Afghanis and introduced reading materials. This would not have met much of a need because the material would have been inaccessible and hence useless. In fact, this is the first major pitfall in the social entrepreneurship process: focusing on supply but not demand—that is, stopping at ideas instead of working all the way through to opportunities.

The nonprofit sector provides many examples of people with big hearts who do not understand this distinction; hence, they work on projects that cannot ultimately come to fruition. In some cases, there is a genuine lack of demand because people truly do not need or want a service. In other cases, a potential social entrepreneur fails to show people why they need a service, so latent demand is never unlocked.

FIGURE 2-1　The Process of Opportunity Recognition

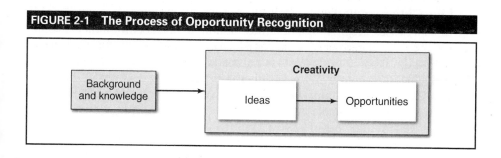

Generating ideas is predicated on having a proper background. This is not limited to a certain type or amount of education (although it may include formal schooling). It also involves experiences, networks of people, and personal attributes. In general, we can break background into two parts: access to information," and utilization of information.

ACCESS TO INFORMATION

Ideas don't materialize out of thin air. The proper background for socially entrepreneurial ideas requires access to information about possible products and services. For example, Martha Rollins did not simply wake up one morning with an idea to soak up unemployed young people in trades and retail professions. She had a background that gave her access to information about how both commercial and nonprofit organizations work.

Access to information can come from many sources, which we can classify into four types: education, work experience, life experience, and social networks.

EDUCATION

Anyone reading a textbook on social entrepreneurship is actively engaged in the process of accessing information on the topic of this book. Formal education is a highly efficient way to provide this kind of access because students are exposed to instructors and materials full of information the students don't already possess. These days, the formal schooling for a social entrepreneur can come in a lot of disciplines: public policy, business administration, law, social work, education, and many others. Each of these fields exposes potential social entrepreneurs to useful information.

WORK EXPERIENCE

Of course, there are some things that formal schooling can't readily teach. Notably, job- or industry-specific skills are not or cannot be translated easily into academic curricula. For example, someone interested in learning about fundraising for Catholic overseas relief organizations would be better advised to seek a job at Catholic Relief Services than in finding these skills in an MBA or MPA program. Many social entrepreneurs spend several years at the beginning of their careers in nonprofit organizations, which is time they view as an "apprenticeship" for the skills they will use in their later endeavors.

LIFE EXPERIENCE

In many cases, access to the best information for social entrepreneurs comes outside both the classroom *and* the workplace—in day-to-day experiences. For example, there is some evidence that traumatic or cathartic life events can provide valuable information. Many social entrepreneurs have served in the Peace Corps in impoverished countries, or come from adverse circumstances. These life experiences provide valuable information on unmet needs and can stimulate the process of generating ideas of a social venture.

SOCIAL NETWORKS

The research shows that successful entrepreneurs tend to have larger-than-average social networks than nonentrepreneurs.[2] This is certainly not coincidental. In fact, social contacts are a key resource for gathering information and "beta-testing" ideas. One scholar calls networks the "most significant resource" of entrepreneurship.[3] Interestingly, researchers have found that the most effective type of network for acquiring information is one that is wider than it is deep; that is, a large group of casual acquaintances is more useful to an entrepreneur than a smaller group of close associates. This is because "weak ties" provide a wider range of experiences because people who are farther apart socially have fewer common experiences.[4] The upshot of this is that aspiring social entrepreneurs do well to cultivate diverse, wide-ranging friendships.

UTILIZATION OF INFORMATION

After social entrepreneurs gain access to information, they have to use it properly to generate the ideas that form the kernel of a social enterprise. Once again, consider Martha Rollins. She had exposure to a lot of information to generate her idea to form Boaz & Ruth, but just as importantly, she was able to use this information effectively.

Knowledge utilization has two components: stocks of knowledge, and cognitive ability.

KNOWLEDGE STOCKS

The ingredients that give you access to information also help you form a stock of information relevant to the generation of social ideas. For example, as education, on-the-job-training, and life experiences expose a person to new information, this information pools, making the person more and more knowledgeable. This is the idea behind a college or graduate curriculum: As a student, you are given access to a lot of different types of knowledge. The curriculum is designed (or is supposed to be designed) in such a way that the classes also have a beneficial effect together—so that you have an integrated knowledge for use in problem-solving. When a difficult job needs to be filled, firms often look for people with a good academic record and lots of varied but relevant job experience because they want the new hire to be able to solve new problems (to him or her) with tools pulled from a stock of prior experiences.

INTELLIGENCE AND ALERTNESS

Knowledge stocks are only useful in utilizing new information if there is appropriate "software" to sort them out. This is where intelligence comes in. I am not talking only about raw cognitive horsepower, or IQ—although studies have shown that successful entrepreneurs tend to score significantly higher on IQ tests than other people.[5] Rather, this is also a question of practical and emotional intelligence, in which some people are naturally likely to make practical choices and to deal well with stress and uncertainty.[6] In addition, research has recently

FIGURE 2-2   The Acquisition and Utilization of Information for Socially Entrepreneurial Ideas

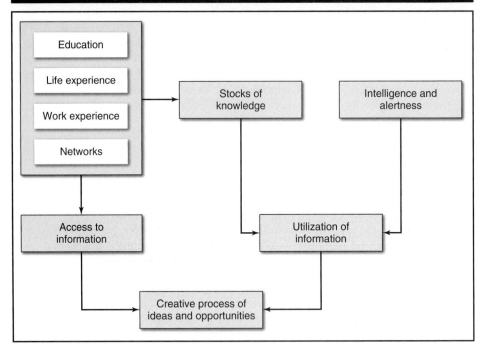

emerged to show clearly that entrepreneurs tend to have an especially acute sense of opportunity, referred to in the literature as "entrepreneurial alertness."[7]

The system of information gathering to generate socially entrepreneurial ideas is summarized in Figure 2-2.

CREATIVITY

Creativity is the generation of ideas that improve the effectiveness of a system. In the case of social entrepreneurship, creativity starts with ideas and culminates in opportunities.

Our stereotypical view of a social entrepreneur's creativity usually involves pure innovation: something from nothing. We find it less intuitive to imagine a social entrepreneur who is *adaptive* instead of innovative. For instance, imagine a school system that drops its arts curriculum because of economic problems. This results in an unmet need. We can easily imagine a social entrepreneur conceiving of a new delivery mechanism for the arts, such as a private nonprofit that uses philanthropic resources to bring music performances and art exhibits back into the schools. However, another kind of idea to solve the problem could be adaptive: to use existing resources in a reconfigured way to reestablish the old programs. For example, a socially entrepreneurial administrator might find a way to use one music teacher in several schools, or integrate the arts into other parts of the curriculum.

Or take the real-life case of the Nehemiah Corporation of America, a non-profit dedicated to helping poor people buy their own homes—an act that has been shown to greatly aid the process of economic mobility.[8] Nehemiah's founder, Don Harris, noticed in 1996 that a slight adaptation of the mortgage system could let whole new classes of people participate in home ownership. What held them back was the down payment, which, for Federal Housing Administration (FHA) loans (which the government makes to poor homebuyers), had to be at least 3 percent of a home's purchase price. Given that the average home seller tends to lower the home's price by at least 3 percent by the time a home is sold, Harris created a system in which sellers effectively paid buyers' FHA down payments (plus a small fee to his agency), in exchange for a firm house price. Nehemiah's social enterprise is fundamentally an adaptive one.

Research shows that entrepreneurial creativity can be manifest in either adaptation or innovation, depending on the problem-solving style of the entrepreneur. One study contrasts the two styles as solving problems either by breaking constraints (innovation) or working within constraints in new ways (adaptation). In the words of one researcher, an innovator "redefines [a] problem by breaking previously defined restraints, aims solutions at 'doing things better.'" In contrast, an adaptor takes a "problem as given and generates[s] ways to develop better solutions for immediate high efficiency."[9] Perhaps not surprisingly, this research shows a natural tension between the two types of entrepreneurs. Innovators see adaptors as "conforming, predictable, and constrained by the system." Adaptors see innovators as "unsound, impractical, risky, dissonance creating, and abrasive."

Research on adaptor-entrepreneurs and innovator-entrepreneurs finds that they naturally gravitate to different tasks.[10] For example, whereas innovators spend the largest percentage of their time (22 percent) on developing new products, adaptors spend the biggest part of their time (45 percent) administering ongoing activities. Clearly these are both important functions. This means that, notwithstanding the tension that tends to exist between innovators and adaptors, a socially entrepreneurial organization usually needs both.

The preceding discussion might make innovation and adaptation sound worlds apart. Yet, in reality, they are simply different ends of the creative spectrum for social entrepreneurship. We can identify various types of entrepreneurial ideas that span this continuum, which is illustrated in Figure 2-3.

- *Invention.* This is the most innovative type of idea: a completely new service or product. For example, a university might establish a brand new program and curriculum for mid-career students.

- *Synthesis.* This combines innovation and adaptation. For example, the university might combine existing programs to create a new executive education curriculum.

- *Extension.* This is the most adaptive type of idea: a new application of an existing product or set of resources. For example, the university might try to serve mid-career students by enticing them to patronize existing course offerings.

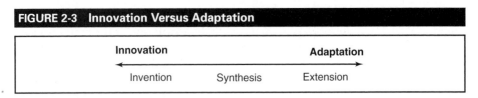

FIGURE 2-3 Innovation Versus Adaptation

IDEAS

Although social entrepreneurs tend to be highly creative individuals, their ideas for social ventures do not just spontaneously occur, as if by magic. For one thing, we have already discussed the importance of having the necessary background to facilitate the creative process. However, there are also techniques for idea generation that most successful social entrepreneurs regularly use. The most common of these are brainstorming, focus groups, and surveys.

BRAINSTORMING

As most of us already know, brainstorming is a process for quick idea generation among a group of people. What is less well-known is that there are a number of established rules to make brainstorming as effective as possible, which can make it useful enough to form a formal part of a social enterprise's growth and planning. First, a brainstorming session should involve a diverse group of people to maximize the variety of ideas generated. Second, it should target a specific topic that is known in advance to the session participants. Third, criticism is not appropriate so as not to inhibit the free flow of ideas. Fourth, the session should maintain a high level of speed so that ideas do not bog down into details. Fifth, a session facilitator should keep a careful record of the session so that no ideas—good or bad—are lost.

FOCUS GROUPS

Because brainstorming usually involves idea generation on the "supply side" of a social enterprise, it is very wise to acquire ideas on the "demand side" as well—among the potential users and clients of a social venture. Focus groups are a good way to get these ideas. Typically, a focus group consists of a few (5–10) people that could have a relationship to a potential enterprise and can thus react to ideas and generate new ones with the perspective of stakeholders. For example, imagine a hospital that is considering the idea of a new program to provide free diabetes screenings to people in poor communities. The right target group for a focus group would be dominated by potential people to be screened, who could be asked to react to various forms and manifestations of the idea. The objective is to gain a sense of the latent demand for some form of a venture. The danger with focus groups is that such a small—and not randomly selected—sample of people can lead to unrepresentative results. This danger can be compounded if the group facilitator has a stake in the group's answers (for example, if the facilitator is asking about his or her own ideas). Focus groups are usually best facilitated by someone with little emotional investment in the ideas.

SURVEYS

In contrast with focus groups, surveys are intended to ensure the representativeness of a target population. As large a group as is feasible, in the population of interest, is asked to answer questions related to the enterprise idea. The survey can be conducted in person, over the phone, or online. For example, a social entrepreneur interested in starting an after-school program for kids might canvass a couple of key neighborhoods, asking the residents a series of questions about their desires and needs for such a program. What surveys gain in accuracy, they pay for in depth, however. For example, in a focus group, an interesting response can be probed, whereas this is not possible in the context of most surveys. One danger in surveys is "nonresponse bias," in which people who do not respond to the survey have an important characteristic in common. (In fact, this is why political polling is frequently so inaccurate: People voting a certain way tend not to answer pollsters.) Online surveys are notoriously inaccurate for this reason because computer skills and access break down fairly clearly on sociodemographic lines.

Generating Direct-Mail Fundraising Ideas

Merkle is a prominent fundraising and nonprofit development firm with offices around the United States and Europe. They are known as the most innovative and creative firm in the field of direct-mail fundraising, and they are responsible for the direct-mail efforts of some of America's most successful nonprofit organizations, including CARE, the Lance Armstrong Foundation, The Nature Conservancy, the American Cancer Society, and Food for the Hungry.[11]

Merkle's approach to idea generation for its clients begins with brainstorming. A fundraising campaign is coordinated by one of Merkle's creative directors, the account director for the client, and a team of writers and designers. Some of the participants are tasked with research on the client, whereas others are brought in with no prior exposure to the account—and hence without any prejudices about what will and will not work for the particular nonprofit.

The group begins with a freewheeling brainstorming session in which all ideas are permissible, and as many new ideas for the campaign are generated as possible. Everything is written down, no matter how improbable the idea. Interestingly, the teams frequently spend the first half hour of these two-hour sessions purposively generating "terrible ideas"—ideas that would have no apparent chance for success based on established wisdom—because the company has found that this exercise generates a surprising amount of useful new material. When the session ends, the participants leave without any clear "winner," just a bundle of possibilities. After the brainstorming session, the creative director and account director look critically at the ideas, selecting the best ones, combining elements between ideas, and further refining them into concrete fundraising plans. Then, they give the resulting one to three campaign concepts to

(continues)

the writers and designers to develop into sample materials, which they present to the client. The client then chooses, makes suggestions, requests changes, or occasionally rejects the ideas altogether (sending the team back to the beginning).

When a campaign is selected, the company sets to work on the finished product for test marketing, which functions like a survey. Generally, the "beta-testing" for a new campaign is done in conjunction with a regular mailing that uses previously established fundraising materials. The test of the new materials might involve 100,000 addresses that are as similar as possible, meaning that they come from the same address lists and the addressees have a lot of demographic similarities (for example, they live in the same region). This group is split in half: 50,000 letters include the test letter (the "test panel"), and 50,000 include the old fundraising materials (the "verification panel"). Using standard statistical techniques, the company compares the response rates and donation rates from these two panels.

In general, Merkle does not rely very heavily on focus groups, having found that focus group participants often contradict test mailing results. Test mailings are more accurate, in their view—and, conveniently, much cheaper than focus groups. One way in which the company *does* find focus groups useful, however, is to ascertain language on specific topics. For example, they have found in recent years that focus group participants have increasingly spoken approvingly of donors "getting bang for their buck" from charities—a phrase they have since incorporated into fundraising materials, with good results.

MOVING FROM IDEAS TO OPPORTUNITIES

The move from ideas to opportunities is essentially a move from supply to demand.[12] The question to ask is: Is the service something people currently want or need, or at least, *potentially* want or need? It is especially critical for social entrepreneurs to answer this question before trying to start the social entrepreneurship process. A handy way to understand the importance of this point—and a tool for guiding the creative process of social entrepreneurship—comes from the work of the famous psychologist Abraham Maslow. Maslow attempted to integrate a large body of knowledge about human motivation and behavior. Prior to his work, most psychologists had viewed behavior from the standpoint of just one dimension, such as biological need or a will to power. Maslow, however, saw human behavior as being motivated by a hierarchy of needs.[13] This hierarchy, from the "lowest" needs through the "highest," is as follows: physiological (hunger, thirst, etc.), safety and security, "belongingness" and love (family and community), self-esteem (achievement and recognition), cognitive and intellectual, aesthetic, self-actualization (self-fulfillment), and self-transcendence (other-focusedness) (see Figure 2-4). According to Maslow, people would not address a higher need until the lower ones were met.

Clearly, every level of Maslow's hierarchy can and does stimulate ideas for social entrepreneurs. Social entrepreneurs focus on feeding the hungry, improving safety, bringing together communities, raising self-esteem, educating, promoting

FIGURE 2-4   Maslow's Pyramid (or Hierarchy of Needs), and Examples of Social Entrepreneurship Potential

Maslow's hierarchy	Example programs that meet different needs
Self-transcendence	Programs to create mentors
Self-actualization	College scholarships
Aesthetic	The arts
Cognitive	Academic programs
Self-esteem	Empowerment programs
Belongingness	Community programs
Safety and security	School and neighborhood safety
Physiological	Proper nutrition

aesthetic experiences, helping people to reach their potential, and teaching people to serve others. The profound implication from Maslow for social entrepreneurs is that social needs or latent social needs that social entrepreneurs can effectively address depend on how and whether lower needs have been met. This helps explain why certain excellent ideas are not viable opportunities and hence not productive social innovations: The target populations are not ready for them. For example, I have met many people who have expressed frustration over the inability to interest poor communities in the arts. According to Maslow, the reason for this inability is not necessarily that taking poor kids to the opera is a stupid idea—it is that the kids have not met their needs up the hierarchy to the point that aesthetic needs are especially salient.

Social entrepreneurs must ask themselves whether the level of their ideas match the level of need in their target communities. To fail to do so is to invite a lack of demand and difficulty in stimulating it.

One way to understand the connection between ideas and opportunities is with what psychologists call Signal Detection Theory.[14] This theory describes the relationship between perception and reality when it comes to opportunity, recognizing that people sometimes see opportunities that are not there or fail to see those that are present. When a person perceives an opportunity that actually exists, this is called a "hit." When someone does not perceive an opportunity that in fact exists, this is a "miss." If the person perceives an opportunity that is actually nonexistent, this is a "false alarm." And when the person does not perceive an opportunity because it does not exist, this is a "correct rejection."[15]

Environmentalism Versus Hunger

Nongovernmental organizations (NGOs) around the developed world have been concerned for decades with environmental degradation in the developing world. NGOs in the United States and Europe have been involved in hundreds of efforts over the years to save the rain forest and various other fragile ecosystems. These can be easy causes to back for most people when the force harming the environment is a multinational petroleum company. The cases have been much harder to make—and thus the causes have been far less successful—when it is poor people themselves who are harming the environment in the course of providing for their day-to-day needs.

One case of this involves the struggle against "desertification," in which overgrazing by livestock increases soil erosion and destroys the ability of lands to support any plant life. In Kenya, for example, NGOs and the Kenyan government throughout the 1970s purposively introduced a plant called prosopis juliflora (also called honey mesquite) to rangelands.[16] This plant established roots very quickly and proved extremely effective at protecting against desertification. Unfortunately, it also lowered the ability of local people—who were overwhelming desperately poor—to support themselves: The plant lowered the supply of drinking water and caused various health problems for livestock and people. Not surprisingly, local people hated the plant and considered it one of the primary culprits for their misery. People have actively fought efforts to introduce it further and have tried to remove it.

Aside from all of the ethical and practical problems this case raises, efforts to introduce honey mesquite to Kenya are a good instance of an idea that was never really a social entrepreneurship opportunity because of a mismatch along Maslow's Pyramid. NGOs were interested in preserving lands for long-term sustainable ranching and protecting habitat as a general principle. Both of these needs were arguably above the ground floor of the hierarchy of needs, while local people were simply worried about staying alive and providing for their families in the very short run. This mismatch is what today has placed the local people in direct opposition to NGOs and the Kenyan government on the issue of honey mesquite and similar plants, making antidesertification enterprises relatively ineffective.

Table 2-1 summarizes the relationship between ideas and opportunities using Signal Detection Theory. When a social entrepreneur has an idea for a venture, and demand (or latent demand) is there, this is a social venture with the potential to succeed. Conversely, an idea for a service people don't want or need is a venture without the potential to succeed. Missed opportunities occur when there is no idea.

TABLE 2-1	The Relationship Between Social Entrepreneurship Ideas and Opportunities	
	Opportunity	*No Opportunity*
Idea	A venture with potential is conceived.	A venture without potential is conceived.
No idea	Missed opportunity.	Correct rejection of an idea.

Table 2-1 suggests that there are several potential strategies for success in beginning the process of social entrepreneurship. First, social entrepreneurs can work on pure idea generation in an effort to maximize the number of hits. Second, they can work on idea discrimination in an effort to minimize the ideas without venture potential. Third, they can search for fruitful areas and then focus on idea generation, in an effort to avoid missed opportunities and stay out of opportunity-poor environments. The research on entrepreneurs suggests that the most successful strategy is one that spends the greatest amount of time on the first and second strategies.[17] That is, successful commercial entrepreneurs—and thus, we can surmise, social entrepreneurs as well—work hard to generate lots of ideas and then scrutinize them as to whether they realistically correspond to opportunities.

SOURCES OF OPPORTUNITIES

What are the main sources of opportunities for social entrepreneurs—that is, the demand and latent demand that can create uptake for a bright idea?

TECHNOLOGICAL CHANGE

We often associate technological change with commercial entrepreneurship—for example, the development of the Internet created an explosion of Web-based products and services. However, technological change also can cultivate the ground for socially entrepreneurial ideas. Consider the case of Howard Dean's bid for the Democratic nomination for president in 2004—a bid largely fueled by a grassroots network linked via the Internet. Dean was a distant contender with relatively little money when his campaign was supercharged by a Web-savvy "Director of Internet Outreach" named Zephyr Teachout, who used a Web tool called Meetup to reach thousands of young, Internet-friendly, politically interested liberals.[18] Meetup is a virtual meeting place, where people with a particular interest find others. Ms. Teachout introduced the idea to mobilize and interconnect Dean supporters, get the word out about campaign events, and fundraise. In fact, as Dean's Internet campaign virtually exploded, the dollars came pouring into his Web site (which accommodated credit card donations): $15 million in the third quarter of 2003 alone, and practically all of it in small sums. This success attracted mainstream press attention, which increased Dean's Meetup popularity still further. The Dean campaign was ultimately unsuccessful in its primary objective but stands as an excellent example of how cutting-edge technology can spur social innovation.

PUBLIC POLICY CHANGES

Changes in public policies can and do stimulate the social entrepreneurship process, as they either create new social needs or make it possible for social entrepreneurs to meet needs in new ways. A good example of this is the federal government's emphasis over the past few years of "faith-based initiatives," services provided by religious organizations with government financial backing. In December 2002, President George W. Bush, fulfilling a campaign promise, issued an executive order guaranteeing the "equal protection of the laws for faith-based and community organizations, to further the national effort to expand opportunities for, and strengthen the capacity of, faith-based and other community organizations so that they may better meet social needs in America's communities, and to ensure the economical and efficient administration and completion of Government contracts." The practical effect of this order was to increase dramatically the amount of government contracts and funding provided to religious nonprofits. Social entrepreneurship followed in quick order as new and existing nonprofits generated ideas to provide services with the new source of revenues.

CHANGES IN PUBLIC OPINION

When the public changes its views in certain areas, it can create a social opportunity. For example, mounting public opposition to a war creates the demand for social entrepreneurs who have the idea to start an antiwar advocacy organization. Or, when public interest increases in improving the performance of the public sector, social entrepreneurs (in government and the nonprofit sector) may have an opportunity to start a movement to "reinvent government." In some cases, social entrepreneurs can help along the public opinion process, creating their own demand. For example, consider Witness, a New York City-based social venture dedicated to filming human rights abuses around the world. Witness broadcasts its videos of gross violations of people's rights on its Web site, which it believes builds popular support for its cause—stimulating political and financial support, and making more work possible.[19]

CHANGES IN TASTES

Similar to public opinion changes, some social innovations become possible because of simple changes in people's tastes. For example, private and public universities find they must change their course and curricular offerings to stay abreast of student wants and needs and continue to keep enrollment up in a highly competitive environment. This can make academic entrepreneurship valuable, as new ideas can lead to innovations that are rewarded with higher application levels and tuition dollars. In many cases, however, changes in taste are "latent," in that a population with certain needs does not exhibit a clear demand for a product or service, but circumstances make it possible that such tastes could be stimulated. For instance, imagine a population in poverty. If the people are starving, a heavy real or latent demand for education and training is not likely. But after the basic needs are met, ideas to introduce human capital innovations might be appropriate.

SOCIAL AND DEMOGRAPHIC CHANGES

In a dynamic society like that in the United States, rapid demographic and social changes are largely the norm rather than the exception. And invariably, they lay the groundwork for social innovations. Take the example of foreign-born immigrants into the United States, the numbers of which have dramatically increased since 1980 (when there were about 14 million immigrants living in the

United States) to the present level of more than 35 million.[20] At least 11 million of these were undocumented (illegal) residents.[21] The single largest group (among both legal and illegal immigrants) is from Mexico, a fact that has led to several interesting socially entrepreneurial ideas. For example, politically conservative groups have noticed Mexican immigrants tend to be family-oriented and religious, leading to efforts to mobilize Mexican-Americans with legal status to naturalize as citizens and vote for conservative politicians. On the other hand, labor unions and various politically liberal organizations have seen the relative poverty of many Mexican immigrants (especially illegal immigrants) as a potential opportunity to launch a renewed workers' rights movement in America.

Summary

- Successfully recognizing a social opportunity is probably the most important part of the social entrepreneurship process. A good opportunity is the seed from which a successful enterprise will grow—or will fail to grow. Attention to this stage can mean the difference between success and failure.
- Opportunity recognition usually requires an appropriate background, which allows the creative process of generating ideas, assessing them critically, and predicting which represent the most promising opportunities.
- Background generally consists of education, life experience, work experience, and personal networks, which provide stocks of knowledge and access to information pertinent to an opportunity. Stocks of knowledge and innate cognitive abilities combine to facilitate the utilization of information.
- Using information, the social entrepreneur generates ideas, which may involve an adaptation or an innovation. Ideas are often generated using brainstorming sessions, focus groups, and surveys.
- An idea is not an opportunity. An opportunity signifies an idea that meets real or latent demand for a particular good or service. The most common reason that social ventures fail is that an entrepreneur attempts to develop an enterprise around an idea where the opportunity is absent.
- Opportunities to meet a social need can exist if "lower-order needs" are met first. Maslow's Pyramid is one way to conceive of the hierarchy of needs that exists in communities.
- Opportunities flow from a number of sources, including changes in technology, public policy, public opinion, public tastes, and demographics.

Key Terms

- Maslow's Pyramid
- creativity
- innovation
- adaptation
- brainstorming
- focus groups
- opportunity recognition
- Signal Detection Theory

End-of-Chapter Questions and Cases

RUBICON PROGRAMS, INC.

Rubicon Programs, Inc., is a California Bay-area nonprofit started in 1973 in response to California's large-scale closing of psychiatric hospitals and the resulting flow of patients into communities. Here is Rubicon's mission statement:

> Rubicon Programs' mission is to create and deliver integrated solutions to profound social problems.
>
> Our purpose is to make a positive and lasting impact on people living in poverty and on people living with disabilities, especially psychiatric disabilities. We empower people to move out of poverty and improve their quality of life.[22]

Rubicon specialized in providing vulnerable populations with job training and life skills, so that they would be able to enter society successfully, not as welfare recipients, but as wage-earners. Many of their clients work in one of the organization's two enterprises, Rubicon Bakery and Rubicon Landscaping Services, which are intended to serve not just as a training ground for clients but also as a source of earned revenues.

Imagine that Rubicon is contemplating an expansion to a new earned-income venture: data-entry for local governments, in response to a statewide mandate to contract out these services. You are in charge of the team to develop this idea and determine whether it is a viable market opportunity.

1. What background would you need on your team to properly develop this idea?
2. Is this new venture idea an adaptive social enterprise or an innovation? Both? Explain.
3. Where in Maslow's hierarchy would you place this idea? What needs must have been met previously with the clients to make the new venture a potentially successful idea?
4. What is the source of this opportunity?

CO-ABODE

As a business women and artist throughout her professional career, Carmel Sullivan was able to put her entrepreneurial skills to work as she discovered an unmet social need as an opportunity for action.[23] It was through an unexpected life experience that she decided to start a nonprofit organization. After her sudden divorce, she felt isolated and overwhelmed with the responsibilities of being a single parent. In an attempt to find some relief, she searched for a roommate, preferably a single mother like herself. She quickly found that there was no service to help single mothers find housing companions, so she placed her own ad and eventually found a match. This gave her the idea to help other single mothers who were in the same situation.[24] She found that there were 14 million single mothers throughout the United States who were struggling financially and emotionally.[25] Carmel thought that finances were the key motivation in single parents wanting to live together, but isolation and loneliness were the reason.[26]

Her background and knowledge, combined with her creativity, allowed her to turn her idea into an opportunity and set her up to become a successful social entrepreneur. She quickly took advantage of this opportunity by using her personal experiences, business expertise, and creativity to create a business plan. Shortly after that, she hired a designer to create a Web site, and Co-abode was launched in 2001. The organization is Web-based and dedicated to helping single mothers find roommates through posted profiles. Single mothers become members of the organization by completing an extensive questionnaire and by giving a minimal donation to help maintain the Web site.

Carmel Sullivan believes in "the idea of community support for families" and that is exactly what Co-abode provides. It gives single mothers "the opportunity to afford a better house or apartment within a safer school district; it halves the cost of rent and overhead expenses, freeing up much needed resources; it lightens the burden of daily chores so that moms are less tired and stressed out and better able to provide for their children and themselves; it allows divorced moms to hang on to the family home by bringing a mom roommate to help cover expenses; and it gives those in abusive situations support and strength so they can escape, knowing there is another mom there to pool resources with and get emotional support." Not only does Co-abode build stronger families, but it also extends beyond the home and builds stronger communities. Today, Co-abode has nearly 20,000 members throughout communities nationwide. These communities benefit by gaining social capital through the trust and relationships that are created through Co-abode.

1. Is Co-abode an innovation or adaptation, or a combination of both? Explain.
2. What are potential threats to this organization, and how can they be resolved?
3. How does the idea of Co-abode fit into Maslow's hierarchy of needs?

End Notes

1. Baron, Robert A., and Scott A. Shane (2005). *Entrepreneurship: A Process Perspective*. Mason, OH: South-Western.
2. Singh, R. P., G. E. Hills, R. C. Hybels, and G. T. Lumpkin. (1999). "Opportunity recognition through social network characteristics in entrepreneurship," paper presented at the 1999 Babson College Conference on Entrepreneurship Research, Columbia, SC.
3. Johannisson, B. (1990). "Economics of Overview—Guiding the External Growth of Small Firms." *International Small Business Journal* 9: 32–44. Quote: p. 41.
4. Granovetter, M. (1973). "The Strength of Weak Ties." *American Journal of Sociology* 78(6): 1360–1380.
5. van Praag, C. M, and J. S. Cramer (2005). "The Roots of Entrepreneurship and Labour Demand: Individual Ability and Low Risk Aversion." *Economica* 68(269): 45–62.
6. Sternberg, R. J., and E. L. Grigorenko (2000). *Practical Intelligence in Everyday Life*. New York: Cambridge University Press.

7. Gaglio, Connie Marie, and Jerome A. Katz (2001). "The Psychological Basis of Opportunity Identification: Entrepreneurial Alertness." *Small Business Economics* 16(2): 95–111.
8. See www.nehemiahcorp.org. Also, Warner, Fara, (November 2001). "Social Entrepreneur: Don Harris." *Fast Company* 52, p. 150.
9. Kirton, Michael (1976). "Adaptors and Innovators: A Description and Measure." *Journal of Applied Psychology* 61: 622–629.
10. Buttner, E. Holly, and Nur Gryskiewicz (1993). "Entrepreneurs' problem-solving styles: an empirical study using the Kirton adaption/innovation theory." *Journal of Small Business Management* 31(1): 22–31.
11. This section follows an interview with Jeff Brooks, creative director for Merkle.
12. For another model of the connection between ideas and opportunities, see Guclu, Ayse, J. Gregory Dees, and Beth Battle Anderson. "The Process of Social Entrepreneurship: Creating Opportunities Worthy of Serious Pursuit." Center for the Advancement of Social Entrepreneurship, working paper, 2002.
13. Maslow, Abraham (1943). A theory of human motivation. *Psychological Review 50*, 370–396.
14. Swets, John A. (1992). "The science of choosing the right decision threshold in high-stakes diagnostics." *American Psychologist* 47(4): 522–532.
15. This terminology follows Baron and Shane (2005), p. 71.
16. Aboud, Abdillahi A., Philip K. Kisoyan, and D. Layne Coppock (December 2005). "Agro-Pastoralists' Wrath for the Prosopis Tree: The Case of Il Chamus of Baringo District, Kenya." *Global Livestock Collaborative Research Support Program* Research Brief 05-02-PARIMA.
17. Baron and Shane (2005) summarize this literature nicely.
18. Wolf, Gary (January 2004). "How the Internet Invented Howard Dean." *Wired* 12(1).
19. See www.witness.org.
20. Camarota, Steven A. (2002). "Immigrants in the United States—2002." Washington, DC: Center for Immigration Studies.
21. Passel, Jeffrey S. (2006). "Size and Characteristics of the Unauthorized Migrant Population in the U.S." Washington, DC: Pew Hispanic Center.
22. See www.rubiconprograms.org/about.html.
23. This case comes from a dossier in the Manhattan Institute's Social Entrepreneurship Awards program and is used with the Institute's permission. Data on the organization and quotes are also taken from its Web site: www.co-abode.com.
24. Taylor, Jonathan R. "Creative Income from Your Hobby." http://careers.articlesarchive.net/creative-income-from-your-hobby.html.
25. Miller, Dan "Passions into Profits." http://48days.faithsite.com/content.asp?CID=17344.
26. Rhule, Patty (April 2002). "Single moms double up to establish new lives." *USA Today*.

CHAPTER 3

DEVELOPING THE SOCIAL ENTERPRISE CONCEPT

INTRODUCTION

In the previous chapter, we met Martha Rollins, founder of Boaz & Ruth, the nonprofit in Richmond, Virginia. After the idea for the organization had been, in Mrs. Rollins' words, "thoughtfully discussed and organized for many years," Boaz & Ruth began to take shape.

The enterprise concept was laid out in the organization's mission—actually, its *missions*.

> The three major missions of the program are 1) to provide job training, life skills, emotional competencies, and entrepreneurship opportunities for individuals seeking to move beyond poverty; 2) to serve as an economic catalyst to the severely depressed Highland Park commercial district; and 3) to provide an opportunity for all residents of Richmond to cross economic, cultural, and geographic divisions that characterize our city. A common thread in all of these missions is our beliefs that change comes best in the context of relationships rather than just with instruction.[1]

Of course, each part of Boaz & Ruth's mission is easier said than done. Mrs. Rollins and her collaborators needed business models for each task, and they met with inevitable difficulties. This chapter deals with the development of a social enterprise—the third step in the process of social entrepreneurship. This begins with the mission that describes the opportunity, envisions the venture, and shapes its development; proceeds with a viable business model; and then describes the mission and model in a business plan for others to see.

THE SOCIAL ENTERPRISE MISSION

The first objective in developing a social enterprise concept involves communication: describing the enterprise in a way that others can understand it and get behind the concept. This is not as straightforward as it sounds. How many times have you heard someone's "bright idea" and were unable to follow it? Ideally, social entrepreneurs are able to express their concept clearly and succinctly, in such a way that anybody can comprehend what the enterprise will do, how it is entrepreneurial, and why it is important. In addition, social entrepreneurs must be able to express what the enterprise is *not,* how they will measure value, and how to know if the enterprise is successful. Altogether, this information constitutes a *social enterprise mission.*

Social entrepreneurs often skip the step of constructing a mission statement at the start of the business planning process. This is a mistake, for two reasons. First, a mission statement focuses social entrepreneurs on what they intend to accomplish and how to measure progress toward the stated goal. A lack of focus in the early stages of a social enterprise is obviously detrimental to the project's likelihood of success. Second, a mission statement provides a marketing tool to bring other interested parties into the enterprise. For example, volunteers and donors are unlikely to support a speculative venture that inadequately expresses its objectives, needs, or success criteria. Even people who might be served by a social venture often need a clear statement of mission if they are to see how it will provide them with social value.

After a social opportunity is positively identified, the next step for social entrepreneurs should be to write a mission statement. The criteria for doing so—or for judging the quality of one that has already been written, for that matter—can be summarized with the following list of questions.

1. What will the enterprise do, and what will it not do?
2. What does "value" mean for this enterprise, and how is it measured?
3. What is this enterprise's unique innovation or adaptation?
4. What constitutes "success" for this enterprise?

Consider the following mission statement for an organization that connects college students in mentoring relationships with low-income inner-city youths:

> The XYZ organization's mission is to provide youths from low-income neighborhoods with the academic skills and learning opportunities they need to succeed and to provide college students with the opportunity to understand and help meet those needs to promote their own development as leaders.

First, this mission statement is successful in describing more or less what the enterprise does, but it says nothing about what it does not do because the service is vague. Second, it does suggest a measure of the social value it creates: at-risk kids mentored and college students involved. Third, it gives no indication of whether the organization is innovative, or how so. Finally, the only definition of success in this statement is meeting the needs of all low-income youths, a goal that is probably unworkable.

If the XYZ organization seeks to portray itself as socially entrepreneurial—and it actually is so—it might rewrite its mission as follows, building on its original strengths and adding the necessary elements:

> The XYZ organization provides low-income youths with the academic skills they need to succeed in life and gives college students the opportunity develop their leadership abilities. The first program of its kind in New York City, XYZ matches at-risk kids with students from local universities who mentor them in basic academics and provide real-life role models of academic success. Our goal, while reaching as many young people as possible, is to create a model for learning and teaching that others will emulate in New York and across America.

While maintaining a manageable length, this mission is specific about what XYZ does (thus bounding it from what it doesn't do). It maintains the original statement's definition and implied measures of social value. The mission states explicitly that the organization's model is an innovation in its area of operation, and it defines success in terms of replication of its enterprise model.

CASE: Ave Maria School of Law

Ave Maria School of Law was founded in 1999 through the generosity of philanthropist Tom Monaghan (founder of Domino's Pizza and former owner of the Detroit Tigers) in collaboration with Bernard Dobranski, then Dean of Catholic University Law School and now President and Dean of Ave Maria. The AMSL project from the beginning has been supported by the Ave Maria Foundation, which has provided the necessary financial assistance for the building and staffing of AMSL. The mission statement for AMSL follows:

Ave Maria School of Law is a Catholic law school dedicated to educating lawyers with the finest professional skills. Inspired by Pope John Paul II's encyclical *Fides et Ratio,* Ave Maria School of Law offers a distinctive legal education—an education characterized by the harmony of faith and reason. Formed by outstanding professional training and a distinctive educational philosophy, Ave Maria's graduates are equipped for leading positions in law firms, corporate legal offices, the judiciary, and national, state, and local government.

Ave Maria School of Law offers an outstanding legal education in fidelity to the Catholic Faith as expressed through Sacred Tradition, Sacred Scripture, and the teaching authority of the Church. University legal education began in Catholic universities, and Catholic law schools have been the bearers of a tradition that safeguards the dignity of the human person and the common good. Ave Maria School of Law affirms Catholic legal education's traditional emphasis on the only secure foundation for human freedom—the natural law written on the heart of every human being. We affirm the need for society to rediscover those human and moral truths that flow from the nature of the human person and that safeguard human freedom.[2]

(continues)

AMSL's mission statement is an excellent example of a social opportunity, manifest in the philanthropic support it received and the immediate uptake among law students (77 of which entered in the first class in 2000). Its mission statement is particularly effective in expressing the enterprise's functions, concept of value and how it is measured, its idea of innovation, and definition of success. Notice the following points about the mission statement:

1. *What will the enterprise do, and what will it not do?* AMSL's plan was to educate lawyers in the Catholic tradition, and it would not deviate from Catholic understanding of Natural Law.

2. *What does "value" mean for this enterprise, and how is it measured?* Value was measured in the spiritual and career success of its graduates.

3. *What is this enterprise's unique innovation or adaptation?* AMSL's unique innovation was a return to classic Catholic legal education, as outlined in Pope John Paul II's encyclical *Fides et Ratio*.

4. *What constitutes "success" for this enterprise?* Success, for AMSL, was determined by fidelity to Catholic principles while graduates received an education that positioned them for top careers in the private and public sectors.

BUSINESS MODELS

After the social mission is defined, expressed, and refined, it is time to formulate a business model. A *business model* is a blueprint for how an organization intends to create value. It is a tangible outline of how the mission will be put into action. As such, it is as important as the mission itself for making a social entrepreneur's opportunity an operational social venture.

The idea of a business model comes from the social sciences, in which complex phenomena are analyzed: Social forces are theorized to function using a model, which is then manipulated to test "what if" questions. Business models in general, including those for social enterprises, follow this same idea. They include the mission, a schema of the operating idea and how its parts link together, and a brief description of the whole venture. A business model usually has four specific components.[3]

- *The core mission.* This is the mission statement, discussed in the preceding section. It includes a brief summary of the organization's activities, definition of value, goals and measures of success, and how the enterprise is innovative or adaptive.

- *Strategic resources.* This is a description of how a social venture acquires its resources, including an idea of its fundraising and earned revenue strategies. It also includes a list of the enterprise's unique competencies and strategic assets.

- *Partnership network.* As subsequent chapters will show in detail, social enterprises do not develop in a vacuum. Social entrepreneurs need partnerships, and the business model must make these partnerships explicit. The network includes donors, volunteers, governments, suppliers, and enterprise collaborators.

- *Service interface.* This is a description of how the enterprise connects with its beneficiaries—those for whom the venture is intended to create value. These beneficiaries include the target clientele, of course, but also the community, staff, donors, and volunteers—all of whom receive positive nonfinancial benefits from their association with the enterprise.

Consider the business model of Boaz & Ruth, which is summarized in the schema in Figure 3-1, whose core mission opened this chapter. Boaz & Ruth's strategic resources include private donations, volunteer time, and support from government. In addition, a major strategic asset is the personal expertise, enthusiasm, and business background of the founder, Martha Rollins. Together, these resources allow the organization to place former inmates in life training and job training programs, and then use their human capital and labor to establish viable commercial enterprises. The partnership network includes local foundations, Richmond residents inside and outside Highland Park, local businesses, and government officials. Together, Boaz & Ruth, with its network, produces benefits for its clients (who are rehabilitated), its community (which is developed), and those providing support (who are enriched).

THREATS TO THE BUSINESS MODEL

There are two major threats to the viability of social enterprise business models. The first was outlined in the previous chapter: an idea that is not an opportunity—or at least, a latent opportunity. The second is financial infeasibility due to costs that cannot be covered from fees, donations, or other forms of subsidy (such as from the government). In other words, threats to the business model can come from the "demand side" or the "supply side."

FIGURE 3-1   Business Model Schema for Boaz & Ruth, Inc.

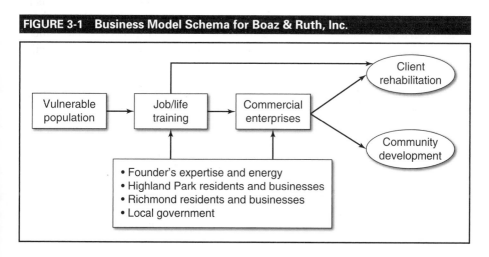

An example of a demand-side failure is any product that people—clients and donors, more specifically—simply do not want. Furthermore, adequate information about the product will not change their minds. This is not an assertion about product quality or the intrinsic value of a service. Many high-quality, high-value ventures exist without any clients or donors. Unfortunately, without clients and donors, they will not be successful.

A supply-side failure is one that might well garner good amounts of revenue but is too expensive to operate on an ongoing basis. This is most often the case for enterprises that are capital-intensive; for example, building projects by organizations without a long track record of fundraising. Once again, this is not to say that supply-side failure indicates terrible ideas—just ideas that do not exist with the range of economic feasibility.

CASE: The Failure of Eastside Neighborhood Arts, Culture, and Technology

In 1996, community activists in Syracuse, New York launched a bold enterprise to transform—they hoped—a run-down section of east Syracuse. The neighborhood, full of turn-of-the-century homes, was once one of Syracuse's most prosperous neighborhoods. At its center stood a massive Victorian mansion built in 1895, known as the Babcock-Shattuck House. For decades, the house had been used as a meeting place for Jewish war veterans. Over the 1970s and 1980s, however, the house fell into disrepair as the neighborhood deteriorated into drugs and crime. In 1996, a local developer sought to demolish the house.

Seizing on the house's historical significance as an opportunity to stimulate the neighborhood's revitalization, a local nonprofit dedicated to affordable housing, Eastside Neighbors in Partnership (ENIP), purchased the house with funds from local lenders. ENIP planned to renovate and convert the house into an arts, culture, and technology center for local youths. They erected a sign out front announcing the future site of ENACT: Eastside Neighborhood Arts, Culture, and Technology.

ENACT was widely reported in the press, and its organizers expected ample support both from the neighborhood's (mostly poor) residents and local donors. Sadly, neither materialized, and after spending tens of thousands of dollars on initial renovations, the project stalled—the house decaying still further and creating a greater blight on the neighborhood than it had been even before the project began. In September 2005, the parent nonprofit itself (ENIP) laid off its staff, dismissed its volunteers, canceled its projects, and closed shop.

What happened to ENACT? On the demand side, ENIP never went through the steps outlined in the previous chapter on assuring that an idea is an authentic opportunity: There was no apparent evidence that the idea was an authentic opportunity. On the supply side, it proved too difficult to raise sufficient funds to finance such a capital-rich project in a relatively impoverished area. ENACT's budget called for $1.3 million to get the center up and running; ENIP only ever raised a small fraction of this amount.

There is nothing in this case to suggest that ENACT's failure was inevitable. Most notably, more aggressive marketing to local residents and creative fundraising might have made the project feasible. But given the efforts actually undertaken, ENACT represented a failed business model on both the demand side and the supply side.[4]

Cases such as ENACT are relatively few and far between because quick exits don't leave much of a trail. But flame-outs are real. According to the nonprofit management consulting firm Fuse, 80 percent of nonprofits fail within their first five years of operation. Furthermore, they find that a lack of "reliable and predictable income" most strongly predicts this failure.[5] Clearly, a lack of income to cover costs can be either a supply-side problem (if costs are too high) or a demand-side issue (if revenues are too low). Either way, the first place to look in understanding the failure is a flawed business model.

Summary

- The mission statement of a social enterprise should express the enterprise idea clearly and succinctly. It should answer four questions: What will the enterprise do, and what will it not do? What does "value" mean for this enterprise, and how is it measured? What is this enterprise's unique innovation or adaptation? What constitutes "success" for this enterprise?
- The business model is a blueprint for how the enterprise intends to create value. It is a tangible outline of how the mission will be put into action.
- The business model has four parts: the core mission, the enterprise's strategic resources, the partnership network, and the enterprise's service interface.
- The majority of nonprofits fail within their first five years of operation. Failure is typically due to a lack of income to cover costs. This can be either a supply-side problem (if costs are too high) or a demand-side issue (if revenues are too low).

Key Terms

- social enterprise mission
- business model
- core mission
- strategic resources
- partnership network
- service interface

End-of-Chapter Questions and Cases

FOOD AND AGRICULTURE ORGANIZATION

Deforestation—the clearing of forests across the Earth—has emerged as a leading environmental problem over the past three decades. In countries in all of the continents besides Antarctica, human populations have cut deeply into forested regions for logging, urbanization, cattle grazing, and farming. The Food and Agriculture Organization (FAO) estimates that 53,000 square miles of tropical forests (rain forest and other) were destroyed each year during the 1980s.[6] Today, 500,000 hectares vanish every week around the world.[7] If the current rate of deforestation continues, the world's rain forests will vanish within 100 years, causing unknown effects on global climate and eliminating the majority of plant and animal species on the planet.[8]

You and several partners are planning to start an enterprise dedicated to replanting indigenous trees in a previously deforested region in southern Mexico.

1. Create a business model for your enterprise.
    a. Write a version of your organization's mission statement.
    b. What are your enterprise's strategic resources?
    c. Describe the enterprise's partnership network.
    d. Describe your enterprise's service interface.
2. Depict a schema of your business model graphically.

CHILDREN FOR CHILDREN FOUNDATION

In 1996, Silda Wall and husband, Eliot Spitzer, wanted to create a way to get children more involved in New York City communities.[9] They felt there was a growing lack of responsibility and giving in young people. As they discussed their concerns with other parents, they found that a large number of parents felt the same way.[10] Shortly after, this group of parents established the Children for Children Foundation, a nonprofit organization with a mission "to promote hands-on youth volunteering and giving programs that teach and instill the value of community involvement and civic engagement in children from all backgrounds beginning at a young age, with an emphasis on providing resources to underserved schools."[11]

Children for Children has involved thousands of New York City children and families of all different backgrounds in giving their time and resources. In its first decade, over a million dollars in funds had been raised to benefit more than 120,000 New York school children, and from 1999 to 2004, the number of youth volunteer hours increased from 180 to 7,394.

The service interface—how Children for Children connects with its beneficiaries—has been established through a variety of programs. These programs are run after school or during out-of-school hours. Even though they focus on serving underprivileged children and their schools, they also serve other populations, such as the disabled.[12] There are a variety of ways in which children can get involved. They can pick one of the many Children for Children programs, or they can go to the Children for Children Web site and join an online community of youth volunteer opportunities that are posted from organizations throughout New York City.

Specific programs sponsored by Children for Children include the Children's Action Board, which enables children to volunteer in other schools; and the Grow Involved Kit Making Program, which allows children to pot flower bulbs and distribute them to nonprofits such as nursing homes. The organization also distributes grants to schools and educators in need. These are just a few examples of how Children to Children reaches out to the community and benefits both the volunteers and the recipients of their generosity.

Of course, to make this all possible, strategic resources are needed. As a nonprofit organization, Children for Children depends on the support of individuals, foundations, and corporations to fund their work. There is no funding from the government. In addition to the financial support, partnership networks are essential to the success of Children for Children. There are 33 volunteers on the Board of Directors, as well as 10 members of the Advisory Board. There are also 8 staff members and 3 Americorps–Vista volunteers working for the organization.[13] Children for Children has thousands of volunteers and donors who also make their programs possible.

1. Based on the four questions that a mission statement should answer, how might Children for Children's mission statement be restated?
2. What are the threats to the business model?
3. What nonprofit partnerships might add to the success of Children for Children?

End Notes

1. See www.boazandruth.com/content.cfm?sec=1&c=0&mpath=2.
2. See http://avemarialaw.edu/home.cfm.
3. Barringer and Ireland provide a similar framework for for-profit enterprises. See Barringer, Bruce, and D. Ireland (2006). *Entrepreneurship: Successfully Launching New Ventures*. Upper Saddle River, NJ: Pearson, p. 108.
4. See Hennessy-Fiske, Molly (December 29, 2005). "Feds Probe East Side Group." *Syracuse Post-Standard*, p. A1; Moses, Sara (September 9, 2005). "City Housing Agency Closes." *Syracuse Post-Standard*, p. B1.
5. www.fuseonline.com/insight.html.
6. http://earthobservatory.nasa.gov/Library/Deforestation.
7. Brown, Katrina, and David W. Pearce. *The Causes of Tropical Deforestation*. Vancouver: UCB Press, 1994.
8. http://earthobservatory.nasa.gov/Library/Deforestation.
9. This case comes from a dossier in the Manhattan Institute's Social Entrepreneurship Awards program and is used with the Institute's permission.
10. Avakian, Monique (March 1998). "Beyond Bake Sales: How Children for Children Improves New York City Schools." *New York Family*.
11. See www.childrenforchildren.org.
12. (July 26, 2006). "Queens Youngsters Can Volunteer This Summer." *The Queens Gazette*.
13. www.childrenforchildren.org.

CHAPTER 4

SOCIAL ENTERPRISE BUSINESS PLANS

INTRODUCTION

The business model described in the previous chapter is the internal blueprint for an enterprise. However, the social entrepreneur needs a way to represent the venture to the outside world as well. The tool for doing this is the *business plan,* which is a document detailing the enterprise. The tendency for social entrepreneurs is to believe they can best express a venture in person, with all the enthusiasm and optimism that stimulated the enterprise in the first place. However, this is a mistake. First, a formal business plan is necessary to cover adequately all the details necessary for key stakeholders to understand the venture as well (or almost as well) as the entrepreneur. Second, it gives the entrepreneur greater reach, in that it can be widely disseminated. Third, it motivates people involved in the venture by summarizing the ideas, opportunities, goals, and objectives. Finally, it forces the social entrepreneur to tie up all of the enterprise's loose ends before launching the venture.

The business plan, therefore, has two kinds of audiences, external and internal. These audiences include several key groups.

External audiences:

- *Actual and potential funders.* These people need full information on a social venture, just as investors do for a commercial enterprise. The business plan provides this information.
- *Government officials.* In the case of enterprises that seek to collaborate with the government or want government support, policy officials are an important consumer of the business plan.

- *The community.* Although a business plan is rarely disseminated to a community-at-large, community leaders and representatives can be important allies (or adversaries), and a business plan can and should be at their disposal. Given the social nature of returns, it is an easy case to make that the community is a true stakeholder in a social venture.

Internal audiences:

- *The social entrepreneur.* The business plan clarifies and codifies all of the most important elements of the enterprise, uncovering rough spots and weak points before they have a chance to impact the venture negatively.
- *Actual and potential staff and volunteers.* People working for a social enterprise—whether they are paid with money or not—are investors of time and energy, and should be treated like the investors in any endeavor. This means they have access to the business plan.
- *Board members.* Nonprofit boards in the United States and many other countries are vested with the legal and moral responsibility to make nonprofits serve the public's interests and use resources wisely. Before responsible persons can make a rational decision to serve on a board, they should read the business plan.

Many authors have listed and described the ingredients of an actual business plan, and a number of excellent texts actually give sample plans.[1] Almost all of the plan descriptions are similar, and list these ingredients:

1. Business plan summary
2. Description of the enterprise
3. The team
4. The market and industry
5. Marketing and fundraising
6. The financial plan
7. Goals and objectives, with a timeline
8. Risk assessment
9. Supporting documents

THE BUSINESS PLAN SUMMARY

This is an abstract of the whole plan that is generally a page or so and answers only the key questions:

- What is the venture?
- Why is it new and important?
- Who will benefit from it, and how?
- How (in general terms) will the idea be executed?

- Who is the social entrepreneur, and what unique skill, service, or background does this person bring to the venture?
- What kind of support for the enterprise is needed, and how much of it?
- What will constitute success?

The summary is the first part of the business plan. As a general rule, however, it is written last, after the other parts.

DESCRIPTION OF THE ENTERPRISE

The main body of the business plan contains the most important information for both the social entrepreneur and the stakeholders. This includes the following elements:

1. *The idea, and why it is an authentic opportunity.* This is the social entrepreneur's chance to make the case that this bright idea can meet an actual or latent social need. This means explaining the genesis of the idea and justifying the claim that it represents an actual opportunity. This is an appropriate time to introduce some details on the data that were used to convince the entrepreneur that the idea is viable.

2. *The mission statement.* This is the place to include the enterprise's mission statement, which bounds the organization, outlines the concept of value, points out the venture's innovation, and defines success.

3. *Definition of value, and how it is to be measured.* After mentioning value in the mission statement, this is the place to develop the definition. List the dimensions of value (financial and nonfinancial), and justify why each is important. Then, using the tools provided in the next chapter on Social Return on Investment (SROI), describe the method for assessing value.

4. *Key innovations or adaptations.* This section gives more detail on how and why the enterprise is an innovation or adaptation that uniquely creates the value described in the previous chapter.

5. *Competitive advantage.* Competition is a subject frequently misunderstood in the social entrepreneurship world. A social venture rarely faces the type of tough market competition that commercial organizations do because the purely financial incentives are not usually present. However, it is not true that competition is absent. On the contrary, competition can be fierce on two dimensions, and both should be made explicit in the business plan.

   a. *Prizes.* Social enterprises rely on donated resources and fees, as well as, sometimes, grants from the government. Generally, there are multiple claimants for these prizes. The business plan should be specific about the support it seeks and the competition for this support.

   b. *Inaction.* The most potent competition that many social enterprises face when it comes to serving clients is inaction on clients' parts. For example, a

---

First Book Marketplace

First Book is a nonprofit founded in 1992 to help poor children own their own books. Since that time, the organization has distributed more than 40 million books nationwide in communities across the United States. In 2004, the organization started a new enterprise called First Book Marketplace to help nonprofits and government agencies acquire books for kids in their communities at a low price.[2]

Here is how the First Book Marketplace business plan summarized the evidence that this idea was an authentic opportunity:

> In July 2004, First Book (FB) quietly launched a pilot of the First Book Marketplace. The pilot has exceeded expectation, generating over $366,000 in sales of 209,000 books to 320 programs. Registration, processing, ordering, and fulfillment were accomplished, and no substantial challenges have arisen.

---

public health clinic does not usually fight other clinics for patients in poor neighborhoods, but rather the tendency of some people who could use services not to seek them. This principle holds for most other parts of the nonprofit and voluntary sector, and social entrepreneurs must explain how they will actively combat it.

6. *The social enterprise's legal structure.* This is a brief description of the venture's legal designation. For example, will the enterprise be a purely voluntary organization, or will it incorporate as a 501(c)(3) nonprofit? The more formal the legal designation of the enterprise, the more detail is necessary in the business plan to show supporters that the social entrepreneur is familiar with the requirements under the law.

7. *Current status of enterprise.* Where is this venture in its planned development? Here, it is necessary to show a trajectory toward the social entrepreneur's goals for the venture.

THE TEAM

Now the social entrepreneur demonstrates that there is a qualified, competent, enthusiastic team in charge of his or her enterprise. This team includes, but is not limited to, four groups:

1. *Management.* Who will run the organization from day to day? In most cases, this is the social entrepreneur but often with the assistance of others. Describe the management team's qualifications and experience, focusing in particular on the education, work experience, life experience, and networks covered in the previous chapter.

2. *Board.* If the enterprise is organized as a nonprofit, it is necessary in the United States and most other countries to assemble a Board of Directors. But beyond legalities, a Board is generally a good thing to have because it provides an opportunity for the social entrepreneur to bring respected leaders

---

Brooklyn Justice Counsel

The Brooklyn AIDS Task Force is a "nonprofit, multi-ethnic, community service program dedicated to providing the HIV-infected and affected individuals of Brooklyn with culturally sensitive HIV/AIDS prevention education, comprehensive social services, and extensive community advocacy."[3] In 2003, the organization launched the Brooklyn Justice Counsel (BJC) to provide low-cost legal services to HIV/AIDS organizations.

BJC's business plan introduced the director, Carol Horwitz, with this description of her background and qualifications:

> Carol Horwitz was hired to direct BJC after managing the feasibility study that yielded BJC and serving as legal counsel and providing technical assistance to and through BATF . . . and other supporting organizations. Along with more than 25 years of legal experience and 15 years of legal supervision and management experience, Ms. Horwitz brings focused expertise in nonprofit legal assistance and securing government benefits. She has received awards for her legal work with HIV/AIDS organizations and legal advocacy. She is also a resident of Brooklyn and brings extensive professional ties to organizations in BJC's target market and to law firms, legal assistance organizations, law schools, and clinics in New York City. (See Appendix One for Ms. Horwitz's resume.)

---

into the venture. Many authors have written about nonprofit Boards, and the consensus is that Board members should be selected with the idea that they can provide one or more of the following services:[4]

- Overseeing the enterprise
- Performing administrative functions
- Lending expertise
- Giving and fundraising
- Enhancing the enterprise's image

This part of the business plan lists the Board's membership and describes its collective background and experience.

3. *Advisors.* A viable social enterprise has advisors that go well beyond the legal Board. This is the place to list the people who give the enterprise guidance.

4. *Early donors.* Ideally, some people have already bought into this venture. This is important to note in the business plan, which appeals to people outside the social entrepreneur's immediate network, giving some tangible evidence that the venture is worthy of support.

THE MARKET AND INDUSTRY

This section describes the industry, the enterprise's target market, and its expected position in this market.

1. *Industry description.* Potential supporters who are not intimately familiar with the enterprise may not be conversant in its market and/or industry. For example, a social entrepreneur starting a literacy organization might need to

---

NPower-Basic

NPower-Basic is "a total IT solution for small nonprofits."[5] The enterprise, started in 2005, runs computer systems for nonprofit organizations. Using labor from its parent organization NPower, which focuses on youth workforce development in New York City's disadvantaged communities, NPower-Basic installs, monitors, maintains, and supports computer systems for New York nonprofits at affordable prices. It can do so because it receives donated software and hardware from manufacturers such as Microsoft and Cisco Systems.

In its business plan, NPower-Basic describes its target market as follows:

New York City has 27,474 registered nonprofit organizations, of which 9,078 file annual reports to the IRS. The 9,078 nonprofits deliver information, products, and services to the public. Although they make up only a share of the total nonprofit universe, they are what are commonly thought of when one refers to *nonprofits*. They include hospitals, day care centers, dance companies, and the entire gamut of organizations serving people on a nonprofit basis. Most notably, approximately 7,000 of the 9,078 nonprofits have budgets of less than $1 million, and a subset of this group represents the target market for NP-Basic.

---

explain the context in which literacy services have traditionally existed—such as within educational institutions instead of within other social service providers. Describe the industry's most important points.

2. *Target market.* This it the first opportunity to explain who exactly will benefit from the enterprise's services. Earlier, the plan described the opportunity; this section puts a face to this opportunity. The plan should be specific about who exactly is benefiting from each service provided. There are two ways to describe the market:

   a. Profiles of people who have received actual services, or are expected to receive services

   b. Summary data on the target market, including the numbers of people in the potential client pool, and client demographics, if appropriate

3. *Expected position and share in target market.* This is the place to describe fully the evidence that the social opportunity is authentic and viable. Did the social entrepreneur conduct a survey? Assemble focus groups? Observe the success of similar organizations in similar circumstances? Based on these data, what are the realistic expectations about initial market position and the position after one year, two years, and so on?

MARKETING AND FUNDRAISING

The business plan now turns to the social entrepreneur's plans to raise resources and publicize the venture.

1. *Fundraising targets and strategies.* It is crucial to lay out concretely the enterprise's plans to raise funds adequate to cover its core activities. The

plan doesn't have to show that the enterprise has raised a lot of money already; only that it has a reasonable plan for doing so. For most ventures, this begins with an outline of the approach to raising private funds. The plan should list all of the fundraising dimensions, such as the following.

   a. Personal relationships. Describe the personal and professional networks the social entrepreneur will rely on for financial support. Reasonably extrapolate from the initial levels of support.
   b. Direct mail. Is the use of direct mail viable for this enterprise? What is the plan to build a mailing list and create mailings? What evidence is there that this might be a successful approach?
   c. Media. Are there realistic media opportunities for fundraising? This does not necessarily mean paid advertisements but rather these opportunities might come from public service announcements or other forms of free media.
   d. Virtual means. In the 1990s, most fundraising experts predicted that direct e-mail and giving through Web sites would revolutionize the fundraising industry and usher in a new era of high giving. This, however, turned out not to be the case, as virtual fundraising means have yielded disappointing results.[6] Still, every social enterprise should develop a plan to communicate with potential donors by e-mail and to accept donations over the Internet for donors who care to give this way. This demonstrates an appropriate comfort level with established technology and is relatively cheap to implement.
2. *Grant-writing plans.* Some enterprises may seek to procure funding from government agencies and foundations. The business plan should describe the grants for which the venture's activities will be eligible.
3. *Pricing plan.* Will the enterprise charge fees for its services? This is appropriate for some organizations but not others; for example, a musical group will probably rely principally on fees, for example, while a counseling service for inner-city kids will probably not. Projecting the role of fees and justifying it is important in the business plan.
4. *For-profit activities.* Related to the earned income from service fees is the idea of engaging in certain activities for the primary purpose of earning income to cross-subsidize the social mission. If this is part of the enterprise, it must be described clearly in the business plan. In particular, the social entrepreneur must explain how it relates to the social mission, and why it will not be unduly distracting to the core mission. For-profit activities by social enterprises are dealt with in depth in a later chapter.
5. *Marketing.* In the social enterprise world, there is not a meaningful line between fundraising and marketing. In fact, nonprofit marketing firms tell their clients that every fundraising effort is an opportunity to market the enterprise, and every marketing effort should help raise funds. The business plan should contain an outline of the venture's marketing strategy, which is the subject of a later chapter.

Providence Home Mortgage, Inc.

Providence Home Mortgage is "dedicated to building better communities through responsive, personal mortgage service."[7] It was launched in 2003 as a subsidiary of Inner City Christian Federation, a nonprofit organization in Grand Rapids, Michigan, which supports families by helping them improve their living situation.

In its business plan, Providence Home Mortgage described its marketing objectives in terms of building bilateral ("channel") relationships with other parties in the housing supply chain, to establish the company as lender to all sorts of borrowers, and to become known for high-level customer service. Here are its three goals:

1. To develop channel relationships with realtors, builders, lenders, nonprofit organizations, and others who will refer business to Providence.

2. To communicate the Providence brand as a high-quality provider of home mortgage products to both the conforming and nonconforming mortgagor.

3. To achieve high levels of customer satisfaction thereby leveraging referral business.

THE FINANCIAL PLAN

Now we reach what many social entrepreneurs consider the heart of the business plan: the finances. The plan should cover several financial areas, including the following, which are described in a later chapter.

- Financial needs for three to five years
- Financial projections
- Income statements
- Cash-flow projections
- Balance sheets

The natural tendency for social entrepreneurs is to assume that this part of the business plan is by far the most important—after all, without a financial plan, there is no way for a venture philanthropist or volunteer force to assess whether the venture is a real opportunity or a waste of time. Right? Wrong, according to one experienced entrepreneur. In his words,

> Most [business plans] waste too much ink on numbers and devote too little to the information that really matters to intelligent investors. As every seasoned investor knows, financial projections for a new company—especially detailed, month-by-month projections that stretch out for more than a year—are an act of imagination.[8]

In other words, the numbers have to be plausible and as accurate as possible. But what really makes a business plan convincing for an experienced donor,

Housing Partnership Insurance, Inc.

Housing Partnership Insurance, Inc. (HPI) is a start-up venture begun in 2004 by several members of the Housing Partnership Network, a national coalition of nonprofits dedicated to providing affordable housing in expensive markets such as San Francisco, California.[9] It was started to provide property and liability insurance coverage to the owners of low-cost housing, who typically have a hard time acquiring insurance coverage. By 2006, it had approximately 35,000 clients across the United States.

HPI's business plan laid out a detailed financial plan, which featured projections of various scenarios, from optimistic to pessimistic. Here is how HPI summarizes its approach:

> [Our] feasibility study examined a number of financial scenarios. Multiyear operating proformas were tested based upon loss projections at various confidence intervals. Each projection incorporated assumptions about how much risk [HPI] would assume and how much would be laid off to other [insurance companies]. [HPI] was ultimately underwritten by our insurance partners and regulators based in large part on . . . an "expected" loss scenario for the portfolio, which was developed and trended upwards from historic levels. Using this analysis, [we] estimated the amount of cash collateral (cash reserves) and equivalents (letters of credit) that were needed for the various exposures, and they stress-tested the company's feasibility in adverse cases.

board member, potential staff member, or volunteer is the venture's core ideas, basic ingredients, and people.

GOALS AND OBJECTIVES, WITH A TIMELINE

The business plan has already defined value and how it will be measured. A business plan might talk about maximizing the number of kids that are exposed to good music, or the percentage of a population vaccinated against a printable disease, or the number of people introduced to a religion. Now it is time to tell potential supporters what success means in terms of this measure—and provide a roadmap for getting there.

1. *Definition of success.* Start by openly stating the enterprise's ultimate goal. If it sounds too outlandish on paper ("our goal is to eradicate world hunger by 2010"), it probably is. Remember: A goal should be motivational but not infeasible. And most importantly in the business plan, it has to be believable. Thus, it should be bounded in scope, time, and geography.

2. *Intermediate goals and success measures.* The ultimate goal is not the only one of interest. Enterprises that create social benefit should have intermediate goals as well, which are important on their own but also should lead in an obvious way toward the ultimate goal of the enterprise. For example, important intermediate goals toward the rehabilitation of a contaminated lake might be the cessation of polluting, the designation as a legally protected environment, and the reintroduction of wildlife.

The Bakery Café

In 1996, Haley House, a Boston nonprofit dedicated to helping the poor achieve economic independence, established the Bakery Café, a bakery-training program for low-income men and women.[10] It is a restaurant open to the public, staffed partly by people training for jobs in high-quality food preparation. After a six-month training period, trainees receive assistance finding jobs in other restaurants and bakeries.

The Bakery Café's business plan listed several performance measures the enterprise would track. They included the following:

- Performance milestones
- The number of businesses where we have outreach coordinators
- The number of community events we have participated in
- The dates and numbers of places we have done literature drops
- The number of customers [who visit] our store each week
- Customer usage of coupons
- Visits to our Web site
- Our weekly retail revenues
- The number and size of wholesale accounts that we add each month

---

3. *Evidence that goals can be achieved.* Supporters need more than an assurance from the social entrepreneur that the enterprise's goals will be met. What evidence is there that the goals are realistic and that this entrepreneur can meet them? This evidence might be the success of related ventures and the success of past ventures by the same social entrepreneur.

4. *Timeline.* The plan should give an anticipated accomplishment timeline that stretches out at least three to five years, if the venture is projected to last that long. This timeline should contain several landmarks:

- Start of the enterprise
- Incorporation date, if any
- Hiring, space, and equipment acquisition
- Start of service delivery
- Beginning of cash flow from fees, grants, and donations
- Enterprise growth milestones
- Goal attainment

RISK ASSESSMENT

Everything up to this point has concentrated on what the social entrepreneur will achieve, *assuming all goes as planned.* The business plan has provided evidence that the venture is realistic, but we all know that nothing is ever sure—risks are involved with any activity. This section lays out the enterprise's risks in a realistic way.

1. *Financial risk.* This is the most obvious risk for any business plan. Answer these questions:
   - How exposed will the enterprise be at various points in the planned development?
   - How much donated and earned money will be vulnerable?
   - What are the financially riskiest individual points in the plan? What is the downside to failure on each point?
   - What is the financial worst-case scenario? If this is especially unlikely, explain why.
2. *Legal risk.* For many enterprises, legal risks are minimal. However, they always exist and require acknowledgment. For example, what happens if the organization's tax status is denied or delayed? How will the enterprise protect Board members from personal legal liability, if at all?
3. *Talent risk.* Social enterprises, like all entrepreneurial endeavors, rely critically on the involvement of the entrepreneur and the team. One of the most important risks, especially early on in a venture, is that the team is damaged when someone leaves. What is the likelihood of this, and why should supporters not worry that personnel changes will derail the whole enterprise? What is the back-up plan if someone leaves?
4. *Environmental risk.* There are many uncontrollable facets of a social enterprise's environment. Environmental risk can usually be classified in three areas:
   a. *Political and governmental risk.* A political or regulatory regime affects the ability of an enterprise to function as planned. This is especially important for enterprises that are highly dependent on public sources of income.
   b. *Economic risk.* The business cycle affects the enterprise because of consumer behavior, demand for services, or the ability of donors to give.
   c. *Demographic risk.* Populations change, which can adversely affect an organization. For example, social welfare enterprises in big cities that serve the poor are often affected by "gentrification," in which urban areas rehabilitate, and the poor are forced out of an organization's service area.
5. *Other risks.* There are other risks that are more specific to each individual enterprise. For example, an enterprise that is reliant on high technology can face risks in the functioning of key technologies.

The assessment of all these risks should include planned workarounds and alternative courses of action to mitigate damage when setbacks inevitably occur.

SUPPORTING DOCUMENTS

An appendix to the business plan should contain supporting documentation that is "optional reading" for the plan. This documentation often includes the following:

- Résumés for the key participants in the enterprise, including the social entrepreneur, other top management, and Board leadership
- Data sources cited in the plan to provide evidence for the plan's viability
- References for the literature cited in the plan, if any

Getting Personal in a Business Plan

Social enterprise business plans can be dull, lifeless documents expressing nothing but facts and projections about a social venture. This is a problem because they are intended to represent the venture to the outside world—and the venture should be something that animates the social entrepreneur on the deepest emotional level. In fact, a social venture is highly personal, expressing entrepreneurs' definition of social value and their attempts to achieve it.

Entrepreneur and Harvard professor William A. Sahlman clearly understands this when he advocates injecting personal information into every business plan. Sahlman provides a guide for putting personality into business plans when he teaches that every plan should answer the following questions:

1. Where are the founders from?
2. Where have they been educated?
3. Where have they worked and for whom?
4. What have they accomplished professionally and personally in the past?
5. What is their reputation within the business community?
6. What experience do they have that is directly relevant to the opportunity they are pursuing?
7. What skills, abilities, and knowledge do they have?
8. How realistic are they about the venture's chances for success and the tribulations it will face?
9. Who else needs to be on the team?
10. Are they prepared to recruit high-quality people?
11. How will they respond to adversity?
12. Do they have the mettle to make the inevitable hard choices that have to be made?
13. How committed are they to this venture?
14. What are their motivations?

See: Sahlman, William A. (1997). "How to Write a Great Business Plan." *Harvard Business Review* 75(4): 98–108.

PITFALLS

Authors Kuratko and Hodgetts provide a list of the most common pitfalls in assembling a commercial business plan.[11] They are failing to communicate realistic goals, failing to anticipate problems, lack of evident commitment or dedication to the venture, lack of experience, and failure to demonstrate market niche. These pitfalls are just as important in the case of social enterprise business plans. Unrealistic goals and a lack of niche generally relate to a lack of adequate demand—and suggest a flawed business model. Failing to anticipate problems and roadblocks stems from an overall lack of experience and a failure to seek the help of someone who can fill this gap. A lack of evident dedication is probably the worst pitfall of all for a social venture because the returns to noncommercial enterprises are usually denominated in nonfinancial terms. Stakeholders expect that one of these nonfinancial returns is fulfillment, even pleasure, from the social entrepreneur. As such, a lack of obvious dedication is tantamount to saying the enterprise will have a low payoff. A business plan should exhibit enthusiasm and total commitment.

Authors Baron and Shane add a few more pitfalls to the business plan mix.[12] First, appearance is important. They note that stakeholders tend to be put off by business plans that are sloppy, or too "slick." Second, potential supporters of a venture lose interest in a business plan that fails to get right to the point of the enterprise or make clear why anyone would want to support it. Third, stakeholders can sense when financial projections are unrealistic or inappropriately optimistic. Fourth, it must be clear where a venture is in terms of its development—whether it has already begun, or is still purely an identified opportunity. Finally, supporters have to understand the qualifications of the venture's leaders before they will become involved.

Summary

- The social entrepreneur needs a way to represent the venture to the outside world. The tool for doing this is the business plan, which is a document detailing the enterprise.
- The business plan is intended for the use of actual and potential funders, government officials, the community-at-large, the social entrepreneur, actual and potential staff and volunteers, and board members.
- Business plans have nine basic ingredients: a summary, a description of the enterprise, information about the management and leadership teams, an analysis of the market and industry, the plan for marketing and fundraising, the financial plan, the venture's goals and objectives, a realistic assessment of risks, and supporting documents.
- The most common pitfalls in preparing a business plan are failing to communicate realistic goals, failing to anticipate problems, lack of evident commitment or dedication to the venture, lack of experience, and failure to demonstrate market niche.

Key Terms

- business plan
- target market
- business plan pitfalls

End-of-Chapter Questions

You and a partner have just come up with what you believe is a brilliant social venture idea, which you have evidence is also an opportunity. Your enterprise is called LearningSite.org, and it is dedicated to providing parents of kids with learning disabilities the learning tools their children can use—but which are often hard to find in public schools. A major foundation has taken an interest in your project and asked you for a business plan before they will provide the enterprise with seed funding.

1. Your partner volunteers to "crank out" the business plan for LearningSite. org—whatever it takes to get the money. Explain why this may not be the best approach.

2. You don't have a business model for LearningSite.org yet, either. Should you try and create one before writing the business plan? Why or why not?

3. Looking at the first draft of the business plan, you see that your partner omitted discussion of the risks from key personnel leaving LearningSite.org, or of not getting sufficient funding after the foundation grant finishes. You point this out, but your partner argues that this would "just open a can of worms." Comment.

4. You are debating whether or not to have LearningSite.org's business plan professionally designed by a graphic design firm. It will be expensive, but it will look great. Should you do it? Discuss the costs and benefits.

End Notes

1. See, for example, Brinckerhoff, Peter (2000). *Social Entrepreneurship: The Arts of Mission-Based Venture Development*. New York: Wiley, pp. 80–93. The social enterprise business plan examples and excerpts in this chapter come primarily from the winners and finalists in the Yale School of Management-Goldman Sachs Foundation Partnership on Nonprofit Ventures' Business Planning Competition (see www. ventures.yale.edu/), which ceased operations in September 2005. All of these business plans are available publicly at www.ventures.yale.edu/competition_winning_business_plans.asp.

2. www.firstbook.org/

3. www.batf.net

4. Oster, Sharon (1995). *Strategic Management for Nonprofit Organizations*. New York: Oxford University Press.

5. www.npowerny.org

6. Hart, T. (2001). "The philanthropy revolution." *Fund Raising Management* 32(3) (May): 22–27.

7. http://www.iccf.org/programs/mortgage.htm

8. Sahlman, William A. (1997). "How to Write a Great Business Plan." *Harvard Business Review* 75(4): 98–108.

9. www.housingpartnership.net/insurance

10. www.haleyhouse.org/about.htm

11. Kuratko, Donald F., and Richard M. Hodgetts (2001). *Entrepreneurship: A Contemporary Approach*. Orlando, FL: Harcourt, pp. 286–287.

12. Baron, Robert A., and Scot A. Shane (2005). *Entrepreneurship: A Process Perspective*. Mason, OH: Thomson South-Western, p. 177.

CHAPTER 5

MEASURING SOCIAL VALUE

INTRODUCTION

Ashoka is a multinational nonprofit organization dedicated to finding and supporting true social entrepreneurs. It formed in 1980 on the belief that, "Rather than leaving societal needs for the government or business sectors to address, social entrepreneurs are creating innovative solutions, delivering extraordinary results, and improving the lives of millions of people."[1] Since it began, Ashoka has supported more than 1,800 social entrepreneurs—called "Ashoka Fellows"—in more than 60 countries around the world. The enterprises they indirectly sponsor range from agriculture to public health.

Ashoka is interested not only in the immediate success of its Fellows but also the enduring social value that these Fellows have years after their Ashoka funding has finished. How should they measure this value?

Each year, Ashoka conducts a Measuring Effectiveness study focusing on the Fellows selected 5 or 10 years prior. The study includes a survey sent to all Ashoka Fellows elected in a given year, as well as a series of in-person interviews with a cross-section of survey respondents. The survey features the following indicators of success and social impact.[2]

1. Original vision: Is the Fellow still working toward his or her original vision? At present, 94 percent of Fellows from five years ago say they are.

2. Independent replication: Are others mimicking the programs started by the fellows? Ninety-three percent of those from five years ago say yes.

3. Policy influence: Has public policy been influenced by the Fellows' programs? After five years, the percent responding affirmatively is 56 percent.
4. Leadership building: Have Fellows developed into leaders in their fields? Fifty-four percent of Fellows have after five years.
5. Leverage: How did Ashoka support help Fellows to succeed? This measure looks at how the stipend, collaboration, communications assistance, and other dimensions of Ashoka support helped the Fellows.

Ashoka's approach is far ahead of the field simply because it desires to measure its long-term social impacts. But are these the best dimensions on which to measure Ashoka's success? How can they be quantified? This chapter seeks to answer these questions and to provide you with concepts and tools for social value measurement. We start by introducing a few concepts of social value measurement, followed by the idea of Social Return on Investment, and a discussion of "efficiency" for social enterprises. Finally, we turn to a full model of organizational effectiveness.

WHY MEASURE VALUE?

Measuring the impact of social enterprises is not straightforward because they have a "double bottom line"; that is, while they must make ends meet financially, they seek—or are supposed to seek, at least—to maximize their social impact, defined by their mission. In fact, no social enterprise can be viable, economically or legally, if its sole purpose is to make money. Think for a moment how different this is from for-profit organizations, which are expected to earn a profit—indeed, the profit earned by commercial organizations lies behind the jobs they create, the tax revenues they generate, and the economic growth they stimulate.

In short, social enterprises have a much harder task measuring their success than for-profit enterprises do. In the past, social enterprises and nonprofits generally made due with purely qualitative arguments about their impact: "We are saving millions of lives each year," or "Our organization has made a major difference in the education of thousands of children" would be typical imprecise claims, with little apology for the fact that these claims leave us unable to quantify the impact or effectiveness of the organizations or compare the effectiveness or impact between enterprises.

Perhaps imprecise measurement sounds like an advantage to a social enterprise, because it takes a huge area of effort out of the picture in trying to raise money. For example, philanthropists, foundations, and governments can hardly ask for precise evidence of impact if this evidence is unavailable, right? On further reflection, however, this is not an advantage to social enterprises because it has really only succeeded in suppressing support, especially to excellent ventures. Think of it this way: Imagine a philanthropist seeking to make a gift that will translate into true social value. Her gift will be more or less equal to her judgment of the expected impact. This expectation, however, will be affected by the wide range of possibilities implied by a lack of evidence, making it harder for the giver to tell the difference between effective and ineffective organizations. Economists call this a "lemons" problem, referring to the fact that consumers who don't know anything about used cars tend to shy away from the market because they can't tell the difference between good cars and lemons—and they tend to underpay for the good cars.[3]

In short, it is in the interest of all good social enterprises to be as precise as possible in the measurement of social value, organizational health, efficiency in meeting mission, and overall organizational effectiveness. What are the measurement tools at a social entrepreneur's disposal?

HOW DO WE MEASURE VALUE?

Throughout the earlier chapters of this book, we have discussed the importance of defining and measuring social value. This is especially important in the concept development phase of the social entrepreneurship process. The idea of measuring social value has four component concepts: accountability, evaluation, outcomes, and effectiveness.

- *Accountability.* Accountability refers to the implicit or explicit social responsibility an enterprise assumes. For example, if I start an enterprise to proselytize for my religion, and you give me money to back my enterprise, I assume responsibility to do—or at least try and do—what I promised in my mission. The concept of accountability has become important all across the public and nonprofit sectors in recent years, due to the perception that bureaucracy and a lack of shareholder input can lead to irresponsible or wasteful behavior. In response, the U.S. Federal Government changed the name of its internal auditing agency, General Accounting Office, to the General *Accountability* Office, reflecting its response to public concerns about government responsibility.

- *Evaluation.* Social enterprises show they are accountable by evaluating their activities. Evaluation is a systematic study of the quality, success, or worthiness of something. For example, the grade you receive in a class is an evaluation, as are the performance reviews that most employees periodically receive. The basic standard for a proper evaluation of any type is that it has four qualities: utility, feasibility, propriety, and accuracy.[4] In other words, an evaluation has to be useful, cost-effective to undertake, and measure the appropriate things accurately.

- *Outcomes and impacts.* What should an evaluation undertake to measure? There is a tendency in the nonprofit and public sectors to measure inputs (e.g., the amount of money raised for a project), activities (e.g., the number of programs we are running), or outputs (e.g., our service volume per month). There is a role for looking at inputs, activities, and outputs, especially as they relate to progress in executing a business plan. However, the end goal of a

FIGURE 5-1 Possible Targets for Measurement in a Social Enterprise

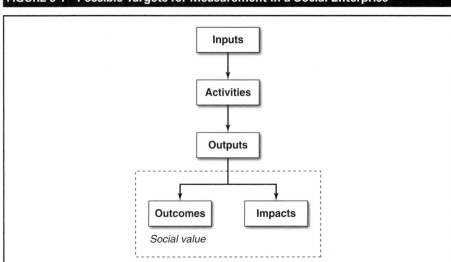

social enterprise is obviously social value, and this means looking at the outcomes of our activities and the impacts these outcomes have.

- *Effectiveness.* An organization that attains desirable outcomes and impacts and does so in an appropriate way is "effective." This is easier to define vaguely than specifically, however, because we need to know what is desirable and what is appropriate. This chapter deals with these questions in depth.

In summary, we expect *accountability* from social enterprises. To show us they are accountable, social enterprises invest in *evaluation* to measure *outcomes* or *impacts*. This informs donors, clients, and the public about the enterprise's *effectiveness.* These concepts are summarized in Figure 5-1.

After we identify them precisely, how do we measure the outcomes and impacts created by social enterprises? Organizational scholars divide performance measurements into three basic types.[5]

1. *Continuous.* In the best of cases, we can measure outcomes precisely and numerically. For example, we might want to know exactly how much in philanthropy a social enterprise raised in its first year. Or, we might seek to count the number of people served by a venture. Continuous measures require precise quantitative data.

2. *Rating scale.* When continuous measures are infeasible, a rating scale can provide a good solution for measuring outcomes. For example, say we want to know people's opinion of the effectiveness of an environmental enterprise. We might ask people to rate effectiveness on a five-point scale, ranging from "very effective" to "very ineffective."

3. *Binary.* These are yes/no measures, which are appropriate if a certain threshold is necessary to attain a measure of success. For example, did a social enterprise meet its stated fundraising goal in the targeted time period? Did an organization seeking to get people off of welfare succeed for a client after two years? For a binary measure to be useful and effective, a clear distinction between the two states is required. It is important that there be little room for doubt as to whether the answer is "yes" or "no."

Many measures are variations, adaptations, or combinations of the basic numeric and binary measures described in the previous list:

1. *Developmental.* Sometimes, outcomes are attained incrementally. For example, enterprise business plans always feature a timeline for the enterprise's progress. An important measure of success indicates whether the venture has reached each of its proposed milestones in the time proposed. Developmental metrics are usually a multistage version of determinate measures.

Can Social and Commercial Returns Be the Same Thing?

One major idea in social entrepreneurship has been to build communities by building economies. It is unambiguously true that social good is derived from providing jobs to families and rescuing communities from financial ruin. Does this mean that commercial entrepreneurs might be social entrepreneurs as well? And does this mean that, in some cases, we might measure social impact (at least indirectly) in the dollars that flow into a community's economy?

Many scholars and writers would say so. For example, Harvard Professor Robert Putnam, author of the bestseller *Bowling Alone: The Collapse and Revival of American Community,* tells the story of Tupelo, Mississippi, which came back from a depressed economy to become a magnet for businesses after conscious efforts to strengthen social networks and create opportunities for self-help and collective action.[6] This was also the idea behind social entrepreneur and Nobel Laureate Mohammed Yunus' Grameen Bank, profiled in the first chapter of this book.

Many other efforts in the United States and other countries have focused social progress on economic growth and development and hence have measured social impact in terms of dollars. Here are a few other examples of cases in which commercial and social entrepreneurship are effectively equivalent.[7]

CDI is a Brazilian social enterprise created to train poor children from *favelas,* the slums surrounding Brazil's cities, in information technologies. Over 80 percent of kids in the programs have attained productive jobs, for their good and the economic development of their families and communities.

ApproTEC works in Africa to develop the most appropriate technologies in local villages to stimulate new industries and economic development. This means processing local products for sale or moving villages from subsistence into commercial farming. The enterprise created 35,000 businesses in Kenya, Tanzania, Uganda, and Mali from 2000–2005.

Sekem is an Egyptian social enterprise dedicated to protecting local plants from pests without using harmful and expensive pesticides. It improved crop yields and established crop export businesses.

2. *Benchmark.* A benchmark is a comparison with a leader of some sort. For example, a new enterprise that provides support for the poor might compare its scale of operations to a larger, more established organization in its area. This kind of measure is usually a continuous or rating measure.

3. *Historic.* Some measures of success are essentially benchmarks of an organization against itself—its past performance. The idea here is to show progress. For example, an enterprise might show that it is X% more successful in fundraising in year two than it was in year one.

Ashoka's performance metrics, introduced at the beginning of this chapter, constitute a mix of binary and continuous measures of success. First, each Ashoka Fellow is asked a series of yes or no questions (which are verified by independent sources): Were they still pursuing their original vision? Had their vision been replicated? Had they influenced public policy? Had they become leaders in their fields? Were they able to leverage Ashoka support? Second, the overall measure for the organization becomes continuous, based on the percentages of yes and no individual responses.

SOCIAL RETURN ON INVESTMENT

In the mid-1990s, the Roberts Enterprise Development Fund (REDF), a San Francisco-area nonprofit dedicated to funding social enterprises that support the poor in acquiring job skills and finding good employment, set out to analyze its "investment" in local organizations.[8] REDF had four specific questions.

1. How can we measure the success of our efforts?
2. How do we—practitioners and philanthropist/investors—know whether we're accomplishing what we set out to do?
3. How can we—practitioners and philanthropist/investors—make informed decisions about the ongoing use of our resources?
4. How can we test and convince others of what we believe to be true: that for each dollar invested in our portfolio agencies' efforts, there are impressive, quantifiable resulting benefits to individuals and to society?[9]

The innovative framework REDF developed to answer these questions is called Social Return on Investment (SROI). It is an attempt to quantify the economic and socioeconomic impacts of social enterprises (see Figure 5-2). REDF broke the benefits of a social venture into two parts: enterprise value and social purpose value. These types of value combined make up what REDF called "blended value." Table 5-1 summarizes how blended value is calculated.

Enterprise value refers to the net revenues from the "business side" of a social venture—the value that constitutes the lion's share of value for a commercial enterprise. This comes from the value of sales, minus the cost of goods and services and operating expenses (e.g., management and labor costs). Obviously, for many social enterprises with little in the way of sales, enterprise value can be permanently negative, which is to say that the enterprise never turns a financial profit.

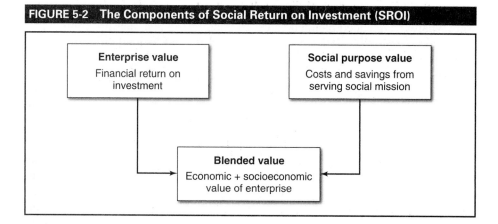

FIGURE 5-2   The Components of Social Return on Investment (SROI)

Social purpose value, on the other hand, refers to the value that the enterprise creates for society—at least, the part that can be measured in terms of costs saved to society or revenues created as a result of positive impact on people's lives. For example, "social cost savings" might include items such as welfare payments averted when a social enterprise moves someone to the workforce. This would also result in an increase in taxes when the person goes from welfare recipient to earner. Of course, there are also special "social operating costs" involved in working with certain populations, such as the high training costs for chronically unemployed people.

Donated revenues in the forms of grants and gifts can go into social purpose value because they represent payments toward an enterprise's social mission. Likewise, fundraising and grantwriting costs represent social operating costs under this standard.

TABLE 5-1   Calculating Social Return on Investment (SROI)

Enterprise value

Value of sales
- Cost of good and services sold
- Operating expenses

Social purpose value
+ Grants and gifts
- Fundraising and grant writing costs
+ Social cost savings
- Social operating costs
+ Increases in Taxes

Debt
- Debt carried by social enterprise

= Blended value

Enterprise value plus social enterprise value, minus an enterprise's debt, were what REDF called blended value. To make blended a measure comparable across social enterprises, REDF went a step further and defined three "indices of value":

- *Enterprise index of return.* Enterprise value, divided by the amount of money given philanthropically to the enterprise.

- *Social purpose index of return.* Social purpose value, divided by the value of the philanthropic investment in the enterprise.

- *Blended index of return.* Blended value, divided by the value of the philanthropic investment in the enterprise.

Using these indices, REDF (or any other donor-investor in a social enterprise) could see how two enterprises stacked up, even if they were greatly different in size and scale.

REDF acknowledged that these concepts of value left out a lot of intangibles in the purely social realm. For instance, a welfare-to-work program might make participants into far happier people when they are engaged in productive work. Nonetheless, REDF's approach represented a major step forward in apprehending the value that social enterprises create and consequently the return on philanthropic investment.

MEASURING THE "VULNERABILITY" AND EFFICIENCY OF SOCIAL ENTERPRISES

Beyond the idea of social impact, social entrepreneurs—and especially their backers—are justifiably interested in understanding the risk to which a venture is exposed. To make rational investments, it is important to measure this.

But is this possible? Some research on the finances of nonprofit organizations provides promising avenues for social enterprise risk measurement. For example, economists Howard Tuckman and Cyril Chang proposed four measures of "financial vulnerability" for social organizations that focused on equity balances, revenue concentrations, administrative costs, and operating margins.[10]

EQUITY BALANCE

An enterprise's "equity" is its total assets minus its liabilities. Higher equity generally lowers financial vulnerability because it facilitates borrowing in capital markets, and equity can generally be converted into cash in hard times. The way to measure the equity balance is by subtracting liabilities L from assets A, and dividing by total annual revenues, TR. That is,

$$Equity\ balance = \frac{A - L}{TR}$$

A higher value of this measure indicates a lower level of financial vulnerability.

REVENUE CONCENTRATION

Financial vulnerability is high when social enterprises receive their revenues from relatively few sources. This is fairly intuitive: One revenue source exposes the venture to problems if that source ends or fluctuates; it is more likely to be able to adjust to changes if the venture has other sources. A common measure of revenue concentration sums the square of each revenue source i, where s_i is a proportion of total annual revenues (so $s_1 + s_2 + \cdots = 1$). That is,

$$Revenue\ concentration = s_1^2 + s_2^2 + \cdots$$

A lower number for this measurement is better, indicating more revenue diversification.

ADMINISTRATIVE COSTS

One way to classify a social enterprise's costs is administration versus operations. That is, money is spent either on the venture's programs directly or on running the enterprise. Administration costs are typically taken to include items such as managers' salaries, fundraising costs, and office expenses. Administrative costs are measured as the ratio of administration $ADMIN$ to total costs TC. That is,

$$Administrative\ costs = \frac{ADMIN}{TC}$$

Although people often think of effective enterprises as spending little on administration—we will discuss this idea in depth later—Tuckman and Chang argue that a high proportion of administration costs lowers financial vulnerability because higher administration costs provide a "buffer" against revenue shocks, in that these costs can be cut back without sacrificing the core mission.

OPERATING MARGIN

An enterprise's operating margin is the money it has to save or invest and, consequently, the insurance it has against future uncertainty. It is measured as the difference between total annual revenues and costs, as a percentage of annual revenues. That is,

$$Operating\ margin = \frac{TR - TC}{TR}$$

A higher operating margin corresponds to a lower level of financial vulnerability.

Nonprofit scholar Mark Hager has extensively tested the usefulness of these four measures of financial vulnerability, especially in the case of the arts.[11] He has concluded that they are generally quite helpful in predicting the success or failure of these types of organizations, noting that, for example, the likelihood that a nonprofit theater company will disappear in a given year is significantly associated with all four measures (and in the expected ways). There has been little scholarly research performed specifically on social enterprises; however, there is little reason to believe that social ventures would vary dramatically in this regard from more established social organizations.

TABLE 5-2 Nonprofit ROI, 2001		
Subsector	*Number of Organizations*	*Average ROI*
Arts	19,383	0.50%
Education	31,918	2.46%
Health	25,553	0.32%
Social welfare	27,878	2.63%
Environmental	4,058	3.41%
International aid	1,707	−1.34%
All nonprofits	187,944	2.33%

Source: IRS Form 990 data (National Center for Charitable Statistics)

One traditional for-profit measure of financial success is return on investment (ROI), generally calculated as revenue's net of total expenditures, as a percentage of net firm assets. That is,

$$ROI = \frac{TR - TC}{A}$$

For many years, social enterprises have labored under the label of inefficiency because they have been subjected, either explicitly or implicitly, to measurement under this kind of standard. For example, consider the data on the simple ROI for total spending by nonprofits in various subsectors from 2001.

Table 5-2 summarizes this calculation for the nonprofits in the United States in 2001 that filed an IRS Form 990 and recorded positive expenditures.[12] These data show that nonprofit subsectors tend to see an ROI that is under 3 percent—and potentially even negative.

Compared to the ROI generated by for-profits, the figures in Table 5-2 are very low. Desai (2001)[13] shows that the ROI enjoyed by American multinational for-profits tends to be about 17 percent, on average. For example, over the period from 1982–1995, annual ROI was 19 percent for chemical firms, 21 percent for food companies, 18 percent for machinery producers, and 23 percent for transport firms.

This discrepancy between for-profits and nonprofits might lead to the intuitive conclusion for many people that nonprofits are somehow "inefficient": If they would just tighten up their operations, make smarter spending decisions, and be held more accountable to stakeholders, the reasoning goes, they would achieve higher ROI levels, indicating a more "businesslike" stewardship of funds. Even some nonprofit insiders seem to share this view. For example, one nonprofit e-commerce consulting firm pitches its services with this statement: "Facing market pressure to become more efficient and less dependent on the government, nonprofit organizations today must find new ways to achieve a leaner, more businesslike operation."[14]

Given this viewpoint, it is especially striking to find a number of scholars who appear to assert that, on the contrary, social enterprises do *not* need to become more businesslike. Paul Light, for example, writes that,

> Just because the nonprofit sector needs to improve its performance does not necessarily mean it has to become more businesslike. Unfortunately, absent a compelling vision of what being nonprofit-like means, it is hard to imagine that individual organizations will be able to resist the pressure to become less like nonprofits.[15]

Similarly, nonprofit scholar Peter Frumkin states that,

> [While] nonprofit and voluntary organizations appear weak, inefficient, and directionless, . . . nothing could be further from the truth. In reality, [nonprofits have] a set of unique advantages that position them to perform important societal functions neither government nor the market is able to match.[16]

Are social enterprises naturally inefficient, or not? To answer this, we have to remember the idea behind SROI, that social enterprises face a peculiar tension between net revenues and adherence to their missions. Assuming for the moment that, as is the case for most social ventures, the "mission service" (for example feeding homeless people) is inherently a loss-making endeavor, the organization must divide its energies and resources between activities (such as selling a more profitable service, or fundraising) that raise net revenues, and core services, which frequently lower them.[17] Many scholars have argued that this is very common all across the nonprofit sector.[18]

Figure 5-3 gives a stylized representation of the relationship between a social enterprise's net revenues, and its level of adherence to its mission. The two axes

FIGURE 5-3 The Relationship Between Net Revenues and Mission Adherence

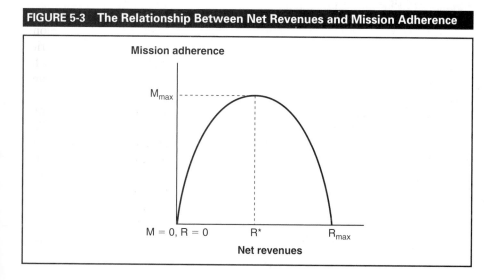

measure the amount of net revenues for operations (R) and the "degree" of mission adherence (M). When net revenues are zero $(R = 0)$, the nonprofit is insolvent and cannot adhere to its mission $(M = 0)$. When net revenues are maximized $(R = R_{max})$, the nonprofit cannot meet its mission either $(M = 0)$, being completely pulled away from its mission services.[19] Thus, there is an optimal point at which the nonprofit raises just enough net revenues $(R = R^*)$ to maximize its mission services $(M = M_{max})$.

An example should help clarify this point. Imagine a dance company that raises a large percentage of its own revenues from donations. It has two kinds of expenses: fundraising and spending on service for performances. Its mission is to provide as much service as possible (with an acceptably high level of quality). To do so means fundraising optimally—up to the point of what economists call "equimarginality," where the last dollar in expenditures earns a dollar in revenues—and then spending its net revenues on core services, without regard for the "return" on this latter type of spending.[20] (Naturally, this is a simplified example. An actual organization has many types of services and expenditures and might elect to save extra revenues some years, if possible.)

For this organization, revenues and mission are related in an interesting way. Without fundraising, if revenues are too low, mission is not met because performances cannot occur. On the other hand, if the organization focuses *only* on raising revenues, it will also be diverted from its mission. What it seeks is the "sweet spot" between fundraising and core services: to raise as much in net donated revenues for service spending as possible. To make this more concrete, imagine the executive director decides that fundraising is peripheral to the core product (dance performances) and eliminates fundraising altogether. If donations are the main source of income, this decision will probably wipe out the ability to engage in the company's mission because there will be insufficient resources to use for performances. Now imagine the executive director decides that fundraising is the company's most important activity, and the staff engages in it to the exclusion of performances. Not only will the mission be neglected, but also probably fundraising will become less effective because donors want to support that mission—not fundraising per se.

The right levels of mission and fundraising exist in a balance, and this balance is achieved by pursuing two simultaneous spending strategies. First, social ventures should fundraise (or write grants, or sell ancillary services) up to the point of equimarginality, which maximizes net donations (or subsidies, or earned revenues). Second, the venture should spend this money in a way that maximizes the mission, notwithstanding the financial return from this spending.

Are social enterprises efficient under this standard? To answer this question means looking at the return from the last dollar spent but only on noncore services. Standard statistical tools exist to test this hypothesis, given data on a sample of nonprofits. The data suggest that, in fact, nonprofits do approach efficient noncore service spending so that they may maximize their level of services. Using data on 190,000 U.S. nonprofits from 2001, for example, we find that the return to the last fundraising dollar spent is $2.91. Good, right? Wrong—this is inefficient: This is telling us that, on average, U.S. nonprofits spend too little on their fundraising. By spending only up to the point that the last dollar brings in about $3, organizations are forgoing net donated revenues that could be spent on their core mission.

What about individual nonprofit subsectors? Let's start with the arts, to get back to the example of the ballet company. Among 20,000 arts firms in 2001, the average return on the last dollar was $1.85. In contrast, for 30,000 education non-profits, the return was $1.32; for 25,000 health organizations, $2.61. In general, U.S. nonprofits spend inefficiently little on fundraising. This is an important point to consider, next time you hear that a social enterprise is efficient because it spends so little raising funds. The only exception to the pattern of inefficiently low fundraising are social welfare organizations. In 2001, for 55,000 welfare orga-nizations, the return on the last fundraising dollar was indistinguishable from zero. In other words, these organizations tended to fundraise all the way to the point that the last dollar spent yields virtually nothing at all. Figure 5-4 summa-rizes these results.

Of course, not all nonprofits are "social enterprises" as we have defined them in earlier chapters (any more than all for-profits are entrepreneurial organiza-tions), and there is really no way with the existing data to pull out these enterpris-es. However, there is not an obvious reason why these data should not be indicative of the patterns among nonprofits that are truly social enterprises.

FIGURE 5-4   The Marginal Returns to a Dollar Spent on Fundraising

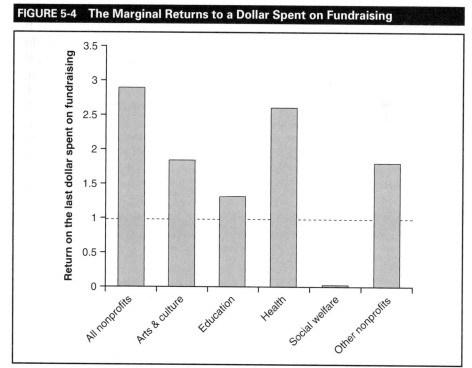

Source: Brooks (2006).[21]

None of this discussion says anything about how well nonprofits use their revenues from fundraising. They might well spend them wastefully—inefficient to be sure. But on the sheer basis of how much they spend, there is detectable inefficiency. Note the irony in the fact that many nonprofits and watchdog agencies have taken to tracking nonmission expenses, especially fundraising, under the belief that the sector can be improved by lowering these expenses. In fact, such efforts generally *decrease* the sector's efficiency and leave nonprofits with fewer resources to spend on their true missions.

For individual social entrepreneurs, the point here is not that organizations cannot understand their efficiency or effectiveness unless they baseline themselves with a million other organizations and employ a set of complicated statistical procedures. Rather, it is simply to advocate that organizations track the returns to their spending on nonmission activities, such as fundraising, and that they aim to maximize the net revenues by looking at the returns to the last dollars of investment. Depending on the type of organization and fundraising technique, this can be achieved in different ways.

To understand this more concretely, consider a nonprofit that raises funds primarily through direct mail campaigns. The search for efficient fundraising levels requires two steps. First, the enterprise organizes its potential donors into as many discrete groups as is practical, for example, by community, by whether and how much people have given in the past, or by some other logical criteria. Second, the nonprofit tracks the returns from each group, as closely as is practical. Each group has an associated cost and will have an associated return. The target in fundraising is dollar-for-dollar (equimarginality), so the nonprofit should classify each donor group as having this return or above. Armed with this information, subsequent campaigns should target those groups with dollar-for-dollar returns or higher.

In practice, this is not an exact science, of course. Measurement is always imperfect, and there are sometimes good investment reasons to focus on groups with a lower-than-equimarginal net return in the short run (building a new mailing list, for example). However, the evidence tells us that, for most nonprofits, this exercise will not lead to less fundraising than at present but rather to more because most organizations tend to stop well before reaching the dollar-for-dollar point.

Even if the results of these practical efforts are messy, nonprofits can use the idea of equimarginality to make real gains in true efficiency—while not wasting their time on pursuit of standards that are either only appropriate for the for-profit sector or that actually push them in the wrong direction altogether.

THE ORGANIZATIONAL EFFECTIVENESS OF A SOCIAL ENTERPRISE

Organization theorists have addressed the problem of multiple social objectives in a different way than economists, and the result is a set of tools social entrepreneurs can use. For example, author Roland J. Kushner's model of nonprofit organizational effectiveness defines the performance of a nonprofit along five lines.[22]

- *Satisfaction of constituents.* An effective organization creates social value not just because it believes this is so; rather, it must satisfy its constituents that this is also the case. This includes the clients, donors, staff and volunteers, and others.

- *Adequacy of funding.* An effective organization requires adequate resources to meet its mission. Although resources are inputs and not outcomes or impacts, successfully identifying and acquiring them constitutes one dimension of total effectiveness.

- *Efficiency of operations.* Having adequate resources is not useful for total effectiveness unless they are used effectively as well. Hence, efficiency is an element of total effectiveness.

- *Attainment of enterprise goals.* The process of social entrepreneurship ends with the attainment of goals. Obviously, therefore, a truly effective social enterprise must reach this stage successfully.

- *Ability to adapt to a changing environment.* A lot can happen to an enterprise between the time that it launches a business plan and when its goals are realized. In a dynamic environment, effectiveness depends on the capability of the organization to stay on the course defined by the social entrepreneur's mission and vision, and this means being able to adapt to changing circumstances.

To ignore any of these dimensions is to possess an incomplete understanding of the performance of the organization. The implications of this model are more far-reaching than just this definition, however. The individual dimensions exist in a positive feedback loop. For example, inadequate resources often lead to operating inefficiently, compromising goal attainment, and thus harming client satisfaction. This in turns leads to a greater crisis in resources, and so on. This is illustrated in Figure 5-5.

Operationalizing an approach to total enterprise effectiveness such as Kushner and Poole's involves the integration of performance metrics, measured in any of the ways discussed earlier. Kushner suggests the following possibilities for each dimension.

Evidence of constituent satisfaction

- A legal status and statutory base that meets the enterprise's needs
- A mission statement that is current, applied, and helps to guide action
- Evidence of responsiveness to beneficiary needs
- Accountability to the community via a governing board
- Involvement of beneficiaries and other stakeholders in program decisions
- Dissemination and communication of results and its needs
- Building of coalitions, partnerships, and networks
- Excellent relationships with principal government departments
- Excellent relationships with principal sources of funds
- A public image of integrity, cooperation, and capability

FIGURE 5-5   Positive Feedback Between the Elements of Overall Organizational Effectiveness

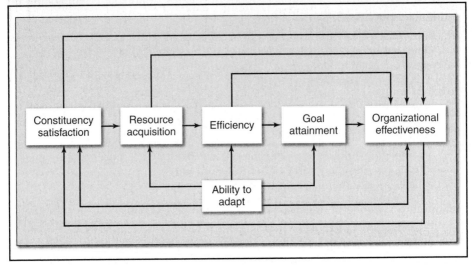

Source: Kushner & Poole (1996).

Resource Acquisition

- Diversified financial resources and resource development programs
- Human resources to deliver service, attract resources, and promote mission
- Leadership resources that provide vision and strategic direction
- Diversity in gender, age, location, and ethnicity consistent with local setting
- Adequate physical resources and infrastructure in headquarters, branches, and sites
- Intellectual capital: knowledge, judgment, unique skills, and/or individuals
- Purchasing and procurement skills to optimize the use of financial resources
- Technology and infrastructure resources: IT, logistics, telecom, MIS
- Ability to exploit interactions between resources

Efficiency

- Recognizable systems of decision making, team development, and conflict resolution
- Effective internal communications
- Logistical capability appropriate to provide services
- Means to develop staff, volunteer, management, and leadership resources
- Processes for organizational learning and development

- Control and reporting via budgeting, planning, reporting, and audits
- Guidance and review by a governing board
- Systems in place for strategic planning and service evaluation
- Evidence of growing productivity with appropriate capacity
- Evidence of resources used in an ethical and just manner

Goal attainment

- Uses long-term, strategic planning to achieve the mission
- Achieves its long-term, strategic goals
- Has a program development strategy to respond to vulnerability
- Achieves its program goals
- Makes administrative plans (operations, structure, budget, resource use)
- Achieves its administrative goals
- Has operational planning to deliver services according to strategy
- Achieves its operational goals
- Evaluates outcomes against goals at strategic, program, administrative, operational levels

Ability to adapt

- Adapts to constituency change
- Adapts to changes in resource availability
- Adapts to changing managerial practices
- Updates goals when appropriate
- Responds to evaluations
- Implements new knowledge and practices

Summary

- Measuring the impact of social enterprises is not straightforward because they have a "double bottom line"; that is, while they must make ends meet financially, they seek—or are supposed to seek, at least—to maximize their social impact, defined by their mission.
- The idea of measuring social value has four component concepts: accountability, evaluation, outcomes, and effectiveness.
- Social Return on Investment (SROI) is an attempt to quantify the economic and socioeconomic impacts of social enterprises. It breaks the benefits of a social venture into two parts: enterprise value and social purpose value, which together make up "blended value."
- Four common measures of "financial vulnerability" for social organizations are equity balances, revenue concentrations, administrative costs, and

operating margins. These measure a social enterprise's financial health far better than many traditional for-profit measures, such as return on investment (ROI).

- The right levels of mission and administrative spending for a social enterprise exist in a balance. Social ventures should fundraise (or write grants, or sell ancillary services) up to the point of equimarginality, which maximizes net donations (or subsidies, or earned revenues). They should spend this money in a way that maximizes the venture's mission, notwithstanding the financial return from this spending.
- The effectiveness of social enterprises can be measured on five dimensions: satisfaction of constituents, adequacy of funding, efficiency of operations, attainment of enterprise goals, and the ability to adapt to a changing environment.

Key Terms

- social value
- double bottom line
- accountability
- evaluation
- outcomes and impacts

- effectiveness
- Social Return on Investment
- equity balance
- revenue concentration
- administrative costs

- operating margin
- return-on-investment
- mission adherence

End-of-Chapter Questions and Cases

BizEthics

Your new social enterprise, BizEthics, is dedicated to assisting for-profit companies in their corporate ethics and social responsibility. Your main source of support will be fees paid by companies for your consulting services on issues ranging from social accountability to corporate philanthropy. Your abbreviated mission statement is as follows.

> BizEthics is a nonprofit organization dedicated to assisting America's most progressive corporations in their efforts to exhibit exemplary corporate ethics, social responsibility, and desire to give back to their communities.

In your business plan, you describe the measures of social value that correspond to this mission.

1. Why should you measure social value?
2. What will you measure?
3. Explain how these proposed measures gauge the true underlying concept of social value.
4. What data should you collect, and how often, to construct your measures?

INSIGHTARGENTINA

InsightArgentina (IA) is a nonprofit organization that seeks to improve the civil society conditions of Argentina by providing opportunities for people to volunteer. IA's mission is to "promote the development of a more engaged, socially aware, and active international community by facilitating experiential education programs that leave a lasting impact on participants and will contribute to the creation of a more sustainable civil and social sector."[23] The organization's mission is accomplished by pairing up volunteers of all ages and backgrounds from around the world to a partnering organization in Argentina that needs assistance. The programs are for those looking for a nonconventional way to experience the life and culture of Argentina and expose them to some of the most important social issues of the area.

IA believes that international volunteering creates social value by benefiting both the volunteer and the host organization. Benefits to the volunteers include meaningful travel experience abroad and specific work training, an awareness of the life and culture of Argentina, and direct foreign language training—all of which are experiences that can also be added to a volunteer's résumé. The host organizations benefit by receiving skills assistance in areas that they lack from volunteers who are dedicated to Argentina and through financial support received through the program fees.

IA also seeks to pursue both financial and social responsibility. It is a social enterprise that works both to achieve a mission and have a self-sustaining business plan. This is an example of the double bottom line, in which they must make ends meet financially, while maximizing their social impact. This allows IA to put its resources directly towards its mission.

Most of the revenues generated by IA come from the program fees that participants pay to be a part of the volunteer operations. The program fees are divided between the host NGO to help fund the project the volunteer will be engaged in, administrative and operating costs, and donations to a partner organization, HelpArgentina.[24] In an effort to be self-sustaining, IA has also established a venture capital fund, which invests both capital and time into projects.

1. Create a chart highlighting InsightArgentina's inputs, activities, outputs, outcomes, and impacts.

2. Which performance metrics are most appropriate for InsightArgentina to measure its social value? Why?

End Notes

1. See www.ashoka.org.
2. Ashoka (2006). *Measuring Effectiveness: A Six-Year Summary of Methodology and Findings.* Arlington, VA: Ashoka.
3. George A. Akerlof, Mani Maun (Aug. 1970). "The Market for 'Lemons': Quality Uncertainty and the Market Mechanism." *Quarterly Journal of Economics* 84 (3): 488–500.

4. See the Joint Committee on Standards for Educational Evaluation, www.wmich.edu/evalctr/jc/.

5. Kushner, Roland J. (2002). "Action Validation Research of an Inventory of Effectiveness Measures." Unpublished manuscript.

6. Putnam, Robert D. (2000). *Bowling Alone: The Collapse and Revival of American Community*. New York: Simon & Schuster.

7. Seelos, Christian, and Johanna Mair (2005). *European Business Forum* 20: 49–53.

8. www.redf.org

9. Gair, Cynthia (2005). A Report from the Good Ship SROI. San Francisco: REDF.

10. Tuckman, Howard P. and Chang, Cyril F. (1991). "A methodology for measuring the vulnerability of charitable nonprofit organizations." *Nonprofit and Voluntary Sector Quarterly* 20: 445–460.

11. Hager, Mark A. (2001). "Financial vulnerability among arts organizations: A test of the Tuckman-Chang measures." *Nonprofit and Voluntary Sector Quarterly* 30(2): 376–392.

12. The data are available from the National Center for Charitable Statistics, at www.nccs.urban.org/.

13. Mihir A. Desai (2001). "Worldwide Capital Shares and Rates of Return to Corporate Capital: Evidence from U.S. Multinationals." Manuscript.

14. See www.openconsult.com/info/news3100.asp (First accessed July 16, 2004).

15. Light, Paul C. (2001). " 'Nonprofit-like': Tongue Twister or Aspiration?" *Nonprofit Quarterly* 8(2). www.nonprofitquarterly.org/section/87.html (First accessed July 16, 2004).

16. Frumkin, Peter (2004). "On Being Nonprofit: The Bigger Picture" Harvard Business School Working Paper. http://hbsworkingknowledge.hbs.edu/item.jhtml?id=3087&t=nonprofit.

17. Of course, there are some lucky nonprofits that produce a profitable core service. But even for those with high earned revenues (arts and culture organizations, universities, hospitals), the core service is not usually profitable.

18. Schiff, J., and B. Weisbrod (1991). "Competition Between For-Profit and Non-Profit Organizations in Commercial Activities." *Annals of Public and Cooperative Economics* 62: 619–640; James, Estelle (1983) "How Nonprofits Grow: A Model." *Journal of Policy Analysis and Management* 2(3): 350–366.

19. It is not necessary for this curve to start at the origin or terminate at $M = 0$. The simple point is that mission adherence is maximized when revenues are neither zero nor at their highest level.

20. If a firm were to spend more than this, the return would be lower than the expense, lowering total profits. If the firm were to spend less than this, it would be forgoing positive net returns on spending.

21. Brooks, Arthur C. (2006). "Efficient Nonprofits?" *Policy Studies Journal* 34(3): 303–312.

22. Kushner, Roland J. and Peter P. Poole. (1996). Exploring Structure-Effectiveness Relationships in Nonprofit Arts Organizations. *Nonprofit Management and Leadership* 7(2): 119–136.

23. See www.insightargentina.com.

24. See www.responsibletravel.com/Wholesaler/Wholesaler100390.htm.

CHAPTER 6

EARNED INCOME

INTRODUCTION

Since its founding in 1995, Pittsburgh's Center for Creative Play (CFCP) has provided a parent-supervised indoor play environment aimed at children of all abilities. CFCP's goals are to create a welcoming, safe, and fun play area for all children; to provide education and networking support for families, and to promote an inclusive community. For many parents, CFCP is one of the few places that they feel welcome and safe as a family.[1]

From its founding, CFCP has recognized the advantages to being self-sustainable, and for this reason, it has concentrated its efforts on earned income. Of CFCP's $1.3 million annual operating budget, 60 percent is earned income through either social ventures or fee-for-service programs, while only 4 percent comes from the government, 10 percent from membership and admission fees, and 26 percent from donations. CFCP seeks to increase its self-sustainability even further, aiming to cover three-quarters of its operating budget with earned income by 2007.

CFCP's earned revenue comes from several unique sources, including an award-winning "Time to Sing" CD series, consulting services for organizations in other locales, leasing and rental opportunities within its building, cause-related marketing, and a Saturday evening camp program. All of these efforts, with the exception of the leasing and rental of space in the building, directly support CFCP's mission of providing inclusive programs to all children while providing a steady revenue stream.

Is CFCP a unique case? Can other social enterprises use earned revenues in such large amounts and innovative ways? This chapter explores the possibilities. After discussing how enterprises mobilize resources and the categories of income, we will focus on fee-based income and its potential to support social ventures.

MOBILIZING RESOURCES

Social enterprises know they need resources—financial, human, and technological, among others. But the questions are how much, and in what combination? Obviously, the business plan requires details in this regard. How do we develop these details? Social entrepreneurship expert J. Gregory Dees suggests the following four-step process to assess resource requirements.[2]

STEP 1. DEFINE THE CAPABILITIES NEEDED FOR THE SOCIAL ENTERPRISE

Social entrepreneurs often prematurely start their planning process by thinking about funding. Instead, they should begin by thinking about their objectives as defined in the mission and the capabilities needed to meet these objectives, as described in the preceding chapters. For example, let's say your enterprise's mission is to improve learning outcomes in your area, and your goal is an after-school tutoring program that has the capacity to serve all the students who want the service. What are the capabilities you will need to make this goal a reality? Here is a possible list of capabilities:

- Tutoring
- Program administration
- Grantwriting, fundraising, and volunteer recruitment
- Clerical support
- Computer support
- Legal support

STEP 2. DEVISE A HUMAN RESOURCE OUTLINE TO MEET EACH CAPABILITY NEED

Often, social entrepreneurs make the mistake of not thinking upfront about how different capabilities might be met, but it is necessary to outline which capabilities will be met and by whom. For example, perhaps your own expertise lies in tutoring, but you are weak in technical areas such as computing. Your partner is better on the technical side; the two of you plan to take on the grantwriting, fundraising, and recruiting of additional volunteer tutors. You plan to hire staff for program administration and clerical support, and contract out for legal advice.

This step is far from mechanical; it actually requires creativity because how capabilities should be assigned is not always clear. Social entrepreneurs tend to be smart, energetic, and incredibly hard working. The tendency is to try to do everything alone—after all, we all know the old saying, "If you want something done right, do it yourself." The reason this approach is usually mistaken has to do with the opportunity cost of a social entrepreneur's time: the value created if his or her time were truly put to best use. Usually, even if you can do a simple task better than someone else, more net value is created by farming it out and concentrating on the things you are truly uniquely suited to.

STEP 3. DEVELOP A RESOURCE PLAN

Each capability requires certain resources to execute, in terms of money, time, expertise, or something else of value. Social entrepreneurs need to map necessary resources into each of the capabilities identified in Step 1 and identify the appropriate sources for these resources. For example, tutoring requires the volunteer time of the social entrepreneur and other qualified people in the community. It also requires space that is either rented or donated, and certain equipment such as computers, which are donated, leased, or purchased. Administrators and staff people will also require some kind of space and compensation.

After a comprehensive resource map is constructed, the social entrepreneur decides where each type of resource will come from. Details on this decision are the subject of the rest of this chapter and include volunteer hours, donated expertise, earned revenues, borrowed revenues, privately donated money, and government funding.

STEP 4. PUT ON THE NUMBERS

Only at this last step is it time to actually start actual financial planning, as outlined in the chapter on business plans. Each capability, with its matching source of resources, requires corresponding figures. How much total volunteer time of each type is needed? How much revenue do we need to earn? What is our fundraising goal? And so on.

Of course, the enterprise's needs have to be based on a particular time frame—the resource needs for the first year of operation are lower than that for the first three years, for example. This means that the resource acquisition plan has to have a dynamic element and answer a series of questions.

1. What are our needs for the first year? The first three years?
2. What resources are already in hand? Which still must be raised?
3. What is the time frame of our resource goals to meet these needs?
4. What are the most important resource milestones that we need to meet?
5. What are our fallback resource strategies in case one source proves more troublesome than expected?

Dees's four-step process essentially asks these four questions:

1. What capabilities do we need?
2. Who will provide them?
3. How will we meet the capabilities?
4. Where will the resources come from?

Figure 6-1 summarizes this model.

FIGURE 6-1 The Capabilities-Resource Model

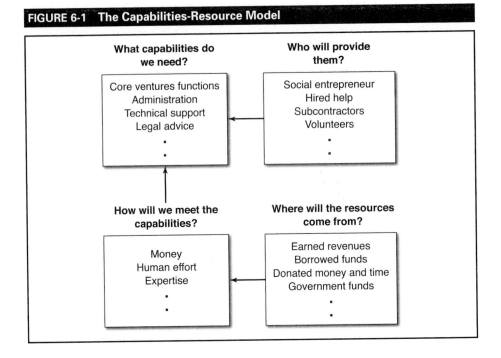

INCOME SOURCES

Income to social enterprises comes from three primary sources: fee income, donations, and governments (see Figure 6-2). In the United States, nonprofits receive roughly half of their income through fees and related earned sources; donations make up a fifth; and the government provides the balance of funding. This pattern, however, hides considerable variation between types of enterprises. For example, social welfare organizations receive, on average, 52 percent of their funds from government and earn less than a third; health organizations depend on donations for just 6 percent; private gifts make up nearly half of all the income of arts groups; sacramental religious organizations rely on donations for 84 percent of revenues and receive no government money.[3]

We will look at each of these funding types in turn and explore the importance of each for social entrepreneurs. This chapter focuses on the varieties of so-called "earned income," and the next chapter is dedicated to donations and government funding sources. The types of earned income are summarized in Figure 6-3.

Fee Income

Social enterprises have a number of ways to earn fee income. The most common route is through sales of a commercial product. Nonsales avenues exist for fee income as well, though. This section covers each.

FIGURE 6-2   Sources of Income for U.S. Nonprofits

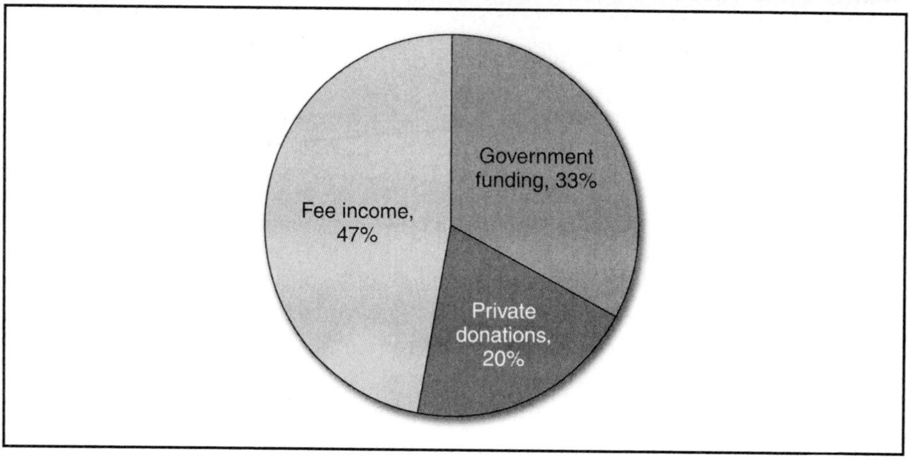

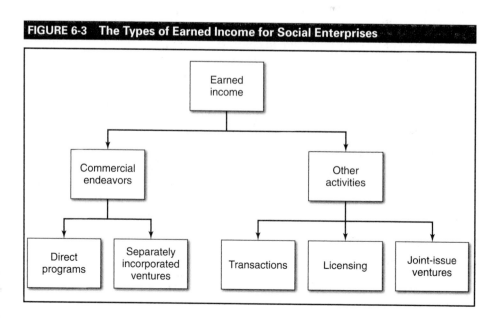

Source: Salamon (2002).[4]

COMMERCIAL FEE INCOME

Social enterprises can earn fee income through endeavors operated directly. For example, the New York City venture Work 101 seeks to help the disadvantaged by addressing a root cause of poverty: low rates of sustained employment. Emphasizing the ability of participants to perform well at their jobs, Work 101 focuses on the confidence of participants and establishing work as a norm in life. To accomplish these tasks, Work 101 established a for-profit business—Imprint

FIGURE 6-3   The Types of Earned Income for Social Enterprises

Cartridge Works—that employs participants on a full-time basis, giving them jobs in production, customer service, sales, or transportation by making high-quality toner cartridges for the New York metropolitan area. After participants spend anywhere from 6 to 18 months working at Imprint Cartridge, Work 101 then helps them find private-sector jobs.[5]

Some fee-based ventures aren't as close to the enterprise's core mission as Imprint Cartridge Works is to Work 101, yet still potentially provides a good stream of useful income. In this case, a social enterprise often chooses to incorporate the endeavor outside the social enterprise. In one famous historical example, friends and benefactors of the New York University Law School purchased the C.F. Mueller Macaroni Company in 1947 and dedicated its profits to NYU. This practice was not unheard of at the time, as colleges and universities invested in numerous for-profit enterprises to get better returns on their endowments. NYU used the profit from Mueller Macaroni to support its law school for more than 40 years. Indeed, prior to 1950, income from wholly owned businesses like this were exempt from corporate taxes as long as the income was used to support the nonprofit's exempt functions, regardless of whether the businesses were related to the activities that qualified the organization as a nonprofit.[6]

How do you decide whether a fee-income program should be direct or separately incorporated? Social enterprise expert Dennis R. Young says, "... ventures intended solely for net-revenue generating purposes are more often separately incorporated (generally as for-profit corporations), while those more intrinsic to mission favor the internal programming format."[7] In other words, the closer a commercial plan is to the mission of an enterprise, the more likely it is to be produced as part of the "core" of the organization. This is summarized in Table 6-1.

For example, a welfare-to-work enterprise might start a commercial enterprise that actually provides on-the-job training for clients. Although this might earn revenues, it is clearly near the core mission of the organization and will probably best be directly provided. In contrast, a museum's café will generally be provided only to raise funds to cross-subsidize the museum's true mission activities

TABLE 6-1 Characteristics of Directly Provided and Separately Incorporated Programs

More Likely to Be Directly-Produced	More Likely to Be Separately Incorporated
Good or service appeals to purchasers' goodwill and sense of charitable support for the enterprise.	Buyers are motivated entirely by self-interest.
The primary motive for production is the mission.	The primary motive for production is revenues.
Sales do not cover program costs.	Sales generate a positive profit stream.
Volunteers participate.	Employees are paid.
Suppliers subsidize operations with donations.	Suppliers charge normal rates.

Sources: Dees (2001); James and Young (2006).[8]

and will likely as not be set up as a separate for-profit enterprise—and may be even subcontracted to an outside firm for a profit.

EARNED INCOME NOT INVOLVING FEE-EARNING ENDEAVORS

Writers about social entrepreneurship have spent considerable energy over the past decade on the ways nonprofits can earn revenues to cross-subsidize their core social missions. These typically involve the relationships and collaborations between nonprofits and for-profits. These relationships come in several basic types:[9]

1. *Transactions* occur between the two sectors when the for-profit purchases or sells services, supplies, or equipment to or from a nonprofit (perhaps at subsidized rates), or when a for-profit includes a nonprofit in the net proceeds from its regular market transactions. An example of a for-profit sharing net revenues is the 1983 campaign in which American Express donated one dollar for every new account (and one cent for every transaction) to the foundation that was renovating Ellis Island and the Statue of Liberty.

2. *Licensing* can be similar to a transaction, except that the nonprofit explicitly sells the use of its name and logo for a fee or a percentage of the sales. Colleges and universities have been licensing their names and logos for decades. More recently, other organizations have entered into this type of relationship. For example, SmithKline—maker of Nicoderm (a smoking cessation product)—and the American Cancer Society have been featured in advertisements as partners to help people quit smoking. The American Cancer Society said that they do not endorse any products but were paid $2.5 million for use of the logo.

3. *Joint-issue promotion* does not necessarily entail a transfer of funds from one to the other. Instead, the nonprofit and the for-profit join forces to combat a single issue, working jointly to distribute products or promotional material.

James Austin, who pioneered much of the thinking on nonprofit/for-profit relationships, believes that social and commercial organizations develop relationships in three stages:[10]

1. *Philanthropic stage.* A business donates money or supplies to a nonprofit. This stage is characterized by a low level of engagement between the two collaborators, a narrow scope of activities, infrequent interaction, and a peripheral importance to the mission of the collaborators.

2. *Transactional stage.* Benefits flow to and from each partner. This stage can also be identified as "commercial" because both partners are focused on a specific transaction. In this stage, the missions and values of the partners begin to overlap, and there is a reciprocal exchange of resources.

3. *Integration stage.* Each organization thinks about not only what is in the best interest for the individual organization but also for the partnership (or collaboration). Through the increased interaction and resource sharing, the organizational culture is interwoven. The chief difference between the second and third stage is that in the third stage, the organizations are combining efforts instead of exchanging resources.

These stages are summarized in Table 6-2.

TABLE 6-2 Stages of Engagement Between Nonprofits and For-Profits

Engagement Type	Examples
Philanthropic stage	Grants Sponsorships Profit-sharing
Commercial/transactional stage	For-profits supply nonprofits Nonprofits supply for-profits
Integrative/partnerships stage	Co-branding and licensing relationships Joint-issue marketing Civic partnerships

Source: Austin (2000).

Earlier, Table 6-1 noted that some fee-based ventures do not earn positive net revenues. There are ample examples of social enterprises losing money on commercial endeavors. The question generally is whether this situation is tolerable due to the proximity of the commercial venture to the enterprise's core mission. Estelle James and Dennis R. Young describe the possible profit outcomes from running a fee-based venture in what they call the "product profile map," summarized in Table 6-3. A venture that is close to a social enterprise's mission and earns a positive profit is a "star." If it is close to the mission but earns a loss,

---

The Dangers of Corporate Partnerships

In 1997, the American Medical Association (AMA) entered into an apparently lucrative licensing agreement with the Sunbeam Corporation, which makes home electrical products. Under the agreement, the AMA would give its famous "seal of approval" for Sunbeam to display on humidifiers, blood-pressure monitors, and certain other devices. In exchange, the AMA would receive millions of dollars in royalties over a five-year period.[11] The trouble is, the AMA had no plans to test or evaluate these devices—so in the minds of some, the endorsement was useless at best and misleading at worst. When the public and members of the AMA found out about the deal, there was such an outcry that the AMA felt compelled to back out of the contract, at which point Sunbeam sued the AMA for $20 million, claiming breach of contract. The suit was ultimately settled for $9.9 million and resulted in several staff firings.

Clearly, this situation is not what an optimal licensing agreement is supposed to do. Licensing is intended to create a mutually beneficial exchange for both partners, in which the commercial entity shows its guarantee of quality with an authentic seal of approval from an enterprise with a social mission that involves the quality of the product. In other words, the nonprofit must have an authentic interest in the product's quality. In exchange for vouching for a good product, the nonprofit receives valuable funding, and the public has greater confidence. The problem in the Sunbeam case was that the AMA was *not* primarily pursuing its mission ("To promote the art and science of medicine and the betterment of public health") in licensing its name.[12]

TABLE 6-3 The Product Profile Map

	High Mission Impact	Low Mission Impact
Positive Profit	Stars	Cash cows
Loss-Making	Saints	Dogs

Source: James and Young (2006).[13]

it might still be worthwhile, so it is a "saint." Profit-making ventures that are far from the mission are "cash cows," whereas those that are not close to the mission but earn a loss are "dogs." Obviously, social entrepreneurs seek stars and want to avoid dogs. Saints and cash cows may or may not be a good idea.

One of the most important pieces of economic theory of fee-based income is the model of cross-subsidy developed by Estelle James in 1983.[14] This model asserts that social enterprises tend to develop at least two products: One that is loss-making but highly mission-oriented, and the other that is less mission-oriented but throws off net revenues to subsidize production of the first. There are many examples of this. Universities cross-subsidize research with tuition revenues; symphony orchestras perform "pops" concerts so they can also perform more challenging symphonic works. The implication of the James model for social entrepreneurs is that a strict adherence to only one activity may not be the norm or even desirable. The question worth exploring is what combinations of products and services are feasible to create a balanced portfolio of mission and solvency?

MEMBERSHIP INCOME

One way some social enterprises earn revenues is through membership fees. There are two types of enterprises that do so. The first are member-serving organizations, which provide benefits primarily to the members themselves. For example, a professional society, such as the American Bar Association, charges membership fees but confers benefits to lawyers who belong to the organization. The second type of membership organization is a public-serving organization with members, which serves both members and the public-at-large. For example, a public radio station solicits gifts in the form of "memberships" but serves all community members regardless of payment.[15]

Many types of social enterprises earn revenues from membership income; however, membership income is most prevalent outside the world of public charities (in the United States, 501(c)(3) nonprofit organizations). The most common nonprofits that earn their revenues from members are professional and trade associations, which are generally associated with particular industries and jobs. Table 6-4 lists the types of nonprofits as well as the percentage of their revenues acquired from membership dues and fees.

Professional and trade associations are an area of substantial nonprofit growth. Between 1996 and 2004, for example, the number of associations grew by more than 4 percent. Even more impressively, from the 1970s to 2005, the

TABLE 6-4	Revenues from Membership Dues for Various Nonprofit Enterprises, 2003	
Enterprise Type	*Percentage of Income from Membership Dues and Fees*
Labor organizations	66.02%
Social clubs	59.61%
Business leagues	40.27%
Public charities[16]	0.90%

Source: Steinberg (2006).

percentage of the adult population belonging to an association grew from less than 15 percent to more than a quarter. Participation is particularly high among younger professionals—those belonging to "Generation X," born between the mid-1960s and mid-1970s. The data suggest that younger adults will also join associations at relatively high rates as they move into their prime earning years. Projections suggest that the number of adults in professional associations will grow by at least five million over the decade from 2005 to 2015.[17]

Given the high growth in professional membership associations (summarized in Figure 6-4) and the interest in these organizations by younger adults,

FIGURE 6-4 Growth in Membership of Trade and Professional Associations

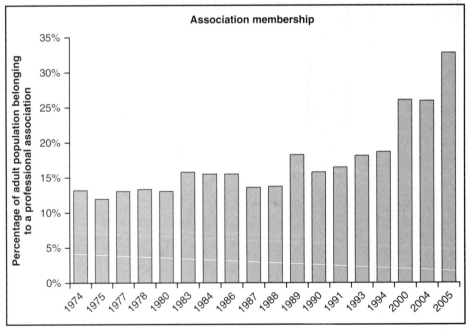

Sources: General Social Survey, 1974–1995[18]; Social Capital Community Benchmark Survey 2000[19]; Maxwell Poll 2004–2005[20].

they are clearly worthy of study by social entrepreneurs. The services that the most successful associations provide professionally for individuals might just be the kind of services different kinds of social enterprises can and should consider in the search for fee-based member income. These services include the following:

- *Benefits.* Association members frequently have access to group health and dental plans, retirement planning services, and outplacement assistance.
- *Career advantages.* Associations can provide career enhancing professional networks.
- *Community.* Members of certain professions seek the communities that associations can provide, particularly in jobs that require frequent moves at the beginning of a person's career.
- *Opportunities to serve.* Younger members of associations frequently look for service opportunities, both to the associations and to related charities. Associations often broker and provide these opportunities.

Summary

- Social enterprises need financial, human, and technological resources. Finding the right type and amount involves a four-step process: Define the capabilities needed for the social enterprise; devise a human resource outline to meet each capability need; develop a resource plan; and put on the numbers.
- Income for social enterprises comes from three primary sources: fee income, donations, and governments. In the United States, nonprofits receive roughly half of their income through fees and related earned sources; donations make up a fifth; and the government provides the balance of funding.
- Social enterprises can earn income through the sales of a commercial product. The two types of commercial sales involve directly and indirectly operated endeavors. Direct endeavors usually involve activities close to the enterprise's social mission.
- Social enterprises can also earn income in other ways. They can profit from transactions in which a for-profit includes a nonprofit in the net proceeds from its regular market transactions; they can license their name or logo for a fee or a percentage of a for-profit's sales; and they can undertake joint-issue promotion in which the social enterprise and the for-profit join forces to combat a single issue, working jointly to distribute products or promotional material.
- Two types of enterprises have members and thus membership income: member-serving organizations and public-serving organizations with members. The most common social enterprises that earn their revenues from members are professional and trade associations.

Key Terms

- resource plan
- Capabilities-Resource Model
- fee income

- licensing
- joint-issue promotion
- membership income

- opportunity cost

End-of-Chapter Questions and Cases

FIRST PLACE FUND FOR YOUTH

The First Place Fund for Youth is an organization founded in 1998 in Oakland, California, that offers services to youth who are emerging out of the foster care system into independent living. The First Place Fund offers significantly discounted housing and assistance in life skills, employment assistance, financial assistance in the form of micro-credit, and education. Having served hundreds of individuals who have "timed out" out of the foster system, The First Place Fund offers a housing subsidy, which gradually phases out over two years. At that time, tenancy is legally transferred fully to the inhabitant, who can live there as long as that person can meet the rent. The First Place Fund boasts a record of participants being six times less likely to be arrested or incarcerated, four times less likely to be homeless, three times less likely to be on welfare, and 50 percent more likely to be employed.[21]

The First Place Fund's mission statement is as follows:

> It is the mission of First Place to promote long-term self-sufficiency among emancipated foster youth by providing them with the skills, resources, and support to make a successful transition to adulthood.

1. Define the First Place Fund's objectives.
2. Define the organization's capabilities.
3. Who will meet these capabilities?
4. What resources will be needed? How will they be spent?
5. Where will the resources come from?
6. Devise both a sales and nonsales earned revenue strategy for the First Place Fund.

ARTISTS FOR HUMANITY

Artists for Humanity is a Boston-based organization that has created a successful model of how a nonprofit organization can be very entrepreneurial in its business approach.[22]

Established in 1991, Artists for Humanity was started by Susan Rogerson as an after-school arts program for middle- and high school students to encourage youth empowerment through art and entrepreneurship.[23] Through the mission "to provide underserved city youth with the keys to self-sufficiency through paid employment in the arts," Rogerson wanted to show that young people could provide tangible services to the commercial world.[24]

Artists for Humanity employs and trains students to build self-esteem and to give them life-long skills. Students receive materials, studio space, and instruction from professionals and artists,[25] and in turn they have to treat the program like any other job: They have to show up on time, treat the work seriously, and function as team members. They also have to fulfill the needs of their customers by listening and responding to their requests. Their instructors not only teach them to become better artists in a variety of mediums but also to become entrepreneurs. Students learn the principles of marketing and selling by working with clients on commissioned work and by exhibiting their art in galleries.

Artists for Humanity has quickly expanded throughout the years, creating not only after-school programs but summer programs as well. As the enterprise has grown, the funding needs have extended beyond the capacity of regular fundraising, and other means of revenue have been incorporated into the organization. For example, the organization has established a membership in which the proceeds help support the organization, and the member receives exclusive benefits and opportunities. In addition to donations from individuals, foundations, and corporations (with limited government support) the students sell their work and services. Both the organization and the artist benefit by each receiving half of the proceeds.[26]

Several years ago, Artists for Humanity recognized the need to bridge urban community businesses and neighborhoods and as a result constructed a facility, the EpiCenter, to house its programs and gallery. As one of the country's most environmentally sustainable commercial buildings, it attracts many, and as a result, Artists for Humanity is able to rent out its gallery space for exhibits, events, and receptions. The gallery rental program exceeded first year projections in just seven months, and the facility had more than 100 bookings in the first year for corporate and nonprofit events, both contributing to additional income. Another benefit of the rental space is that it brings in a captive audience to view the students' work, leading to opportunities to create more work and more program income. Furthermore, the students are now selling their art online at the organization's Web site.

Even with declining funding from the government,[27] Artists for Humanity has shown that it can generate revenue and maintain a sustainable social enterprise through fundraising, selling memberships, selling artwork and services, and providing rental space for exhibits and events.

1. Outline the Capabilities-Resource Model for Artists for Humanity by answering the following questions: What capabilities do they need? Who provides them? How will they meet the capabilities? Where will the resources come from?

2. What are some other ways in which Artists for Humanity could generate income not involving fee-earning endeavors? Be specific.

End Notes

1. See www.centerforcreativeplay.org/.
2. Dees, J. Gregory (2001). "Mobilizing Resources." In Dees, J, Gregory, Jed Emerson, and Peter Economy (Eds.). *Enterprising Nonprofits: A Toolkit for Social Entrepreneurs.* New York: Wiley, pp. 63–102.
3. Brooks, Arthur C. (2004). "The Effects of Public Policy on Private Charity." *Administration & Society* 36(2): 166–185.
4. Salamon, Lester M. (2002). "The Resilient Sector: The State of Nonprofit America." In Salamon, Lester M. (Ed.). *The State of Nonprofit America.* Washington, DC: Brookings Institution Press: pp. 3–61.
5. From "Success Story: Ethan Wohl: From Wall Street Attorney to Non-Profit Entrepreneur." JDBliss Web site. www.jdbliss.com/e_article000316579.cfm?x=b11,0,w.
6. Hansmann, Henry B. "Unfair Competition and the Unrelated Business Income Tax." *Virginia Law Review*, Vol. 75, No. 3. (Apr. 1989): 605–635.
7. Young, Dennis R. (2006). "Wise Decision-making for Nonprofits in Uncertain Times: An Overview." In Young, Dennis R. (Ed.). *Wise Decision-making for Nonprofits in Uncertain Times: Using Nonprofit Resources Effectively.* New York: The Foundation Center Press, 2006.
8. James, Estelle, and Dennis R. Young (2006). "Fee Income and Commercial Ventures." In Young, Dennis R. (Ed.). *Financing Nonprofits: Putting Theory into Practice.* Lanham, MD: AltaMira Press, pp. 93–120.
9. Andreasen, Alan R. (1996) "Profits for Nonprofits: Find a Corporate Partner." *Harvard Business Review, 74,* 47–59.
10. Austin, James E. (2000). "Strategic Collaboration between Nonprofits and Businesses." *Nonprofit and Voluntary Sector Quarter, 29,* 69–97.
11. Bartling, Charles. E. (1998) *Strategic Alliances for Nonprofit Organizations.* Washington, DC: American Society of Association Executives; *The New York Times* (August 3, 1998): "Broken Deal Costs AMA $9.9 Million." *The New York Times,* A12.
12. See www.ama-assn.org/ama/pub/category/1815.html.
13. James, Estelle, and Dennis R. Young (2006). "Fee Income and Commercial Ventures." In Young, Dennis R. (Ed.). *Financing Nonprofits: Putting Theory into Practice.* Lanham, MD: AltaMira Press, pp. 113.
14. James, Estelle (1983), "How nonprofits grow: a model." *Journal of Policy Analysis and Management* 2(3): 350–366.
15. Steinberg, Richard (2006). "Membership Income." In Young, Dennis R. (Ed.). *Financing Nonprofits: Putting Theory into Practice.* Lanham, MD: AltaMira Press, pp. 121–155.
16. These are all 501(c)(3) nonprofit organizations.
17. See Brooks, Arthur C. (2006). *Generations and the Future of Association Participation.* Chicago, IL: William E. Smith Institute for Association Research.
18. Davis, James Allan, Tom W. Smith, and Peter V. Marsden (2002). *General Social Surveys, 1972–2002: Cumulative CodeBook.* Chicago: National Opinion Research Center; *Giving and Volunteering in the United States* (2001).
19. *Social Capital Community Benchmark Survey* (SCCBS). www.roper.com.
20. Maxwell Poll on Civic Engagement and Inequality. Campbell Public Affairs Institute (2004). Maxwell Poll on Civic Engagement and Inequality [Computer File]. Syracuse, New York: the Maxwell School at Syracuse University.

21. Source: "About Us." The First Place Fund for Youth Web site. (www.firstplacefund. org/about/index.html); Shirk, Martha. (July 5, 2006). "New Homes for Foster Care's Old Folks." *Youth Today*. (www.youthtoday.org/youthtoday/July05/ story2_7_05.html).
22. This case comes from a dossier in the Manhattan Institute's Social Entrepreneurship Awards program and is used with the Institute's permission.
23. Gould, Kira L. (November 6, 2004 Third Edition). "Picture of efficiency—Artist space for teens draws on renewable technologies." *The Boston Globe*. Real Estate, pg. E8.
24. See www.afhboston.com
25. Jain, Vinay. (Summer 2003). "Not-So-Starving Artists – Artists for Humanity students are also employees." Stanford Social Innovation Review.
26. (Jain, 2003).
27. (Jain, 2003)

CHAPTER 7

DONATIONS AND GOVERNMENT INCOME

INTRODUCTION

Bill Gates is the world's richest man, with a net worth of more than $50 billion. He is also the most philanthropic: The Bill & Melinda Gates Foundation, formed in 2000, has (as of 2006) an endowment in excess of $33 billion and is growing quickly. In fact, it will almost double in size when another of the world's richest men, Warren Buffett, fulfills his pledge to give more than $30 billion to the Gates Foundation. With an endowment that will soon be as big as the entire GDP of Ukraine, the Gates Foundation is the largest in the history of the world. It is clear that the Foundation must operate differently than others have in the past—and indeed, it claims that it does. From its inception, the Gates Foundation has prided itself on being unique, adopting an entrepreneurial approach to donations reflecting the background of its founder.[1]

What is the entrepreneurial approach? First, the Gates Foundation concentrates on a just a few areas of giving—rather than trying to flood the field, it specializes in education and third-world health issues. The objective here is to ensure that the Foundation's efforts have an impact. Second, the Foundation insists on measuring its impact. As we have already discussed, the process of social entrepreneurship relies on the definition and measurement of social value, and the Gates Foundation assesses its impact as assiduously as would any for-profit entrepreneur. Third, the Gates Foundation regularly works in partnerships—with governments, businesses, and other nonprofits—to make sure that their efforts lead to a real, lasting change. Developing better schools, for instance, can require the work of parents, teachers, administrators, the school district, and a whole host of other actors. The Gates Foundation tries to work with and coordinate the actions of these groups, providing funding (or other assistance) up front to create changes that will last well after the departure of the Gates Foundation.

Is the Gates Foundation an aberration, or is its approach the future of charitable giving? What do social entrepreneurs need to understand about philanthropy in this rapidly changing world, as well as that from governments? How can entrepreneurial service providers and entrepreneurial givers work together? These are the issues we will probe in this chapter.

PRIVATE GIVING

Most U.S. social enterprises and other nonprofits rely critically on donated support. For example, donations make up 16 percent of the revenues to nonprofit education organizations (and far more to private universities), 20 percent to human service charities, 44 percent to the arts, and 84 percent to religious institutions.[2] Small, grassroots enterprises rely even more heavily on donated support because government grants and earned revenues are frequently not available to them. The bottom line is that, without private charitable giving in the United States, many critical services would simply disappear, and many needs would go unmet. It is inconceivable that the U.S. public sector could or would step in to provide all the funding that private citizens currently donate to charities and causes across the country.

Charitable donations come from four basic sources: individuals, foundations, bequests, and corporations. Table 7-1 shows that, by far the largest source is living individuals, who privately give more than three quarters of all gifts.[3] This comes as a surprise to many social entrepreneurs, who see foundations and corporations as especially promising gift sources. In reality, foundations provide less than 12 percent, and corporations give about 5 percent of the total. The lesson from this is that social entrepreneurs should not neglect individuals in their fundraising efforts; rather, private donations should be central to any serious fundraising effort.

WHO GIVES?

A large majority of U.S. citizens give money each year. Most estimates place the percentage of American households that make money contributions each year at 70 to 80 percent, and the average American household contributes more than $1,000 each year. Among those households that make positive contributions, the

TABLE 7-1 Source of Donations to American Nonprofits, 2005	
Living individuals	76.5%
Foundations	11.5%
Bequests	6.7%
Corporations	5.3%

Source: Giving USA 2005.

FIGURE 7-1   Average Annual Contributions to Various Types of Causes and Charities Among Those Making Positive Contributions to These Types of Causes, 2003

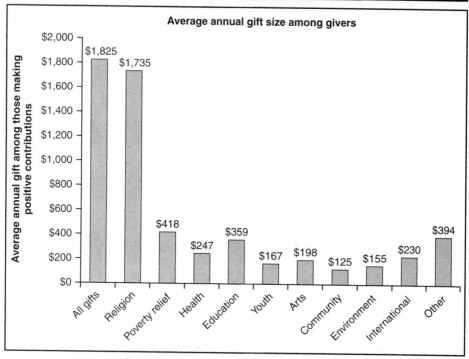

Average annual gift size among givers

Source: 2003 COPPS/PSID[4].

average amount given is about $1,800.[5] For these families, this represents an annual sacrifice in excess of 3 percent of total household income. Figure 7-1 summarizes how large the average annual gift to each type of cause was in 2003, among households that gave to each type of cause.

Contrary to what we often hear, American giving does not go all—or even mostly—to religion. About a third of all individual gifts go toward purely religious activities, such as support for houses of worship. The rest goes to secular activities (some of which are undertaken by religious organizations), such as education, health, and social welfare.[6]

Between 50 and 60 percent of American households formally volunteer their time each year, volunteering an average of almost 50 hours annually.[7] About 40 percent of volunteer hours go to religious causes, followed by about 30 percent for youth-related activities, such as the PTA and children's sports. Poverty-related causes, health charities, and activist causes also receive significant amounts of volunteer time.[8]

The Americans, who give money, volunteer, or both, are the people most likely to behave charitably in informal ways as well. As Table 7-2 shows, formal

	People Who Give Money Formally to Charities	People Who Don't Give Money Formally to Charities
TABLE 7-2 Americans Who Give Money Formally to Charity Give Informally as Well		
Activity (Annual)		
Give blood	18%	8%
Return mistaken change to a cashier	51%	33%
Help a homeless person	67%	48%
Give up seat to another person	43%	36%
Let someone cut ahead in line	89%	76%
Give directions to stranger	90%	78%
Express concern for the less fortunate	73%	66%

Source: 2002 General Social Survey.[9]

money donors are nearly three times as likely to give money informally to friends and strangers as nondonors. People who give to charity at least once per year are twice as likely to donate blood as people who don't give money. They are also significantly more likely to give food or money to a homeless person on the street.[10]

No developed country approaches American giving and volunteering levels. Many studies show that Americans give charitably more money per capita than the citizens of other developed countries. Volunteering follows the same pattern: In 1998, Americans were 15 percentage points more likely to volunteer than the Dutch, 21 points more likely than the Swiss, and 32 points more likely than the Germans. These differences are not attributable to demographic characteristics such education, income, age, sex, or marital status. On the contrary, if we look at two people who are identical in all these ways—but one is European and the other American—the probability is far lower that the European will volunteer than the American. For example, an Austrian who is otherwise identical to an American will be 32 percentage points less likely to volunteer, a Spaniard will be 31 points less likely, and an Italian will be 29 points less likely, on average.[11]

In sum, it is indisputable that the nonprofit sector in the United States is one of the dominant features of the American economic landscape, that voluntary support for the sector is abundant in the form of money and time, and that the United States is exceptional in both these ways, compared with other developed nations. U.S. social entrepreneurship is inseparable from private giving.

Why Do People Give?

Four major demographic effects predict giving better than others: income, wealth, religious participation, and the structure of families.

The most common way to measure the relationship between charitable giving and income is by looking at the percentage increase in donations associated with a 10 percent increase in income. Most research has found this to be in the neighborhood of 7 percent, even after controlling for other factors, such as education, age, and race. For example, imagine a family, who earns $100,000 per year and gives $3,000 to charity. If they receive an income increase of 10 percent, to $110,000, the data suggest that they will most likely increase their giving to something like $3,210. Conversely, an income decrease down to $90,000 would mean a giving drop to about $2,790. This is a good news–bad news story for social enterprises. On the one hand, it means that donations tend to grow more slowly (in percentage terms) than the whole economy. On the other hand, it means charities tend to be hurt less than the economy as a whole when there is a recession and incomes decline.[12]

Charitable donations are also affected by changes in wealth (the value of people's savings, investments, and property). Economists estimate that a 10 percent increase in the amount of wealth people have increases their giving by about 3 percent. Most economists believe that wealth affects giving less than income because people protect their savings to ensure an income source in the future for themselves or their heirs. Still, the wealth effect on giving can be important for social enterprises. For example, from 1995 through 2000, inflation-adjusted GDP per capita increased by just 12 percent, whereas average household giving exploded by 54 percent, due to a run-up in average household wealth caused by the stock market boom and increases in house values.[13]

Religious behavior is the single biggest predictor of American charity in general. Whether they are religious or nonreligious themselves, social entrepreneurs need to understand the connection between faith and giving. In the year 2000, religious people (the 33 percent of the population who attend their houses of worship at least once per week) were 25 percentage points more likely to give away money than secularists (the 27 percent who attend less than a few times per year, or have no religion). They were also 23 points more likely to volunteer.[14] When considering the average dollar amounts of money donated and time volunteered, the gap between the groups increases even further: Religious people gave nearly four times more dollars per year, on average, than secularists ($2,210 versus $642). They also volunteered more than twice as often (12 times per year, versus 5.8 times).[15]

Naturally, these differences could be due to religion itself, or rather to some other personal characteristics such as race, education, gender, or income. Controlling for all these demographic differences, we still find an enormous charity gap between religious and secular people. For instance, imagine two people who are identical in income, education, age, race, and marital status. The one difference between them is that, while one goes to church every week, the other never does. Knowing this, we can predict that the churchgoer will be 21 percentage points more likely to make a charitable gift of money during the year than the nonchurchgoer and will also be 26 points more likely to volunteer. Furthermore, the churchgoers will tend to give about $1,400 more per year to charity and volunteer on about six more occasions.[16]

The differences described here are not a simple artifact of religious people giving to their churches. Religious people are more charitable in every measurable nonreligious way—including secular donations, informal giving, and even acts of kindness and generosity—than secularists. For example, in 2000, religious people were 10 points more likely than secularists to give money to explicitly nonreligious charities and 21 points more likely to volunteer. The value of the average religious household gifts to nonreligious charities was 14 percent higher than the average secular household's.[17] Religious people were also far more likely than secularists to give in informal, nonreligious ways. For example, in 2000, people belonging to religious congregations gave 46 percent more money to family and friends than people who did not belong.[18] In 2002, religious people were far more likely to donate blood than secularists, to give food or money to a homeless person, and even to return change mistakenly given them by a cashier.[19]

Family life in America is deeply connected with giving behavior as well. First, people who have children give more than people who don't. Perhaps the act of having children stimulates giving, or givers are more likely to have children (researchers don't know for sure), but we find that, for example, a household with four members is more likely to give and volunteer each year than a household with only two members. If two married adults are identical in income, education, religion, race, age, and political views—but the first has one more child than the second—the odds are that the first parent will be more likely to give and will give away more dollars each year.[20]

A second fact about giving and families is that children tend to learn giving habits from their parents. In one large survey from the year 2000, a sample of Americans was asked about their parents' volunteering, as well as their own volunteering. People who said they saw their parents volunteer when they were children were 28 percentage points more likely to do the same when they grew up than people whose parents did not volunteer. This difference persists even after correcting for other demographics. For example, if two people had the same income, education level, gender, race, and marital status—but the first had volunteer parents while the second did not—the first person would be 12 points more likely to volunteer as an adult than the second.[21]

We tend to assume that charitable giving is a very good thing, of course. But some Americans would question the assumption that private charity is actually a positive phenomenon; in fact, some social entrepreneurs have made this very case. The author John Steinbeck sums up the reason for this viewpoint.

> Perhaps the most overrated virtue in our list of shoddy virtues is that of giving. Giving builds up the ego of the giver, makes him superior and higher and larger than the receiver. Nearly always, giving is a selfish pleasure, and in many cases is a downright destructive and evil thing. One has only to remember some of the wolfish financiers who spent two thirds of their lives clawing a fortune out of the guts of society and the latter third pushing it back.[22]

This viewpoint is generally accompanied by the opinion that governments should provide basic goods and services to those in need. According to one scholar on private charity, "By harnessing a wealth of volunteer effort and donations, [charities make] private programs appear cheaper and more cost effective than

Who Really Benefits from Charitable Gifts?

Donors give to charity for very specific, personal reasons usually having to do with the needs of the activities and causes they support. But a good deal of emerging research indicates that donors themselves experience a tremendous amount of benefit from giving. Economists and psychologists have found that charitable giving makes people healthier, happier, and even more financially successful. Giving is, in and of itself, a source of value for those who donate to charity.

Evidence suggests that charitable giving may be an element in the business cycle — where strong charity fuels expansions, and weak charity reinforces recessions. At the individual level, givers and volunteers have been found to experience positive long-term financial returns to their donations, and enjoy better mental and physical health after serving others. People are even more likely to act as good citizens (voting and participating in their communities) after volunteering. Why is this? Scholars point to several explanations:

- When people give and volunteer, they improve their sense of control over their environment, which leads to higher personal effectiveness — and ultimately, greater personal success.

- Giving provides a great source of meaning in people's lives, improving happiness and probably health.

- There is evidence that people recognize leaders at least partly through their giving behaviors. In other words, when people give they may be lifted into positions of success.

- Giving to those in need raises the overall level of prosperity, which benefits all.

- "Social capital" theory suggests that such charitable acts create trust and social cohesion within a community, which leads to happiness, health, and prosperity in the community as interpersonal networks are strengthened.

Effective giving depends on worthy causes that use resources optimally — which is where social entrepreneurship comes in. Historically, the problem of where to donate one's time and money has been solved by the wealthy via the establishment of foundations and managers who administer their charitable activities. Givers who are not wealthy have to rely on reputable charities to use donations wisely. Unfortunately, many charities do not actively pursue donations, relying instead on government funds. Effectively, this creates a situation where social entrepreneurs and charities overlook the willingness of individual charitable donors, who receive a great value when they are connected to worthy causes through the natural conduit of charitable organizations. Social entrepreneurs can create social value not just by providing an important service but also by connecting givers to the provision of this service.

FURTHER READING

Brooks, Arthur C. (2006). *Who Really Cares: The Surprising Truth About Compassionate Conservatism.* New York: Basic Books.
Post, Stephen, and Jill Niemark (2007). *Why Good Things Happen to Good People: The Exciting New Research that Proves the Link Between Doing Good and Living a Longer, Healthier, Happier Life.* New York: Broadway.

their public counterparts, thus reinforcing an ideology of voluntarism that obscures the fundamental destruction of rights."[23] This is surely a minority viewpoint, however. As evidenced by their exceptionally charitable behavior, most Americans value voluntary charity as an important virtue. Social entrepreneurs, regardless of their political views, should keep this in mind.

VENTURE PHILANTHROPY

Venture capital refers to funds provided by outside investors for financing of entrepreneurial, for-profit businesses. Venture capital investments are usually high in risk, but offer the potential for high returns. A venture capitalist is the person who makes such venture capital investments.

Earlier, we distinguished commercial entrepreneurship from social entrepreneurship only in terms of the denomination of returns—financial versus social. The philosophical and practical fundamentals of entrepreneurship are the same in both systems. Not surprisingly, venture capital also has an analogous concept: *venture philanthropy*. Venture philanthropy refers to the philanthropic funding for social enterprises and is usually associated with new wealth accruing to commercial entrepreneurs who have experienced high returns in their businesses and are comfortable with relatively high risk. These donors, naturally, are known as *venture philanthropists*.

WHO ARE VENTURE PHILANTHROPISTS?

According to venture philanthropy pioneer Mario Morino, founder of the organization Venture Philanthropy Partners,

> If new wealth creates new philanthropy, then what does new philanthropy create? It creates dialogue, in public and private, reflecting vigorous, animated soul-searching on how such precious new resources can be best put to improve schools, health care, and the other delivery systems for basic human needs. And, hopefully, it leads to transformational change.[24]

One question many people ask is, "Does venture philanthropy really differ from traditional philanthropy?" Authors Kuratko and Hodgetts answer the analogous question in the for-profit case by identifying several common myths about venture capitalists.[25] The lessons they develop also apply to venture philanthropy.

1. *Venture capitalists take over enterprises and tell people how to run businesses.* This is not true in the commercial world, generally, because venture capitalists have no time or desire to be company managers. Similarly, venture philanthropists are not generally looking to micromanage social enterprises.

2. *Venture capitalists are content with a "fair" rate of return.* Wrong—venture capitalists seek extraordinary returns, which is why they provide capital to ventures with relatively high levels of risk. Similarly, venture philanthropists

Venture Philanthropy Partners

Venture Philanthropy Partners (VPP) is "a philanthropic investment organization that helps great leaders build strong, high-performing nonprofit institutions. It concentrates money, expertise, and personal contacts to improve the lives and boost the opportunities of children and youth of low-income families in the National Capital Region."[26] VPP was created in 2000 by two entrepreneurs and a former politician, who pooled $30 million in donated funds from other entrepreneurs and business leaders to invest aggressively in social ventures with high potential for growth. Each year since its founding, the organization has funded a small number of high-growth, high-potential nonprofits in the Washington, D.C. area.

Two of VPP's projects are the Asian American Leadership, Empowerment, and Development (AALEAD), and the Boys and Girls Clubs of Greater Washington (BGCGW).

The Asian American Leadership, Empowerment, and Development defines its mission as promoting "the well-being of Asian American youth and families through education, leadership, and community-building" in the Washington, D.C. metropolitan area. In this regard, it offers a variety of after-school programs for elementary school students; mentoring, leadership development programs for high-school age students; and services aimed to increase parents' knowledge about the American educational system. In 2002, VPP committed $425,000 to build AALEAD's organizational capacity. VPP believes that, as the only organization in the community with the specific objective of helping students achieve academic success, the growth potential is high. VPP estimates that AALEAD is still at a formative stage; with the right continued improvements to its management, infrastructure, and programs, AALEAD could by 2010 dramatically increase the quality of services provided and the number of recipients.

The Boys and Girls Clubs of Greater Washington provide after-school and summer academic and athletic activities for approximately 36,000 children annually in the Washington D.C. area. While there is significant diversity in the types of programs offered, all attempt to provide a safe place to learn and grow through ongoing relationships with adult professionals and life-enhancing and character development programs. As one of the largest institutions serving youth in the D.C. region, even a slight change in benefit and value for children will produce a significant Social Return on Investment (SROI). Given its history of positive performance, and a belief that VPP's investment can positively impact 5,000 to 10,000 children in the next decade, VPP has committed $898,962 to the organization since 2004. This money has been used to help the BGCGW increase its focus on deepening the impact on children served and on opening several new sites.

understand that social enterprises are riskier "investments" than long-established nonprofits. They give anyway because of a promise for explosive social returns.

3. *Venture capitalists jump impulsively into investments.* In reality, successful venture capitalists are highly schematic in their approach and study candidate ventures in great detail. Only a small percentage of proposals are ever funded. Social entrepreneurs should expect nothing less from venture philanthropists, who are (ideally) just as careful in their giving approach.

4. *For venture capitalists, management quality is less important than innovation.* Any experienced venture capitalist understands that a new venture is only as good as its execution, and that means high-quality management. Social entrepreneurs can expect venture philanthropists similarly to look for efficient, creative administration.

5. *Venture capitalists don't need more than basic information before investing.* The chapter on business planning argues that, on the contrary, all enterprises—commercial and social—require a clear and complete business plan.

VENTURE PHILANTHROPY AND RISK

The perceived risk of a social enterprise for a venture philanthropist revolves largely around the development of the venture, as well as the depth of its management. In theory, the riskiest venture—and thus least likely to be funded—is one in which the social entrepreneur is working alone, and in which the venture is still in the planning stage. The least risky—and thus most likely to be funded—is an enterprise that is already operating at some reasonable capacity, serving clients, and has a management team in place, if appropriate. This implies a two-dimensional measurement of risk and a matrix (illustrated in Table 7-3) that social entrepreneurs can use to predict their likelihood of receiving funding from a venture philanthropist.

What do venture philanthropists look for when supporting a social enterprise? Social entrepreneurs might be tempted to assume that it is nothing more than the quality of the venture concept. This no doubt is important in all cases, but research on venture capital suggests that it probably goes much further than

TABLE 7-3 Perceived Risk for Venture Philanthropists				
	Social Entrepreneur Working Alone	*Partners Working Together, But No Management Team*	*Management Team Identified*	*Management Team in Place and Working*
Venture in the planning stage, not yet operable	Greater risk———————————————————→ Less risk			
Venture in pilot stage				
Venture launched but not developed				
Venture operating at working capacity	Less risk			

Source: Adapted from Kuratko and Hodgetts (2001).[27]

this. In fact, data on venture capitalists show that they look for four things before funding an enterprise:[28]

1. *Favorable characteristics of the entrepreneur.* Venture capitalists look for high education but not necessarily older entrepreneurs or more experience.

Andrew Carnegie, Venture Philanthropist

Andrew Carnegie was one of the most successful American businessmen in the latter half of the nineteenth century. Born into a poor Scottish family, Carnegie was able to work his way up in American society, eventually investing heavily in railroads and related industries in pre-Civil War America, and ultimately becoming one of the preeminent investors of his time. By the late 1880s, Carnegie shifted some of his attention to philanthropy, arguing that industrialists should distribute the wealth that they had acquired to benevolent causes. In 1892, with the founding of the Carnegie Steel Company (later renamed US Steel), Carnegie became a dominant figure in the steel industry. Its sale in 1901 brought Carnegie $480 million, which he spent his last 15 years giving away to charitable causes. Carnegie particularly favored giving to libraries and universities.

In 1889, Carnegie made a general call to other wealthy industrialists to distribute their money for the betterment of society. Noting that "the problem of our age is the proper administration of wealth, so that the ties of brotherhood may still bind together the rich and poor in harmonious relationship," Carnegie urged that the wealthy put their money back into society to achieve the greater good.

Particularly worrisome for Carnegie was the pattern of the wealthy passing on their fortunes to heirs, who often wasted them without doing any good for society. Yet for Carnegie, even giving one's wealth to a charity was no guarantee that it would ultimately be used wisely and in accordance with the wishes of the benefactor. Therefore, Carnegie called for the creation of a new form of charity that operated on the principle of "teaching a man to fish" rather than simply "giving him a fish." By supporting the creation of public libraries and universities, Carnegie provided people with tools needed to better themselves, while also requiring the locality to support ongoing operational costs after the initial grant was used up, thereby ensuring that the investment was a wise one.

Andrew Carnegie is often considered a traditional philanthropist, a man who accumulated vast wealth in America's gilded age and gave large sums to elite institutions. In reality, his approach to giving was highly entrepreneurial: betting on enormous returns and fraught with risk. Carnegie sought to create social value not directly, but indirectly by letting others lift themselves up. In this way, he aimed to leverage his giving not by placing a short-term patch over a societal problem with direct aid, but rather by making people more able to take care of themselves. This was a risky strategy, of course, because he had little control over the behavior of those to whom he was extending his philanthropy—success depended on *their* initiative, not his. Yet, as we now know, his philanthropic venture was hugely successful, raising the educational attainment of millions of Americans.

FURTHER READING

Andrew Carnegie (June 1889). *The Gospel of Wealth.* North American Review 148(391): 653–662.

2. *Favorable enterprise characteristics.* Venture capitalists seek ventures that are developed enough to show promise and are in growing parts of the economy.

3. *A good request.* Venture capitalists tend to fund proposals with a high-quality, believable business plan that asks for an appropriate amount of funding.

4. *Good advice.* Venture capitalists require that entrepreneurs they fund are getting good financial, management, and technological advice.

Venture philanthropists look for approximately the same qualities in a proposal. Social entrepreneurs should thus emphasize these points as they look for funding.

DONATIONS OF TIME

The discussion so far has focused mostly on donations of money. Yet most social entrepreneurs also rely heavily on time donations—volunteering—as well, so we need to spend a bit of time understanding what motivates volunteers and how best to stimulate their generosity.

Let's start by reviewing the benefits and costs of using volunteers. Most social entrepreneurs are interested in getting volunteers to help provide their services, so the benefits are well-known: The use of volunteers lowers the costs of delivering services and allows social entrepreneurs to embed themselves into the community. The use of volunteers also involves costs, however.

• Because volunteers are unpaid, they feel less beholden to an organization. That is, they are harder to control and are less likely to be reliable.

• Volunteer recruitment can be difficult and expensive.

• Competition between volunteers and paid staff can develop.

Typically, these costs come up after the fact, and social entrepreneurs can and should anticipate them to ameliorate these problems that may develop.

The objective for social entrepreneurs, then, is to maximize the benefits while minimizing the costs. Experience and research reveal the following six principles in designing a volunteer program:[29]

1. A social enterprise's paid staff must be behind the activities of the volunteers. If staff feel that volunteers are an ineffective mechanism to deliver services compared to the efforts they (the staff) carry out or that the volunteers are infringing on tasks that they (the staff) should be carrying out and producing less either quantitatively or qualitatively, there is likely to be internal resistance.

2. Volunteers must have clearly defined job expectations. They should never be brought in and not given specific instructions on what to do. For example, if a social enterprise trying to teach children to read does not lay down pedagogical guidelines, the nonprofit would at the very least have significant inefficiencies. Such job expectations require three elements:

   a. Volunteers must fall into job categories, so they know what they are expected to do.

The Taproot Foundation[30]

The Taproot Foundation is a social enterprise that solves many volunteering dilemmas for other social enterprises. The Foundation matches business professionals with the nonprofit community, matching skills to needs, and thus obviating the need for several steps in effectively engaging volunteers. Taproot uses the skills of professional IT workers, marketing professionals, HR professionals, and people from other high-value professional backgrounds to help nonprofits with pro bono donations of their time. Founded in 2001, the Taproot foundation has attracted support from employees at the world's leading consulting firms and some of the world's largest corporations, including Deloitte, Time Warner, and Microsoft.

Today, the Taproot Foundation serves nonprofits operating in the San Francisco Bay Area, New York City, Chicago, and Boston, and has matched more than 5,700 volunteer applicants to more than 400 unique nonprofits. Nonprofits have been able to use this professional help to do everything from designing their Web sites, to creating brand identities, to developing new models of performance management.

---

b. Volunteer assignments must be meaningful and significant tasks. If not, volunteer attrition could become a problem.

c. Volunteer assignments must fit with the overall strategic goals of the organization.

3. An effective volunteer program requires an effective recruitment campaign. This requires an efficient use of marketing, which we will discuss in the next chapter.

4. Effective volunteer programs make use of interviewing and matching. Although every organization interviews staff, it is surprising how few vet volunteers formally and thus effectively create organizational representatives unknown to the venture.

5. Volunteer training is key to make sure that the individual volunteer knows how to carry out the job.

6. Volunteers require supervision, just as staff members do. This means that a clearly delineated chain of command must be in place where volunteers report to direct supervisors. In addition, there must be a policy in place for dismissing volunteers who are deemed unfit for one reason or another.

GOVERNMENT SUBSIDIES

Individuals, foundations, and corporations are not the only entities that can donate to social enterprises, of course; governments can do so as well. Governments regularly provide social enterprises and other nonprofits with subsidies, payments, and other kinds of grants. Governments also provide support in the form of tax advantages.[31]

TABLE 7-4	Government Funding to Various Nonprofit Subsectors in the United States		
Subsector	*Portion of Nonprofit Sector*[1]	*Government Funding*	*Percentage of Revenues to the Sector*
Education	18%	$22.7b	19%
Social welfare	12%	$41.5b	52%
Health	49%	$136.9b	42%
Arts	2%	$1.3b	10%
Religion	12%	$0	0%
Total	100%	$219.4b	33%

[1]*Source:* Independent Sector (2002); Salamon (2002).

Direct government subsidies to American nonprofits came to $208 billion in 1997.[32] At 31 percent of total nonprofit revenues, direct government subsidies were actually higher than private donations (but lower than earned revenues). Government subsidies have grown since the mid-1970s in real terms, and, despite much political rhetoric, have never fallen over any sustained period. This source of revenues has almost always exceeded or kept pace with the overall growth of the nonprofit sector.

Individual nonprofit subsectors receive different levels of support from governments. Table 7-4 shows that although health-related nonprofits clearly received the lion's share of all government subsidies to nonprofits (about two-thirds), this funding comes to about 42 percent of total health nonprofit revenues. Social welfare organizations, which make up a smaller subsector in dollars, rely on government subsidies for more than half of their revenues.

How does the American nonprofit sector compare with that of other countries, with respect to the percent of its revenues that come from direct government subsidies? The U.S. figure of 31 percent is slightly below average by world standards. In general, Western European governments cover larger parts of their nonprofit sectors' budgets than in the United States. For example, direct subsidies come to 77 percent in Ireland and Belgium, 64 percent in Germany, 59 percent in Holland, and 58 percent in France. Not coincidentally, this is accompanied by very low percentages of total revenues in these countries from donations.[33]

Direct subsidies are fairly easy to comprehend, but they do not comprise all of the government funding to nonprofits. In many areas of the nonprofit sector, *indirect* subsidies make up a substantial portion of total revenues. Indirect subsidies come in three basic varieties: tax payments foregone on corporate activity and tax-deductible contributions, tax credits, and funding through nonprofit partnerships with government.

In the United States and many other countries, qualified nonprofit social enterprises and other nonprofit organizations are exempt from paying corporate taxes.[34] This is the effective *quid pro quo* that nonprofits enjoy for agreeing not to distribute profits to corporate owners. The nonprofit form of organization solves different sorts of market failure by removing profit motives, and the favorable tax policies are the means by which government can enhance the attractiveness of nonprofit status.[35] The implicit subsidy in this system is the tax foregone on either net or gross revenues (depending on the tax system). In other words, it is the money that would have been paid to the government if the firm had been organized as a for-profit organization.

Although this may seem like a lot of money, given the scale of the nonprofit sector (approximately $1 trillion), keep two caveats in mind. First, a sector that has low net revenues because of its inability to distribute profits may be foregoing relatively little corporate tax. Second, were it not for tax exemption, some (perhaps much) nonprofit activity might be infeasible in the first place, so there is actually little opportunity cost to government from exempting the activity.

A more important source of indirect subsidy comes in the form of government revenues foregone on tax-deductible contributions.[36] Many governments, including the U.S. federal and many state governments, allow donors to qualified charities and causes to deduct their contributions (generally up to some level of total income) from taxable income. That is, if the marginal income tax rate — the tax rate that applies to one's last dollar of earnings and because of our progressive tax system is generally higher than the *average* tax rate (total taxes paid divided by total income) — is, say, 30 percent, then each dollar donated to charity consists of a net cost to the donor of only 70 cents, and an indirect subsidy from the government to the nonprofit of 30 cents. The size of indirect subsidies from tax-deducted donations is huge. The U.S. Internal Revenue Service, for example, estimates that in 2002, individuals donated and deducted $142.4 billion in money and in-kind gifts. (Note that this does not represent total private giving, much of which is not deducted for tax purposes.) Breaking this figure down by income class and applying 2002 marginal tax rates for these classes, this represents foregone income tax revenues — and hence a government subsidy — of about $37.2 billion, which is nearly a fifth as important as direct subsidies to nonprofits. In some areas, indirect subsidies are especially large. For example, in the area of arts and culture, indirect subsidies outstrip direct subsidies by about $14 to $1 at the federal level.[37]

How do donations tend to respond to changes in marginal income tax rates (the tax rate on the last dollar of income earned)? An increase in tax rates lowers the effective cost to the donor for giving. The "tax price of giving" is the cost, after taxes, of donating a dollar to charity. If the marginal tax rate is 30 percent ($t = .30$), the tax price of giving is 70 cents ($p = 1 - t = .70$). Economists have found that the "tax price of giving" — the percentage that private donations increase when the price increases by 1 percent — is about 1.2. This means that a 10-percent increase in the tax price of giving will lower giving by 12 percent, all else constant.[38] To understand this better, imagine that a person donates $1,000 per year to charity and has a 20-percent tax marginal income tax rate. The price of giving, therefore is .80 — for each dollar in donations, this person deducts 20 cents from the tax bill (meaning that the charities receiving the gifts get a 20-cent indirect subsidy).

Imagine the tax rate decreases to 12 percent. This would mean an increase in the price of giving from .80 to .88, or a 10-percent increase. An elasticity of 1.2 means this person will decrease giving by 12 percent, or $120, to $880.

Notice the slightly counterintuitive fact that giving tends to decrease when taxes go *down*. This is because, even though decreased taxes mean more disposable income, the "price effect" tends to dominate giving decisions, at least in the short run.

THE RELATIONSHIP BETWEEN GOVERNMENT SUBSIDIES AND PRIVATE DONATIONS

Social entrepreneurs disagree as to the whether or not government funding to their organizations is a good thing. Naturally, some are attracted to the money. Others note that government funding can threaten the independence of their organizations.

Another social and fiscal threat in these relationships is less obvious. A classic case of the "Law of Unintended Consequences" involves government subsides to nonprofits and an accompanying displacement of private philanthropy. Economists refer to this phenomenon as "crowding out": As government subsidies to nonprofits increase, the perceived need of the recipient organizations declines in the eyes of potential donors. Furthermore, there is evidence that organizations tend to spend less effort on private fundraising when the government provides support. The end result is that government subsidies knock out some part of private giving.

Statistical studies show that the amount of private giving displaced by a dollar of government funds is positive but less than a dollar. For example, Table 7-5 reflects the average effects reported in seven major economic studies conducted on the U.S. nonprofit sector from 1982 to 1998. Depending on the type of nonprofit activity, a dollar of government funding to nonprofits tends to result in the displacement of between 15 and 40 cents in private giving.

What does all this mean for social enterprises? First of all, note that crowding out, which is only partial, means that a dollar of subsidies still leaves a nonprofit richer—just by less than the full dollar. At least in the short term, therefore, crowding out doesn't represent a strong financial case against government

TABLE 7-5 Crowding Out of Private Gifts by Government Subsidies			
Nonprofit Subsector	*Social Welfare*	*Health*	*Arts and Culture*
Amount of private donations crowded out by $1 in government subsidies	$0.36	$0.18	$0.27

Source: Brooks, Arthur C. (2000).[39]

intervention in the nonprofit sector, nor a good argument for social entrepreneurs to avoid government money all together.

There might be other concerns about government funding worth taking into consideration by social entrepreneurs, however. At the political level, any displacement of philanthropy means that some nonprofit funding decisions are turned over to the government. Is a social entrepreneur confident that the government is better placed and informed than private donors to make funding decisions?

There are social concerns as well. For example, studies on the nonprofit sector show unambiguously that philanthropy and voluntarism are positively associated. If we agree that voluntary participation is a mainstay in the development of civil society, we might expect harmful social effects when the government short-circuits this mechanism. In the end, social entrepreneurs need to keep these arguments in mind as they assemble a portfolio of resources. The bottom line is that no source of support is costless.[40]

Summary

- Most of the American social enterprises and other nonprofits rely critically on donated support. Charitable donations come from four basic sources: individuals, foundations, bequests, and corporations. By far, the largest source is living individuals, who privately give more than three quarters of all gifts.
- The percentage of American households that make money contributions each year is 70 to 80 percent, and the average American household contributes more than $1,000 each year. About a third of individual gifts go toward religious activities, such as support for houses of worship. The rest goes to secular activities.
- The four major demographic effects that predict giving better than others are income, wealth, religious participation, and the structure of families.
- Venture philanthropy refers to the philanthropic funding for social enterprises and is usually associated with new wealth accruing to commercial entrepreneurs who have experienced high returns in their businesses and are comfortable with relatively high risk.
- Venture philanthropists typically look for four characteristics in a social enterprise: favorable personal characteristics of the entrepreneur, a good idea with promise for explosive social value, a good philanthropy request, and assurance that the entrepreneur is getting good advice.
- A social enterprise's paid staff must be behind the activities of the volunteers. If staff feel that volunteers are an ineffective mechanism to deliver services compared to the efforts they themselves carry out, or that the volunteers are infringing on tasks that they (the staff) should be carrying out and producing less either quantitatively or qualitatively, there is likely to be internal resistance.
- There are six principles in designing an effective volunteer program: A social enterprise's paid staff must be behind the activities of the volunteers;

volunteers must have clearly defined job expectations; a volunteer program requires an effective recruitment campaign; volunteers should be interviewed like staff; volunteers should be trained; and volunteers require supervision.

- Governments regularly provide social enterprises and other nonprofits with subsidies, payments, and other kinds of grants. Governments also provide support in the form of tax advantages. Direct government subsidies to U.S. nonprofits exceed $200 billion per year.
- An indirect government subsidy to social enterprises comes in the form of government revenues foregone on tax-deductible contributions. This represents about $40 billion per year.
- As government subsidies to nonprofits increase, the perceived need of the recipient organizations declines in the eyes of potential donors. Furthermore, there is evidence that organizations tend to spend less effort on private fundraising when the government provides support. The end result is that government subsidies displace between 15 and 40 cents in private giving.

Key Terms

- venture capital
- venture philanthropy
- venture philanthropist
- marginal income tax rate
- direct government
- indirect government subsidy
- crowding out

End-of-Chapter Questions and Cases

DONOR RELATIONS AT THE FOOD BANK

"I just don't understand those people," the executive director of the local Food Bank told you, "and frankly, I don't like them very much." She was referring to her donors. Actually, she was complaining about her donors, as she tended to do in each interview.

The Food Bank has retained you as a philanthropy consultant, and you have been trying to get to the bottom of their inadequate development of private gifts. According to the director and senior staff, the major donors (who are also board members, in some cases) are fickle, demanding, and unable to see the vision of the Food Bank. The Bank wants to change the conditions leading to hunger in their city, but donors are only apparently interested in alleviating the symptoms of hunger.

1. Write a memo that helps the Food Bank think in a socially entrepreneurial way about charitable donations and donors.

SOCIAL VENTURE PARTNERS

Social Venture Partners (SVP) is a venture philanthropy organization that creates a community of social investors to fund social ventures or enterprises that bear more risk than others. Divided into chapters around the world, the Boulder, Colorado chapter has a mission to "maximize social impact by assisting nonprofit organizations in strengthening organizational capacity and sustainability through the creative use and leverage of our partners' skills and resources."[41]

Founded in 2000, Social Venture Partners Boulder County is a donor-advised fund within the local community foundation.[42] The investor-donors, or "partners" who provide the funds, make a minimum three-year commitment of at least $5,000 per year, participate in a voting process to select which nonprofit to invest in each year, and volunteer their time and expertise to the funded nonprofits. The advantage for an individual to make a donation to SVP versus making a direct donation to the organization is that the money can be pooled together to create a big and fast impact, similar to venture capital. The donors also get to be directly involved with grant recipients to ensure that funds are being used in the proper manner and as efficiently as possible, creating results in terms of value and social impact.

The focus of SVP is funding the areas of youth development during out-of-school time, early childcare and education, and strengthening educational and economic opportunities for Latinos. An example of this is the support of Growing Gardens; an organization dedicated to cultivating community through gardening by teaching sustainable agriculture, leadership, entrepreneurial, and life skills to youth.

SVP's support of Growing Gardens is directed towards Cultiva! Youth Project, a youth-operated organic market garden. Youth between the ages of 11 and 20 plant and nurture a 2-acre garden, harvest the produce weekly to sell at the Boulder County Farmer's Market, and donate a portion of what is harvested to those in need in the local community. In 2006, SVP gave Growing Gardens $15,000, including $10,000 for general operating support of the Cultiva! Youth Project and $5,000 designated to support implementation of an earned income strategy. SVP partners have personally assisted in earned income strategy development and implementation, improving management systems and strategic planning.

1. What are the advantages for a donor of participating in a venture philanthropy organization versus traditional philanthropy?
2. What types of recipient organizations are best-suited to SVP-type funding? If all philanthropy were to move to this model, would any nonprofits be hurt?
3. Is there any down side to a recipient organization taking a grant from a venture philanthropy fund such as SVP?

End Notes

1. See www.gatesfoundation.org/AboutUs/.
2. Brooks, Arthur C. (2004). "The Effects of Public Policy on Private Charity." *Administration & Society* 36(2): 166–185.

3. *Giving USA 2005* (Giving USA Foundation, Center on Philanthropy at Indiana University, 2005).
4. Center on Philanthropy Panel Study (COPPS) (2003). In the Panel Study of Income Dynamics (PSID) Wave XXXII Computer File. Ann Arbor, MI: ICPSR
5. 2003 PSID. Center on Philanthropy Panel Study (COPPS) (2003). In the Panel Study of Income Dynamics (PSID) Wave XXXII Computer File. Ann Arbor, MI: ICPSR (http://simba.isr.umich.edu).
6. *Giving USA 2005*.
7. These are the estimates from the Independent Sector's 2000 Giving and Volunteering Survey (GVS) and the 2003 COPPS/PSID. *Giving and Volunteering in the United States* (2001). Independent Sector, Washington, DC, www.IndependentSector.org.
8. 2003 PSID.
9. 2002 General Social Survey (GSS), 2000 GVS.
10. 2002 General Social Survey (GSS), 2000 GVS. Davis, James Allan, Tom W. Smith, and Peter V. Marsden (2002). *General Social Surveys, 1972–2002: Cumulative Code-Book*. Chicago: National Opinion Research Center.
11. 1998 International Social Survey Program (ISSP). Zentralarchiv für Empirische Sozialforschung. *International Social Survey Programme, 1998*.
12. The discussion here closely follows that in several chapters of Brooks, Arthur C. (2006). *Who Really Cares: The Surprising Truth About Compassionate Conservatism*. New York: Basic Books; Richard Steinberg, "Overall Evaluation of Economic Theories," *Voluntas* 8 (1997): 179–204; McClelland, Robert, and Arthur C. Brooks, "Comparing Theory and Evidence on the Relationship Between Income and Charitable Giving," *Public Finance Review* 32, no. 5 (2004): 483–497.
13. *Giving USA 2005*.
14. 2000 SCCBS. *Social Capital Community Benchmark Survey* (SCCBS). www.roper.com.
15. 2000 SCCBS. This analysis compares the effects of religious participation and secularism on giving and volunteering. The analysis relies on the estimates of marginal effects generated by probit models, where giving is regressed on dummies for religion and secularism, as well as a full battery of demographics.
16. 2000 SCCBS.
17. 2000 SCCBS.
18. 2000 GVS.
19. 2002 GSS.
20. 2000 SCCBS. The model here regresses dollars given annually to charity, and the number of occasions volunteered, on one's family size and the other demographics mentioned. I estimated the model using the Tobit procedure.
21. 2001 Giving and Volunteering Survey. *Giving and Volunteering in the United States* (2001). Independent Sector, Washington, DC, www.IndependentSector.org. The model here is a probit estimation of the likelihood of volunteering on a dummy variable for parental volunteering as well as the demographics listed. A similar difference exists for strictly informal volunteering.
22. Quoted in Nielsen, Waldemar A. (1972). *The Big Foundations.* New York: Columbia University Press, p. 311.
23. Poppendieck, Janet, (1998). *Sweet charity? Emergency food and the end of entitlement.* New York: Penguin, p. 6.
24. Morino, Mario (2004). *High-Engagement Philanthropy: A Bridge to a More Effective Social Sector.* Washington, DC: Venture Philanthropy Partners, p. 10.

25. Kuratko, Donald F., and Richard M. Hodgetts (2001). *Entrepreneurship: A Contemporary Approach*. Orlando, FL: Harcourt, pp. 286–287.
26. See www.vppartners.org.
27. Kuratko, Donald F., and Richard M. Hodgetts (2001) p. 446, Figure 14-1.
28. Hustedde, Ronald J., and Glen C. Pulver (1992). "Factors affecting equity capital acquisition: The demand side." *Journal of Business Venturing* 7(5): 363–374.
29. This discussion follows that of McCurley, Stephen (1994). "Recruiting and Retaining Volunteers." In Herman, Robert D. (Ed.). the *Jossey-Bass Handbook of Nonprofit Management and Leadership*. San Francisco: Jossey-Bass, pp. 511–534.
30. This example comes from a dossier in the Manhattan Institute's Social Entrepreneurship Awards program and is used with the Institute's permission; see also www.taprootfoundation.org/.
31. Rushton, Michael, and Arthur C. Brooks (2006). "Fee Income and Commercial Ventures." In Young, Dennis R. (Ed.). *Financing Nonprofits: Putting Theory into Practice*. Lanham, MD: AltaMira Press, pp. 69–92.
32. Independent Sector (2002). *The New Nonprofit Almanac and Desk Reference*. Hoboken, NJ: Jossey-Bass.
33. Brooks, Arthur C. (2003). "Charitable Giving to Humanitarian Organizations in Spain." *Hacienda Pública Española/Revista de Economía Pública (Spanish Journal of Public Economics)*. No. 2: 9–24.
34. Weisbrod, Burton A. "Tax Policy Toward Nonprofit Organisations: An Eleven Country Survey." *Voluntas* 2, no. 1 (1991): 3–25.
35. Brown, Eleanor, and Al Slivinski. (2005). "Nonprofit Organizations and the Market." In *The Nonprofit Sector: A Research Handbook*, edited by Walter Powell and Richard Steinberg. New Haven, CT: Yale University Press.
36. Brooks, Arthur C. (2004). "In Search of True Public Arts Support." *Public Budgeting & Finance* 24, no. 2: 88–100.
37. Brooks (2004).
38. Steinberg, Richard (2004). "Does Government Spending Crowd Out Donations? Interpreting the Evidence." In *The Nonprofit Sector in the Mixed Economy*, edited by Avner Ben-Ner and Benedetto Gui. Ann Arbor, MI: The University of Michigan Press, pp. 99–125.
39. Brooks, Arthur C. (2000). "Is There a Dark Side to Government Support for Nonprofits?" *Public Administration Review* 60(3): 211–218.
40. Brooks, Arthur C. (December 2004/January 2005), "Can Governments Kill Nonprofits with Kindness?" *Fraser Forum*, 5–6.
41. See www.svpbouldercounty.org.
42. (December 10, 2004). "Social Venture Partners Awarded Fast Company Magazine's Social Capitalist Award," www.svpbouldercounty.org/news/award.htm.

CHAPTER 8

ENTREPRENEURIAL FUNDRAISING AND MARKETING

INTRODUCTION

DonorsChoose.org is a Web site that is designed to bring donors together with teachers needing small donations to facilitate small projects (see the case study at the end of Chapter 1). For example, one teacher in the South Bronx in New York City recently requested $802 through DonorsChoose.org to provide school children their own dictionaries. Since its inception in 2000 by a high school social studies teacher, these small grants have added up to large sums: over $12.5 million donated to nearly 600,000 students across the country (and world) from more than 27,000 individuals.[1]

DonorsChoose.org was a social enterprise founded in response to very real fundraising problems. First, it had been difficult to match people with small needs to individual donors. Second, in cases where only small grants were needed, there were few feedback mechanisms to provide assurances to donors that their gifts were being used wisely and appropriately. This was not an issue of negligence by grantees or nonprofits; it was a question of cost-effectiveness. In the past, it simply had not made financial sense to look for individual small donors and spend money exhaustively informing them about the use of their contributions. But this resulted in a disincentive for some potential donors to give.

DonorsChoose.org saw the growing power of the Internet as a way to find and provide information to small donors at low cost. With little overhead and no mailing costs, the enterprise was able to interface givers with recipients; screen all projects before posting them online; purchase the materials needed and ship them directly to the school; and compile photographs, thank you notes from students, and teacher feedback. Included in this feedback is an expenditure report, assuring donors that the donations were spent exactly as claimed. Today, thanks to these efforts, DonorsChoose.org has won awards for innovations in fundraising online and has attracted major corporate sponsors, including Yahoo!, Lehman Brothers, and Bank of America, while earning press coverage worldwide.

DonorsChoose.org is an example of social entrepreneurship "turning in on itself," that is, being part of its own resource-acquisition process. This chapter shows how social entrepreneurs can and should think about the process of acquiring resources. It lays out the basics of fundraising and marketing for nonprofits but goes beyond to ask how social entrepreneurship principles themselves can be applied to raising funds.

TYPES OF FUNDRAISING

Fundraising is the effort designed to stimulate the donated revenues discussed in the preceding chapter. It has become a large part of the operations of many social enterprises and other nonprofit organizations and now represents an entire profession. It has even stimulated a distinct field of study, and one major university—Indiana University—now even offers a PhD in Philanthropic Studies.

Fundraising generally encompasses six broad categories of activity.

PERSONAL RELATIONSHIPS

The most important avenue for most nonprofits' fundraising stems from personal relationships. One of the most important markers of fundraising success is the ability of individuals in a social endeavor to get others on board with their vision, and this usually requires personal contact. Personal relationships are especially critical for social entrepreneurs because a new venture frequently has a lot more *vision* than *history*. In other words, social entrepreneurs must share with others—venture philanthropists, regular donors, small community supporters, and anyone in between—what they "see," and a fundraising letter may be insufficiently personal for doing so. Personal relationships include everything from one-on-one conversations with donors, to organized tours.

DIRECT MAIL

Fundraising letters may seem to some social entrepreneurs like an antiquated phenomenon. But, in fact, this approach is still not only prevalent but highly profitable for many organizations and is an area frequently contracted to for-profit fundraising firms. Some well-known nonprofits, such as the Easter Seals and St. Jude's Children's Hospital, rely on direct mail for millions of dollars of support each year. Social entrepreneurs without an established fundraising base often have a somewhat harder time with this technique because the profitability depends so much on whether someone has given in the past. For example, a typical rule of thumb for an American nonprofit is that somewhere in the neighborhood of

1 to 3 percent of people contacted for the first time respond to direct mail. Among those that do, approximately 20 percent will give again subsequently. In other words, the profitability for a list of established donors is probably somewhere around 10 times higher than that of a new list.

FUNDRAISING EVENTS

Many established nonprofit organizations rely on fundraising events to raise awareness, goodwill, and money. These events range from awards banquets to cocktail parties to auctions; the central ingredient in all of them is getting donors together in the same place for the cause. The theory is that this will engender social capital and stimulate "peer effects" to give. Social entrepreneurs can consider the use of events. However, it is worth noting that some fundraising experts question the cost-benefit ratio of this fundraising strategy because events generally require a huge amount of time and attention on the part of staff.

TELEFUNDING

Few people like to engage in telephone fundraising (telefunding), and most people say they dislike being telemarketed, even by nonprofits. Yet this is a technique that works quite well. There are several distinct kinds of telefunding to raise donations. The first is calling lists of nondonors for small contributions. The second is telefunding former donors to attempt to renew their giving. As in the case of direct mail, the second type is not necessarily practical for social entrepreneurs, especially at the beginning, when all the donors are new. Furthermore, telefunding requires a certain level of fundraising infrastructure—people to make the calls, and the means to call—that many social ventures do not possess. Many telefunding firms have recently stepped in to provide these services for a commission. However, there are obviously substantial risks involved in allowing low-paid telefunders to represent (or misrepresent) a social enterprise's all-important social mission.

TRADITIONAL MEDIA

Radio, television, and print are important fundraising vehicles for nonprofits. Radio in particular has been a traditionally good means to reach certain audiences in a cost-effective way. For example, many Christian organizations have been hugely successful raising funds by way of Christian radio stations, which are common and popular around the United States. Obviously, this means of fundraising will be more effective for some organizations than others. Social enterprises should not rule out traditional media, however.

VIRTUAL MEANS

Many social entrepreneurs see virtual means of publicity—e-philanthropy, Web site giving, and direct e-mail—as a potential panacea. So far, things haven't worked out this way: Donors (even younger donors) have not rushed to e-giving;

TABLE 8-1 Nonprofit Use of E-mail and the Internet	
	Percentage of Nonprofits, 2001
Use e-mail	88%
Have Web access	88%
Have a Web site	66%
Accept donations through a Web site	17%
Sell merchandise through a Web site	15%

Source: Zimmer 2002.[2]

direct e-mail solicitations have gotten caught up in the storm of general e-mail "spam," rendering it a nuisance to receivers (whereas direct postal mail is generally not); and Web sites do not guarantee any Internet traffic at all in a World Wide Web consisting of millions of sites. Although social entrepreneurs should not neglect virtual means, they should also not rely on them for substantial support.

One surprising fact about nonprofits in general is how far behind they have been in adopting relatively inexpensive virtual technologies. In many cases, the problem for virtual fundraising is not that a social venture that tries it finds it ineffective, but rather that social entrepreneurs do not have the necessary sophistication to employ e-mail and the Internet optimally. There is evidence from the early part of this decade that a third of nonprofits did not even have a Web site, and only a small minority was equipped to accept donations through the site even if they had one. Nonprofit scholar Eric Zimmer estimated in 2001 that more than 10 percent of nonprofits did not even use e-mail—this at the height of the e-commerce boom (see Table 8-1). No doubt this has improved since 2001, but there is undoubtedly still a lot of technical progress to be made in the worlds of nonprofits and social entrepreneurship.

A general implication from the preceding discussion is that social entrepreneurs should focus initially on a fundraising approach centered on relationships and engage in (but not overemphasize) virtual means of fundraising. Direct mail is an approach most appropriate as an enterprise matures or if it has access to the fundraising base of an established nonprofit. Traditional media must be evaluated for its cost-effectiveness but shouldn't be ruled out.

HOW SHOULD WE SPEND FUNDRAISING DOLLARS?

An earlier chapter made the case that most social enterprises actually underspend on their fundraising, the evidence being that the returns to each dollar are "too high." They could efficiently spend more and raise a lot more money. This point, however, doesn't tell us *how* social entrepreneurs should spend their fundraising dollars. Although successful entrepreneurship involves "pursuing opportunities without limitation by resources currently in hand," social entrepreneurs still must make decisions—including fundraising decisions—that use scarce resources in the most efficient way possible.

FIGURE 8-1   Spending Tradeoffs in Fundraising

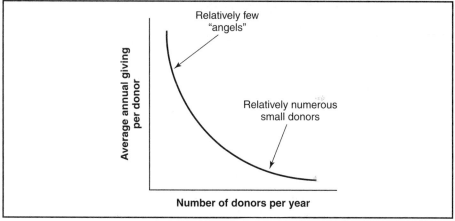

The first fundraising tradeoff is between the number of donors and the size of donations. Social entrepreneurs often have a "mental picture" of donors: Some see a single millionaire bankrolling a project; others see large numbers of small donors supporting the venture from the grassroots up. This represents a tradeoff in the focus of fundraising; energy and resources can be expended in either direction. Figure 8-1 depicts this tradeoff. The right strategy depends on the function of the fundraising efforts and the pool of prospects. For example, a student-run organization might focus on young people with relatively little philanthropic capacity but see fundraising as an important vehicle to build awareness of the organization. Note that this has the potential to generate a lot of money. Many national organizations rely very heavily on inexpensive direct mail and lots of small checks to support massive organizations. In contrast, a new venture within an established nonprofit might look to an existing donor base. In some types of organizations, this might involve the support of major donors or venture philanthropists. The alternative fundraising strategies are summarized in Table 8-2.

A second tradeoff involves differentiating donors themselves. A frequent and serious error that social entrepreneurs make when they are inexperienced in

TABLE 8-2   Choosing a Fundraising Strategy

	Focus: New Donors	*Focus: Established Donors*
Purpose: Raise money	Strategy: mix of large and small gifts	Strategy: larger, fewer donations
Purpose: Raise visibility	Strategy: smaller, more numerous donations	Strategy: mix of large and small gifts

---

Understanding the Tradeoff Between Donor Numbers and Donation Size

Easter Seals, a nonprofit organization originally founded in the United States in 1919 as the National Society for Crippled Children, is an example of an organization that has prospered in its fundraising by relying on numerous, small donations.

Easter Seals provides assistance for individuals with special needs and disabilities, as well as their families. Launching an Easter "seals" campaign in 1934 to raise funds, the organization—renamed in 1967—received so much public support that they were able to expand nationwide, as well as provide many more services. Today they offer medical rehabilitation, job training, childcare, adult day services, and camping and recreation opportunities, to name just a few. In addition, the organization has actively lobbied on behalf of the interests of the disabled and was instrumental in the 1990 Americans with Disabilities Act.[3]

Easter Seals has been remarkably successful in cultivating and retaining donors. In the organization's history, at least 26 donors have made contributions of $1 million or more, 14 have donated over $500,000, dozens more over $100,000, and 3,800 have contributed between $1,000 and $25,000. However, these large contributions are no match for the small checks that pour into Easter Seals each year in response to the organization's extensive direct mail campaigns, making up the bulk of the $150 million the charity raises annually.[4]

---

fundraising is to focus only on winning new donors. In fact, there are six basic donors types, and effective fundraising means addressing each one.

1. *Potential donors.* These are potential donors who have not given but have been identified as possible givers. For example, they are on a mailing list or an alumni database. Social entrepreneurs almost invariably have to start with a focus on these possible givers because social ventures obviously do not have past donors, except when the venture stems from an older endeavor.

2. *New donors.* These are donors who have given for the first time.

3. *Transition donors.* After a second year giving, people are transition donors, moving from being "new" toward being part of the social enterprise's "core."

4. *Core donors.* These are the most loyal donors—the heart of a social venture. They have given three or more years in a row.

5. *Lapsed donors.* These are donors who have given in the past but not over the past year. After two years, they are "deeply lapsed."

6. *Lapsed but reactivated.* These are donors who gave in the past and stopped for a year or more but have started giving again.

The data on each of these types of donors is very revealing about their differences and the importance of paying attention to various types of donors. Data on social service nonprofits' mailing lists from Merkle, a major direct-marketing firm specializing in nonprofits, makes this point vividly clear (see Figure 8-2). First, a typical mailing list is dominated by inactive donors—those who are

FIGURE 8-2   The Dimensions of a Typical List of Active Donors

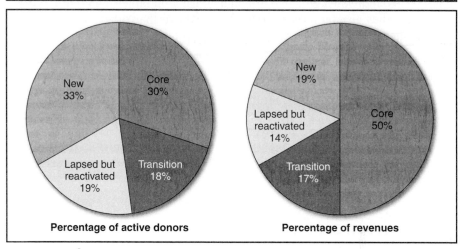

Percentage of active donors   Percentage of revenues

Source: Merkle.[5]

lapsed, deeply lapsed, or who have never given in the first place. The percentage of donors who are inactive can be as high as 80 percent. The active donors of an organization fall in four categories—new, lapsed but reactivated, transition, and core—of similar size. Despite similar proportions in numbers, the revenues from each group are not similar at all (see Figure 8-3). Core donors make up at least 50

FIGURE 8-3   Gift Size Among Active Donors

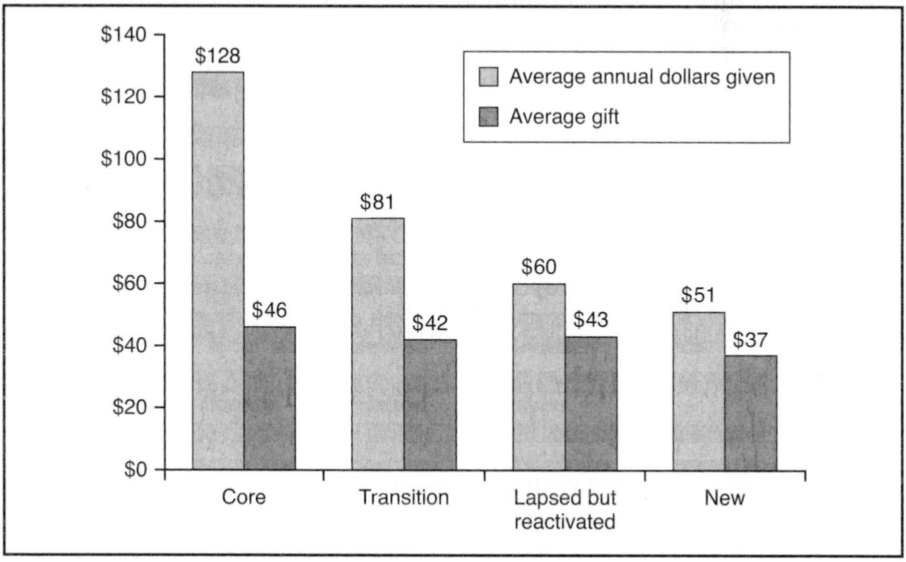

	Average annual dollars given	Average gift
Core	$128	$46
Transition	$81	$42
Lapsed but reactivated	$60	$43
New	$51	$37

Source: Merkle.[6]

percent of revenues and frequently a much higher percentage than this. Core donors make individual gifts that are on average a bit larger than those of other groups, and they give far more total dollars each year than others. The main take-aways from this are as follows:

- Core donors are the most productive for a nonprofit organization. Social enterprises should spend fundraising time and energy building this core.
- New, lapsed but reactivated, and transition donors are critical in large part because they have the potential to enter the core.
- Truly lapsed donors are not a very productive focus for most enterprises, yet many organizations chase their former donors for years and leave them on donor lists. The data show that truly lapsed donors are no more likely to give than people who have never given at all.

FUNDRAISING STRATEGIES

There are three strategies social entrepreneurs must understand to acquire new donors, bring them to the core, and lift the giving by the core donors. These strategies can be summarized as *win, keep,* and *lift.*

WIN

This is all about gaining new donors or regaining lapsed donors. Most fundraising pitches we see are geared toward this strategy. These pitches can be simple or amazingly innovative.

One especially innovative organization in winning donors is Habitat for Humanity, the international organization that builds simple housing for families in need. Habitat makes extensive use of houses of worship to both recruit volunteers and gain financial donations.[7] As an ecumenical Christian housing ministry, HFHI encourages churches and affiliated religious organizations to become involved first as volunteers or advocates in the community. After enough interest, HFHI asks churches to encourage donations in their mission work by making regular donations or setting up special offerings for the organization. HFHI has found that people who experience a project physically are far more likely than they otherwise would be to donate money, and in this way, Habitat uses volunteering as an effective "gateway" contribution to win new money donors.

KEEP

Winning donors is important but will do little to sustain an enterprise if they do not stay active, as the preceding data show vividly. It is simply impossible to generate meaningful amounts of donations on the basis of new donors alone; every philanthropically successful venture requires a "core." This means keeping the donors we have won.

One nonprofit that has taken this truth to heart and developed strategies accordingly is World Vision, an international relief organization focusing on child

FIGURE 8-4   The Percentage of Donors Retained from One Year to the Next

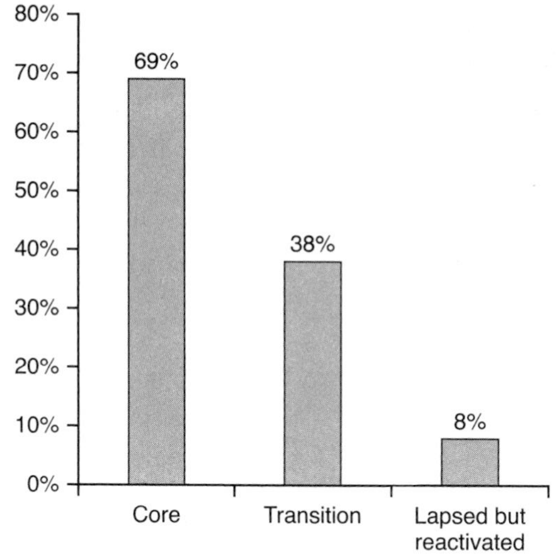

Source: Merkle.

poverty. World Vision has begun surveying the satisfaction of about 600,000 donors with the organization's work. Using this information, WV tailors its communications strategy to the preferences of each donor, rather than bombarding them with generalized direct mail flyers like many other organizations do. The result is that World Vision donors now stay active, on average, for two-thirds more time than they did before the donor retention strategy was implemented.[8]

What predicts keeping a donor? The answer to this is whether the donor has given in the past. Giving predicts giving, pure and simple. More than two-thirds of core donors give in a new year versus a third of transition donors and just 8 percent of lapsed but reactivated donors. This is shown in Figure 8-4.

LIFT

Core donors give not just most frequently and over the longest period of time but the largest amounts of money as well.

MAP International, a medical assistance organization that provides medical services and medicines in poor communities around the world, recently integrated its fundraising and marketing efforts in an effort to target donors that might be willing and able to contribute more than they had in the past. MAP tracked individual donations that came in to better understand the motivations, interests, and giving trajectory of each donor. Using this information, MAP International was able to target the best prospects for higher giving, which lead to increased average gifts.[9]

FIGURE 8-5 The Fundraising Ecosystem

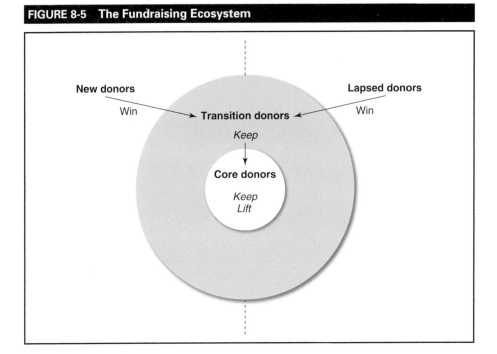

The win-keep-lift strategy defines, along with the four donor types, a fundraising ecosystem depicted in Figure 8-5. New giving prospects and lapsed donors are won, at which point they become transition donors. At this point, work has been done to keep them so they enter the core. The approach to the core is not just to keep these donors but also to lift them to higher giving levels. Typically, social entrepreneurs start out by winning but must quickly adopt keeping and lifting strategies as well, if they are to prosper.

Losing Donors

It would certainly be convenient if, once a donor were won, social entrepreneurs could just sit back and let them fall into the core as long-term supporters. As it has been seen, however, donors can and do lapse. Why is this? Little research has gone into asking this question, but what little there is, is provocative.

First, let's dispense with a popular myth about donor attrition—the idea that donors tend to "fatigue" after too many asks from an organization. Most social entrepreneurs worry about going to the same sources too often for support, and as a result, alienating their core donors. This results in infrequent asking, sometimes as infrequent as just once per year. No doubt that some donors have stopped supporting organizations for this reason, but there is no evidence to support the idea that it is normal or frequently the case. For example, one dataset shows that core donors to social welfare organizations give, on average, 2.8 times per year, and

FIGURE 8-6 **Average Number of Donations by Different Donor Types**

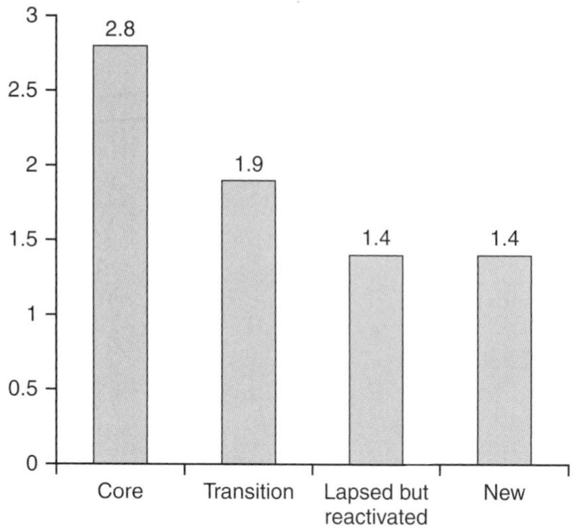

Source: Merkle.

even new donors give more than once, on average (see Figure 8-6).[10] In fact, people respond to multiple appeals with multiple gifts.

So what are the real reasons why donors "defect" from a cause they have supported in the past? There is a surprising lack of data on this subject from American nonprofits, although British nonprofit scholar Adrian Sargeant has conducted surveys in Great Britain that are illuminating.[11] Sargeant's survey questioned lapsed donors and assembled a list of the most common reasons that donations stopped. The reasons are summarized in Figure 8-7.

Some reasons for donor lapse might seem beyond a social entrepreneur's control. For example, 27 percent of lapsed donors say they found other organizations more deserving. Similarly, 22 percent say they simply could not afford to continue to support the organization. On reflection, however, a worthy entrepreneur should never take these as forces beyond their control. If other organizations are not *truly* more deserving, what did they do to poach our venture's donors? And it is a simple fact that nearly everybody can afford to support an organization at some level, or with some resource, even if it is not money. (Note that many studies find that the U.S. working poor give more generously—relative to their income—than the rich.[12]) If donors lapse because they cannot afford to give, it probably means that they were not aware of a wide enough array of options to support the venture.

Other reasons for lapse are inexcusable. Eleven percent do not remember giving in the first place, certainly meaning that the organizations established no ongoing relationship with them. Similarly, 3 percent stop because they are not

FIGURE 8-7 The Main Reasons Donors Lapse

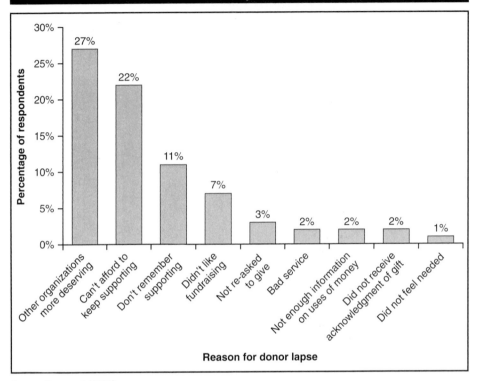

Source: Sargeant (2001).

re-asked to give. In the world of social entrepreneurship, in which personal relationships are key, these errors should not occur.

All of the techniques and strategies reported here require a certain amount of administrative capacity. One reason social entrepreneurs and nonprofit managers are often reluctant to expend the necessary resources on administration is because they fear reprisals from donors. In fact, a common lament of social entrepreneurs is that they feel the need to neglect operations costs—the costs of running an office, for example—to satisfy donors, government officials, and other constituents that they are sufficiently efficient. There is a fear that administrative spending will "crowd out" gifts because it is seen as inefficient. The result is insufficient investment in capacity.

The research indicates that fears about the reaction of donors and others to administrative expenses is not well-founded. Nonprofit scholars Peter Frumkin and Mark Kim found that fundraising spending is strongly related to higher giving to all types of nonprofits, and other kinds of administrative spending are unrelated to donation levels.[13] The most likely explanation for this is that the majority of donors have no idea how much a social entrepreneur or nonprofit

---

Donor Defection

United Way of America is a coalition of charitable organizations that works to create "lasting, positive changes" in individual communities. From its founding in Denver in 1887, today there are more than 1,300 chapters across the country. In each community that the United Way operates, it attempts to engage the community to find the most significant local issues, such as helping children and youth, supporting families, providing access to health care, and promoting economic independence.

Throughout the 1970s and 1980s, the United Way prospered and was often seen as a model for successful fundraising with its workplace-based approach, in which employers and labor unions would collaborate on fund drives to encourage employees to give through direct deductions from their paychecks. By the 1990s, however, the United Way's fundraising was faltering. From 1991 to 1996, even as the economy was taking off, the UW experienced an 11 percent decrease in donated revenues. Over 4.5 million people—an astonishing 20 percent of United Way's donors—had stopped contributing to the organization; the remaining 17.7 million were giving less than before. Thomas A. Ruppaner, president of United Way of the Bay Area, said, "we are going out of business unless we fundamentally change."[14]

There were at least two causes of the decline in donations to United Way during the 1990s. First, the organization was battered by scandal. William Aramony, the president of United Way until his resignation in 1992, was convicted of fraud in 1995. Second, some claimed that giving patterns in the United States changed during the 1990s, as corporate downsizing and declines in union membership significantly impacted United Way's traditional base of large corporations and unions.

---

manager is spending on overhead unless it is truly egregious, and that fundraising expenditures really do lead to more and better donor appeals. The implication for nonprofit managers is that there is no reason to fear responsible spending.

VOLUNTEER RECRUITMENT AND ATTRITION

In general, donors of time are similar to donors of money in the fact that they must be won, kept, and lifted. What differs about volunteers are the techniques needed to win them in the first place. The literature on volunteer recruitment suggests that there are three basic types of volunteer appeals that social enterprises and other nonprofits should understand: warm body recruitment, targeted recruitment, and concentric circles recruitment.[15]

Warm body recruitment focuses on developing a large volunteer force without much regard for specific skills. This technique is ideal if the nonprofit is looking for support conducting major events or staffing ongoing low-skill operations. Nonprofits that use this approach typically work through other organizations that bring large groups of people together, such as houses of worship or schools, and do not need to know the volunteers well. A noteworthy example of a nonprofit that uses this sort of recruitment is Habitat for Humanity, which approaches

---

Innovative Volunteer Recruitment at Help the Hospices

Help the Hospices is a British-based charity that seeks to provide support for hospice organizations (which provide aid and services to the dying) in the form of training, education, information, grant assistance, and advice for fundraising.[16] One great need that hospices have is that of volunteers, and Help the Hospices developed an innovative program to meet this need. Working with an existing British nonprofit that connected volunteers with charities, Help the Hospices developed a campaign called 13 Days, referring to the average stay of a patient in a hospice program.[17]

13 Days conducted a large, well-publicized survey in which respondents were asked what they would do if they had only 13 days to live, and what they would stop worrying about. The resulting information attracted the attention of the British media, which covered the survey results extensively. As a result of the media, nearly 2,000 people—nearly three quarters under the age of 35—inquired about volunteering for hospices.

---

churches to get volunteers willing to help construct houses for lower-income individuals.

Targeted recruitment focuses on a smaller number of individuals who have specific skills needed for the organization's operations. For instance, if an organization wants to teach immigrant children to speak English, it needs to recruit volunteers who have some skills teaching English to nonnative speakers. As a general rule, targeted recruitment is good at getting longer-term volunteers. An example of an organization that uses this approach is Teach For America, which recruits graduating college students to teach in economically underprivileged schools for a period before beginning their regular careers.

Concentric circles recruitment focuses on keeping a steady flow of volunteers involved in an organization. Typically, current volunteers are relied upon to find new volunteers when they leave an organization. Such a policy, obviously, can only be launched after the nonprofit is established and has had some success in volunteer recruitment.

Just as social enterprises lose donors, they also lose volunteers, and much volunteer attrition is avoidable. Many nonprofits treat volunteers as a "free" resource, which inevitably results in misuse of volunteer time and a falling desire to support the organization. The key principle to keep in mind to avoid volunteer attrition is that, even if a manager does not recognize the value of volunteers, the volunteers themselves do—or at least think they do. Generally volunteers look at three elements in calculating their own value—determining whether what they get in return from volunteering is higher or lower than the cost of volunteering. These are the elements that social entrepreneurs should consider as well as they engage and work with volunteers.

1. *Market work value.* What volunteers might be earning if they were putting their energies into the labor market. When volunteers are put into tasks with a market value far below their foregone wages, they recognize that the opportunity cost of volunteering is higher than the benefit.

2. *Next-best volunteering effort.* For many volunteers, there is no market-work equivalent; however, they virtually all have alternative volunteer opportunities. When these alternate opportunities are comparatively more attractive, they degrade the value of the volunteer assignment at hand.

3. *Leisure time value.* Volunteers value their leisure time, presumably, time with which volunteering generally competes. So even if market work and alternate volunteer opportunities are irrelevant, a volunteer's time still has value.

SOCIAL ENTERPRISE MARKETING

Fundraising efforts are part of a much broader category of social enterprise activities: marketing. Marketing involves *planning, pricing, promoting,* and *distributing* a venture's programs and products.

Whereas for-profit entrepreneurs obsess on marketing, social entrepreneurs often neglect it in their fundraising or efforts to increase demand for their products and services. Why? The reason for many is that it seems so alien to the concept of the social mission. "I'm trying to save the world," many social entrepreneurs might lament, "So how can I be expected to pay attention to the grubby world of advertising?" This attitude is naïve for several reasons. First of all, marketing goes beyond advertising to encompass many tasks. Second, the fact is that without public knowledge of a venture's services, no mission can be met. Marketing, properly understood, is important.

The tasks of marketing are to define target markets and link to the people in these markets.

- *Define target markets.* The key question for social enterprise marketing is: Who should our clients (or donors) be? For example, the marketing plan for an urban literacy venture has to spell out whom it intends and hopes to reach: kids in poor city neighborhoods. This gets us back to the discussion much earlier in the book about connecting *supply* and *demand,* or equivalently, *ideas* and *opportunities.*

- *Link to the clients (or donors).* The key questions for enterprise marketing are:
  - How do we reach the clients?
  - What "price" attracts them?
  - How do we communicate with them?

Imagine a social service enterprise dedicated to improving literacy among adolescents. This organization is only effective if it can reach potential clients and their families. Then, it needs to "price" the services in the right way—almost certainly meaning that the service has to be sufficiently convenient to draw people to it (price here not being denominated in dollars, obviously). Finally, it has to be able to communicate with the kids and their families about its offerings.

Marketing in the commercial sector is not controversial; it is taken for granted that marketing is necessary if a product is to have any customers at all. In the social sector, however, there are frequently cultural barriers to marketing. First, there is frequently a bias in the world of social ventures and nonprofits against "commercialization," and other "free market" phenomena. Social entrepreneurs often rebel against the idea that they must compete for clients, donations, or grants in free markets, and they are reluctant to undertake marketing practices as a result. Second, many social enterprises have human resources that are difficult to use in an effective marketing campaign. For example, an enterprise that is staffed largely by volunteers may be ill-equipped to mount a marketing effort.

In the first case, social entrepreneurs have to realize that they exist as a feature of market economies, not in opposition to them. This is not the same thing as saying that social ventures must celebrate the virtues of market capitalism, but it is a fact that social entrepreneurship—like every other kind of entrepreneurship—tends to bloom in market-based environments. As such, rebellion against the forces of supply and demand by neglecting marketing is inherently self-destructive. In the second case, social enterprises ill-equipped in human resources to execute a marketing plan can look outside their organizations for help. Today, a vast array of nonprofit marketing firms and consultants are available, and not all are expensive.

STEPS IN BUILDING A SOCIAL ENTERPRISE MARKETING STRATEGY

A social enterprise marketing strategy is a five-step process (see Figure 8-8).

EXTERNAL ANALYSIS

We begin by looking outside the venture, asking many of the same questions that went into turning ideas into opportunities earlier in the social entrepreneurship process.

- Who are my constituents? A marketing plan must be focused on clients, donors, government officials, or whomever we serve or seek resources from. Identifying them specifically makes marketing focused and effective. For example, an urban church offering a new program to feed the hungry starts its external analysis by identifying the homeless in its area and concerned parishioners.

- Who are my competitors? Social entrepreneurs frequently live in a "bubble" when it comes to competition, especially when there is no clear profit motive, and the venture is created in reaction to an unmet social need. Yet competition is still real. As we discussed in an earlier chapter, one of the main sources of competition is actually *nothing:* In many cases, people forego social services due to ignorance or disinterest. A chamber music ensemble can play to an empty auditorium not because another ensemble is playing across the street, but because people prefer to stay home. All sources of competition must be explicitly considered for the time and resources of clients and donors.

FIGURE 8-8   The Social Enterprise Marketing Strategy Process

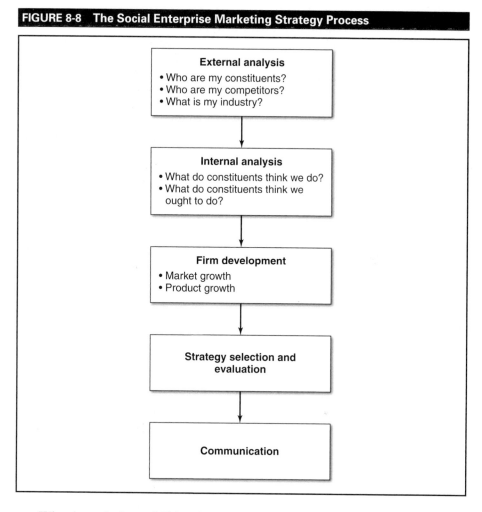

- What is my industry? This might sound like an obvious question, but is it? Is a university's art museum in the education business or the arts? Is a welfare-to-work program in job training or poverty relief? Identifying our principle industry helps in identifying competition as well as sources of resources.

INTERNAL ANALYSIS
We continue with a look inside the venture, asking three questions:

- What do we do? There is nothing more lethal to a social enterprise than hesitation in answering the question, "So, what does your organization do?" Every venture is complicated and nuanced, but the social entrepreneur must be able to describe it succinctly to constituents. This was made plain in the discussion about business planning, but it is even truer as we look for smaller donors who will give us mere seconds of their time and attention.

CARE International Rebrands Itself

What do constituents think we do? Frequently, the perceptions of social-purpose organizations and their constituents differ, making marketing difficult. A classic example of this is CARE International, one of the most important humanitarian relief organizations in the world. Here is the beginning of CARE's description of itself:

> CARE tackles underlying causes of poverty so that people can become self-sufficient. Recognizing that women and children suffer disproportionately from poverty, CARE places special emphasis on working with women to create permanent social change.[18]

A major problem for the organization is that many people still tend to see CARE as merely a distributor of food relief—passing out the famous "CARE packages." To fight this mismatch between perceptions, CARE changed its logo in recent years, from a stencil on the side of a food crate, to one featuring a circle of hands.

CARE International's Old and New Logos, Reflecting an Effort to Match the Organization's Real Mission with its Publicly Perceived Mission

Old logo   New logo

- What do constituents think we do? This is the critical question that motivated the rebranding of CARE International (see the accompanying box feature) from an organization that provides food aid, to one that fights root causes of world poverty. It is virtually impossible to succeed when our perceived mission is out of alignment with our true mission.

- What do constituents think we ought to do? It is an even tougher problem when there is a mismatch between what we think we do and what our constituents think we *ought* to do. This makes effective marketing virtually impossible because our efforts will publicize something clients and/or donors think is the wrong product. Obviously, this situation goes beyond a marketing problem.

FIRM DEVELOPMENT

The next chapter discusses the fact that social enterprise growth can occur in two ways: a growth in markets or a growth in products. The former is an expansion in the client or donor base; the latter is an expansion in the range of product offerings. Both of these growth strategies must also be part of the enterprise's marketing strategy.

STRATEGY SELECTION AND EVALUATION

After a marketing strategy is selected, it is necessary to establish a way to measure its effectiveness. Chapter 5 outlined the means to gauge effectiveness, including effectiveness of a marketing strategy.

COMMUNICATION

Only in the last step of a marketing strategy do we turn to communications—the actual contact with constituents. There are two types of communications: explicit and implicit. Explicit communications take many forms. Enterprises communicate with constituents with brochures, media, direct marketing, special events, and direct mail, of course, but there are many other means as well. Every contact with constituents should be viewed as an opportunity to communicate and raise constituents to a higher relationship level. This includes annual reports, newsletters, and press releases.

Implicit communications with constituents are less open but not necessarily any less effective. These include the pricing of products, the actual products offered, and their distribution, all of which communicate with constituents in many ways. For example, a performing arts organization that gives away free tickets is communicating something very different to its audience than one that charges a high entrance fee. What it chooses to program likewise communicates with the audience. As obvious as these points may seem, they often elude social entrepreneurs, who do not stop to think what message they are sending through these implicit means.

SOCIAL ENTERPRISE MESSAGES

Much has been made of targeted marketing for social enterprises: the idea that messages should be tailored to a client or donor with particular characteristics. The appeal to a young person is not necessarily the same as that to someone who is older. This is obviously not a revolutionary idea—the for-profit world has done it for decades—but the nonprofit world has often neglected this point.

Targeted marketing is the core of effective social enterprise messages. It emphasizes the benefits of social enterprise that are most important to various groups in the population. A large body of statistical research demonstrates that people respond to different sorts of appeals; in an environment in which we can gain access to high-income prospective donors, women, political conservatives, or practically any other specific group by renting mail and e-mail lists from other organizations, it is senseless to neglect targeted messaging.

Using Newsletters for Social Enterprise Marketing

Social enterprises should treat every communication with constituents as a marketing opportunity. A good example is an organizational newsletter. Traditionally, nonprofits have used their newsletters as a vehicle for fairly esoteric information about the venture: an employee training program, for example, or some personal background on new additions to the leadership. Professional marketing firms have found, however, that newsletters are an ideal opportunity to introduce clients, donors, and other constituents to new ideas and programs. CARE International's newsletters contain news not about the organization's employees but about the people CARE serves, thus giving supporters the information they really want and need and pushing the organization's mission forward.

A Newsletter from CARE International Profiles a Real Beneficiary of CARE's Services

Table 8-3 demonstrates how targeted messaging can work to raise funds.[19] Based on a large survey of Atlanta-area residents, the matrix matches reasons for giving that people state with their demographic characteristics. It shows that tax-based appeals ("Your donations are fully tax-deductible") are particularly effective among high-income people, young donors, married people, and women.

TABLE 8-3   Targeting Demographics

Demographics to Target	Sense of Community	Charities Are More Effective Than Government	Sense of Duty	Helped You in Times of Need	Tax Benefits	Religious Reasons
	Fundraising Focus					
High Income					X	
Low Income			X	X		
Younger					X	
Practicing Faith			X			X
Married					X	
Single						
Nonwhite		X	X			
Women		X	X		X	X
Conservatives		X				
Volunteer	X	X	X	X		X

Source: Van Slyke and Brooks (2005).

Arguments that a charitable cause is more effective than government programs — and hence deserving of private charitable support — are especially effective among minorities, women, conservatives, and those who volunteer for charity. Appeals to duty ("Won't you do your part to help?") work best among those with lower incomes, religious people, minorities, women, and volunteers.

The targeted messages in Table 8-3 are positive in nature — they look for the reasons people give or might give. But targeted messages can also exploit negative information, seeking to refute the reasons people do not give. Table 8-4 shows how

TABLE 8-4   Using Negative Information in Marketing

Target Group	Show How Aid Helps Those in Need	Show That Aid Reaches Those in Need	Show That Even Small Gifts Can Be Useful	Improve Awareness of Organization
	Strategy			
Young				X
Older	X			
Men				X
Unmarried			X	
Low education		X		X
Small family				X
No religion	X	X		
Big city			X	

Source: Brooks (2003).

this can be done.[20] A survey of Spanish citizens in the 1990s asked people who did not contribute to charities why they failed to do so. Besides the claim that they were financially unable to give, the most common responses were disbelief that those in need were actually helped by the aid; disbelief that the aid reached those in need; skepticism that a small donation made any difference; and a lack of awareness of giving opportunities. This information was then matched against the demographics of survey respondents and implied targeted messages. Young people needed to have their awareness of giving opportunities increased; older people needed to be shown that aid really impacts people in need; and so on.

Social enterprise communications can be categorized in two ways: abstract versus concrete, and promotional versus refutational. Understanding these dimensions is important for designing optimal appeals.

Abstract appeals do not focus on particular cases or specific issues. When a fundraising letter asks you to "do your part," it is making an abstract appeal. In contrast, *concrete appeals* draw attention to something specific. "Help us feed 100 hungry men and women today" is obviously a concrete appeal. *Promotional appeals* proactively ask people to do something. For example, "Please volunteer to help us build a home" is a promotional appeal. *Refutational appeals* are designed to counter implicit barriers, and as such are related to the negative messages described earlier. "We know you're busy, but can't you spare an afternoon to help us build a home?" is a refutational appeal. Table 8-5 summarizes the resulting four types of appeals: abstract/promotional, concrete/promotional, abstract/refutational, and concrete/refutational.

Fundraising research shows that social enterprises do best when they use concrete/promotional and abstract/refutational appeals.[21]

- *Concrete/promotional.* A typical concrete/promotional appeal is intended to give a potential supporter or client an idea that he or she wouldn't otherwise have had. Toys for Tots provides a good example of this. Founded in 1947 and run by the U.S. Marine Corps Reserve, Toys for Tots is an independent charitable organization in the United States that donates toys to lower-income children who would otherwise not be able to receive a Christmas gift. In 2006, with the support of a major donation from Learning Resources, Toys for Tots offered to match any gift purchased online by a customer with a second gift, offering individuals the opportunity to "buy once, give twice."

TABLE 8-5   Types of Messages

	Promotional	Refutational
Abstract	"Giving is vital for society."	"Your gift might be small, but you are doing your part."*
Concrete	"Your $10 gift will feed a child for 10 days."*	"$10 might seem like a pittance, but it will feed a child for 10 days."

*Messages found to be most effective.
Source: Clary, et al. (1994).

The effect was immediate: By mid-December, the company had donated over 42 tons of toys.

- *Abstract/refutational.* The classic abstract/refutation appeal is along the lines of, "Your gift is small but can do important thing nonetheless." A social enterprise that has effectively used this approach is Kiva, a Web-based microcredit organization that provides small loans to small businesses and entrepreneurs in the developing world to help the working poor more toward economic independence. Accepting donations on their Web site of as little as $25, Kiva allows donors to monitor the business they are helping, enabling individual donors of all sizes to see how effective their donations are.[22]

PRICING

How should a social enterprise price its services? This is a complicated question, because—unlike most commercial enterprises—net revenues are not the primary objective for most social ventures. In general, economists offer five pricing schemes to social enterprises, which are summarized in Table 8-6.[23]

For-profit organizations tend to set prices at such a point that profits are maximized. An airline looks for the price point at which—it hopes—the passengers multiplied by the average ticket price (total revenues) most exceeds the cost of transporting them. This does not mean maximizing the number of customers, generally, and even less does it imply that the price should be as high as possible.

Nonprofits occasionally price in this profit-maximizing way. For a subset of students, for example, private universities definitely maximize profits. Although only a small percentage of students at most private universities pay the "rack rate"—the published tuition—schools are always on the lookout for the students who can and will. These customers are sought to cross-subsidize the students who cannot or will not pay full price but whom the university wants nonetheless. Most nonprofits, however, pursue an objective that explicitly rules out profit maximization. It is far more common to maximize the number of clients served or the quality of service.

To maximize the level of service or service quality, how should a social enterprise price its services, if at all? One common technique is to implement a "sliding

TABLE 8-6   Pricing Options

Strategy	Description
Profit maximization	Maximize net revenues
Mixed pricing	Cross subsidize favored clients with fees from others
Classical price discrimination	Charge prices that vary by client characteristics (age, race, income, etc.)
Voluntary price discrimination	Charge a low price but augment with voluntary donations elicited at time of sale
Intertemporal price discrimination	Charge according to time or day

scale" of prices, in which some clients pay the profit-maximizing price so that others can pay less, without an enterprise falling into debt.

A system of prices that differ by a client's characteristics is called "classical price discrimination," and it is common not just among nonprofits but in the for-profit world as well. Children and adults pay different prices of admission to the movies; business and leisure travelers pay different transportation ticket prices, and so on. But while price discrimination in the commercial world is designed to get the most money out of each market segment, social ventures use it to cross-subsidize clients that are desirable but (usually) money-losing. Hospitals committed to treating the poor and uninsured will inevitably lose money on them and finance these losses with profit-generating fees charged to the insured nonpoor.

There are two variants of classical price discrimination that are useful to social enterprises. The first is "voluntary price discrimination," in which clients are offered a loss-making price but asked for a voluntary donation. This is a very common strategy in the arts, and you have probably experienced it yourself: The price of entrance to an arts event is low, but you are asked to donate whatever you can on top of the ticket price.[24] It has been shown to be an exceptionally effective fundraising strategy for many social ventures because it allows people to autodiscriminate according to information the social entrepreneur may not have—willingness and ability to pay. Although it might seem like people will tend to hide their ability and underpay, this is usually not the case.

A second innovation is "intertemporal price discrimination," in which the price depends on the time or day of service. Most nonprofits face uneven demand over time; for example, museums are packed on Saturday but empty Tuesday mornings; hospital emergency rooms are crowded Friday night but not Sunday morning. Service demand that is "clumpy" presents an opportunity to social entrepreneurs: Build demand during the down times—when there is no competition for service with others—with reduced pricing.

Summary

- Fundraising generally encompasses six broad categories of activity: personal relationships, direct mail, fundraising events, telefunding, traditional media, and virtual means.
- Social entrepreneurs still must make decisions—including fundraising decisions—that use scarce resources in the most efficient way possible. One major fundraising tradeoff is between the number of donors and the size of donations.
- Donors are not all alike. There are six basic types of donors: potential donors (who have not given but have been identified as possible givers); new donors (who have given for the first time); transition donors (who have given twice); core donors (who have given three or more years in a row); lapsed donors (who have given in the past but not over the past year); and lapsed but reactivated (who gave in the past and stopped for a year or more but have started giving again).

- Core donors are the most productive for a nonprofit organization. Social enterprises should spend fundraising time and energy building this core.
- There are three strategies social entrepreneurs must understand to acquire new donors, bring them to the core, and lift the giving by the core donors. These strategies can be summarized as win, keep, and lift.
- Donors lapse for many reasons, some of which are under the enterprise's control. Improved fundraising can prevent many lapses.
- Research indicates that fears about the reaction of donors to administrative expenses is not well-founded. There is no reason to fear responsible administrative spending.
- There are five basic steps in building a marketing strategy: External analysis, which studies the circumstances outside the venture; internal analysis, which asks what the venture does, what people think it does, and what it should do; a decision on firm development or how the organization will grow; strategy selection and evaluation; and communications with the public.
- There are three basic types of volunteer appeals that social enterprises and other nonprofits should understand: warm body recruitment to develop a large volunteer force, targeted recruitment to acquire a smaller number of individuals with specific skills, and concentric circles recruitment, where current volunteers recruit future volunteers.
- Volunteers consider three elements in calculating their own value: their value in market work foregone (i.e., wages), the value of the next-best volunteering opportunity, and the value of their leisure time.
- Communications take two forms: explicit and implicit. Explicit communications with constituents use brochures, media, direct marketing, special events, direct mail, and so on. Implicit communications include the pricing of products, the actual products offered, and their distribution.
- There are four basic types of appeals: abstract/promotional, concrete/promotional, abstract/refutational, and concrete/refutational. The second and fourth have been shown to be most effective for social enterprises.

Key Terms

- fundraising
- potential donors
- new donors
- transition donors
- core donors
- lapsed donors
- "win" fundraising strategy
- "keep" fundraising strategy

- "lift" fundraising strategy
- warm body recruitment
- targeted recruitment
- concentric circles recruitment
- abstract appeals
- concrete appeals
- promotional appeals
- refutational appeals

- profit maximization
- classical price discrimination
- voluntary price discrimination
- intertemporal price discrimination

End-of-Chapter Questions and Cases

HEALTHY LIVES

You have just accepted the position as the executive director of a medium-sized human service nonprofit called *Healthy Lives,* which promotes healthy living habits to the inner-city poor in your region. The agency was a start-up five years ago, and the social entrepreneur had significant initial success raising support from foundations and private donors. However, her interest in fundraising gradually waned, donors were neglected, and most fell into lapse. In looking at the file of former donors, you see that approximately 90 percent are currently inactive, and only 5 percent are the core. The rest are either new, transition, or reactivated lapsed.

1. Who are this organization's target donors?
2. Outline a strategy to win—or win back—these donors.
3. Outline a strategy to keep these donors.
4. Outline how the current and future core can be lifted to higher donation levels.

SYRACUSE SYMPHONY ORCHESTRA

The Syracuse Symphony Orchestra (SSO) is a full-time performing ensemble in Central New York State.[25] Like most other arts nonprofits, it relies heavily on donated income and has adopted a multidimensional fundraising approach.

Personal relationships are built primarily through events and receptions related to specific concerts. Relationships are also built around phone calls and personalized handwritten notes, whether as a thank-you or extending an invitation. Furthermore, assigning donors to a staff person to assist with any help regarding donations or ticket inquiries further develops these relationships. The focus of personal relationships is the core donor.

Direct mail is used year round and includes core, transitional, nonrenewed, lapsed, and nondonors. There are about five cycles that occur throughout the year with personalized letters going out to each of these groups. Further segmentation of these groups is done as well to enhance the personalization of the letter. For example, people who have attended a single concert receive a different letter from those who are concert series subscribers.

Telefunding is outsourced to a for-profit company and focuses on lapsed and nonrenewed donors, as well as single-ticket buyers who have never given in the past. After each concert, a list of single-ticket buyers is segmented into nonrenewed, lapsed, and nondonors. These people then receive a phone call from a representative who emphasizes what a great concert they had just attended. The SSO finds that this personal touch produces a good response: The group with the highest response rate is the nondonor group, with average gifts of $100. Before telefunding, average gifts among this group were only around $30, showing that this technique helps both in acquiring new donors and also increasing the average gift amount.

Traditional media is not used directly for fundraising efforts but rather for ticket sales marketing. Radio, television, and print ads are the main means of advertisement for the Symphony and as a result create a greater audience to be solicited. The Symphony also uses virtual means. SSO officials believe that the Internet, even though it does not bring in many donations, is an effective way for potential and current donors to learn more about the Symphony, its programs, and fundraising opportunities.

1. Given ways on how the Symphony segments its constituents, what might be some other examples as to how they could segment their ticket buyers and solicit them?

2. Given the techniques used by the Symphony, what might be some specific strategies as to how donors and potential donors could be won, kept, and lifted?

3. The more engaged someone is with an organization, the more likely they are to invest into the organization. Using volunteers is a great way to turn a non-donor into a donor. How might the Symphony engage its volunteers to assist in each of the fundraising activities?

End Notes

1. "How it Works." DonorsChoose.org Web site. (www.donorschoose.org/about/about. html); (March 7, 2005). "It's Raining Pencils." *Time Magazine*.
2. These data were provided to the author by Eric Zimmer, SJ.
3. See www.easterseals.com/site/PageServer.
4. Easter Seals (2006). 2005–2006 *Annual Report*.
5. These dimensions come from data on social welfare nonprofit agencies. Some social enterprises have different dimensions of course—especially when they are so new that no "core" exists, or they are aggressive about dropping lapsed donors—but this represents a fair representation of many donor lists. These data are used with permission from Merkle.
6. These data are not representative of all nonprofits or social enterprises but rather those from a sample largely of social service organizations. The numbers here should be interpreted in relationship to one another.
7. "Church Partnership Opportunities." Habitat for Humanity Web site. (www.habitat. org/cr/opportunities.aspx).
8. Hall, Holly (November 23, 2006). "The Vanishing Donor." *The Chronicle of Philanthropy*.
9. Press Release "MAP International Uses Convio to Strengthen Constituent Relationships, Accelerate Fundraising and Drive In-Kind Donations." July 31, 2006. www.convio.com/site/News2?abbr=news_&page=NewsArticle&id=2603392&news_iv_ctrl=2600054.
10. Merkle-Domain Corporation.
11. Sargeant, A. (2001) "Relationship Fundraising: How To Keep Donors Loyal." *Nonprofit Management and Leadership* 12(2): 177–192.
12. See Brooks, Arthur C. (2006). *Who Really Cares: The Surprising Truth About Compassionate Conservatism*. New York: Basic Books, Chapter 4.

13. Frumkin, Peter; and Mark T. Kim (2001). "Strategic Positioning and the Financing of Nonprofit Organizations: Is Efficiency Rewarded in the Contributions Marketplace?" *Public Administration Review* 61(3): 266–275.
14. Sources: Johnston, David C. (November 9, 1997). "Charity Pleading Poverty; United Way Losing Donors." *New York Times*.
15. See McCurley, Stephen (1994). "Recruiting and Retaining Volunteers." In Herman, Robert D. (Ed.). *The Jossey-Bass Handbook of Nonprofit Management and Leadership*. San Francisco: Jossey-Bass, pp. 511–534.
16. "Who We Are." Help the Hospices Web site. (www.helpthehospices.org.uk/whoweare/index.asp).
17. "Help the Hospices: 13 Days Campaign." TimeBank Web site. (www.timebank.org.uk/services/portfolio_detail.php?id=1).
18. See www.care.org/careswork/whatwedo/index.asp.
19. Van Slyke, David M., and Arthur C. Brooks (2005). "Why Do People Give? New Evidence and Strategies for Nonprofit Managers." *American Review of Public Administration* 35(3): 199–222.
20. Brooks, Arthur C. (2003). "Charitable Giving to Humanitarian Organizations in Spain." *Hacienda Pública Española/Revista de Economía*.
21. Clary, E. Gil, Mark Snyder, John T. Copeland, and Simone A. French (1994). "Promoting Volunteerism: An Empirical Examination of the Appeal of Persuasive Messages." *Nonprofit and Voluntary Sector Quarterly* 23(3): 265–280.
22. See www.kiva.org/.
23. Brooks, Arthur C. (2006). "Nonprofit Performing Arts Firms." In Ginsburgh, Victor, and C. David Throsby (Eds.). *The Handbook on the Economics of Art and Culture*. North Holland Handbooks in Economics. Amsterdam: Elsevier Science, pp. 473–506.
24. O'Hagan, J., and M. Purdy (1993), "The Theory of Non-Profit Organisations: An Application to a Performing Arts Enterprise." *Economic and Social Review* 24(2): 155–167.
25. This case is based on information shared with the author by the Syracuse Symphony Orchestra.

CHAPTER 9

LAUNCH, GROWTH, AND GOAL ATTAINMENT

INTRODUCTION

The Bronx Preparatory Charter School is a middle school chartered by the state of New York in April 2000. It started with 102 fifth and sixth graders and seven teachers and planned to add an additional grade each year until the initial class graduated from high school. Bronx Prep promised to prepare economically underprivileged students for top colleges with a rigorous academic environment and extended school days and years.[1]

Although Bronx Prep possessed a promising business model, its success depended on its growth. The school limited its size to 200 by 2002 but planned a rapid expansion as it moved into becoming a high school as well. Plans called for the school's enrollment to quadruple to 800 students. To do this, however, Bronx Prep needed to significantly increase its funding—under New York state law, charter schools receive 80 percent of the per-pupil funding from the government that public schools receive, but no funding is provided for building new facilities or purchasing old ones.

During the school's first year of operations, expenses were approximately $1.5 million (including costs incurred prior to the opening of the school), and the state provided approximately $960,000. The projected costs for the necessary growth were $12.5 million. This meant that a growth plan had to rely on good strategy and proactive fundraising. It enjoyed both and was successful. The school raised about $900,000 in its first year, much of it prior to the opening of the school. Reviewed by the State of New York in 2004, Bronx Prep received a full renewal for five years to continue operating. Several donors contributed significantly toward the expansion, including the Merrill Lynch Corporation, which contributed $1 million. Today, Bronx Prep serves more than 500 students.

For every successful social enterprise like Bronx Prep, there are others that never navigate through the launch and growth stages in the social entrepreneurship process. What do we need to know about these stages? What are the biggest pitfalls and opportunities social entrepreneurs need to understand to reach the successful attainment of their goals?

PREPARING FOR GROWTH

Before launching a venture, a social entrepreneur assesses the likelihood of a high social return. What impacts the likelihood of this return? One popular conceptual framework in the literature on commercial enterprises is known as the Five Competitive Forces Model.[2] This model predicts that commercial firms that can diminish these forces have a better chance of earning positive profits.

1. *Substitutes.* Firms with a product that have few substitutes will do better, on average, than those with lots of substitutes.
2. *Ease of entry.* If it is difficult to enter an industry, profit margins can be protected. Easier entry means competitors will tend to take profits off the table.
3. *Market power of buyers.* In some industries, the consumer has a lot of power to set prices, either because there are few buyers or because sellers are so competitive with one another. More buyer power means less profits to sellers.
4. *Market power of sellers.* In other industries, few sellers, or lots of competition between buyers, means that sellers can drive up their prices and profits.
5. *Competitive pressure.* These first four forces all determine the degree of rivalry in an industry: If there are many rival firms, price competition will tend to drive down profits.

Is there a parallel model to the Five Competitive Forces in the case of social entrepreneurship? We can conceive of a framework in which we evaluate the biggest threats to social value creation—threats that social entrepreneurs must assess before launch just as commercial entrepreneurs assess the competitive threats. Threats to social value creation come primarily in four forms (see Figure 9-1).

SUBSTITUTES FOR SERVICE

Some mission-based social ventures may worry little about new organizations serving their clients. For example, a soup kitchen in one part of town is rarely threatened because another food provider to the poor opens up. Other enterprises, however, feel a distinct competition with existing nonprofits for donations, other revenues, or clients. Here are two examples.

- *Competition for donations and other revenues.* The American Red Cross is one of the most well established charities in the United States. With a

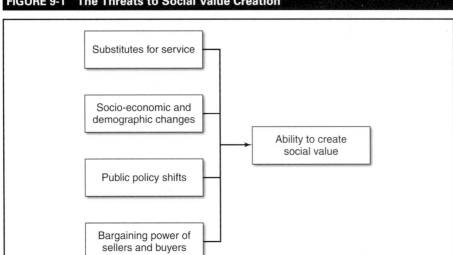

FIGURE 9-1   The Threats to Social Value Creation

budget of nearly $2 billion, and more than 1.3 million volunteers, the ARC provides services to 150,000 people per year, primarily through its blood distribution network and disaster relief services. With numerous organizations taking an increasingly active role in disaster relief—from well-established charities such as the United Way and the Salvation Army to various church-based organizations, to name just a few categories—ARC has witnessed gradually declining donor revenue in recent years, with the notable exception of 2005, which is likely attributable to the outpouring of donations in response to Hurricane Katrina. This trend is almost certainly due to the proliferation of social enterprises doing many of the same things that the ARC has traditionally done.[3]

- *Competition for clients*. The December 26, 2004 Indian Ocean tsunami was one of the most devastating natural disasters in history and brought a wide range of relief agencies, both new and established, seeking to provide assistance to the region. These agencies included international NGOs, national governments, and for-profit corporations. Even here, though, social enterprises competed for "clients." Throughout the relief efforts, various actors in the region tussled over how to coordinate their activities so as not to duplicate services, who was to run various shelters that had been constructed by other parties, and how best to spend the massive resources that had been contributed.[4]

Beyond competition for revenues and clients, social enterprises frequently compete against something entirely less defined: inaction by clients. The biggest threat many social ventures face is the decision to forgo services among those they hope to serve. Many organizations to help the homeless, for example, describe people sleeping on the street rather than using shelters. Free concerts have empty seats in the audience; free health clinics frequently go underused; and so on. This fact takes us back to the discussion in an earlier chapter about the difference between good ideas and real opportunities and the difference between supply and demand—or at least between latent and actual demand. Social entrepreneurs need to understand, anticipate, and cope proactively with inaction as a substitute for their service.

SOCIOECONOMIC AND DEMOGRAPHIC CHANGES

One of the greatest sources of opportunities for a social entrepreneur is demographic change. Recall that where many people see problems, social entrepreneurs see opportunity, especially socioeconomically: a neighborhood in decline, a sudden influx of poor immigrants, a loss of income when a factory closes, and so forth. But these very kinds of changes can also work against the social entrepreneur and hence are potential threats to anticipate. There are two main types of socioeconomic threats to anticipate.

- *Need.* Economic or demographic shifts can lower the need for an enterprise's services. For example, a neighborhood can redevelop or gentrify, which can drive a social enterprise serving the poor out, along with the poor themselves.

- *Interest.* When economic or social circumstances change, communities can become less interested in a social enterprise, resulting in a loss of clients or support. For example, if a disease is eradicated in America, it can lower the interest of Americans in supporting its treatment in other, poorer countries. There are many cases of transnational NGOs finding insufficient support in the United States for fighting diseases in the developing world that Americans never face.

PUBLIC POLICY SHIFTS

With the stroke of a pen, public policymakers can radically change the landscape for social entrepreneurs—for better or worse. Governments create social opportunities all the time when they offer contracts for services or increase tax incentives to give. But governments can also threaten the success of social ventures. The most common threats are from regulation and public funding decreases.

- *Regulation.* Nonprofit social enterprises face a rash of government regulation, from financial reporting requirements to mandated labor practices. Social entrepreneurs must understand these regulations before launch. But even more, they need to predict the most likely threats from new regulation. For example, an acute current challenge to the autonomy of foundations coming from the U.S. Congress is the Pension Protection Act of 2006. It was passed to ensure that grant-making organizations could not be used for the private benefit of an individual person. However, it directly threatens the ability of donor-advised funds to purchase goods and services to carry out charitable activities.[5]

- *Funding decreases.* Just as the government giveth, so can it taketh away—that's what many social entrepreneurs have learned over the years. In an earlier chapter, we saw that the rate of bankruptcy is very high in certain parts of the nonprofit sector, and there is some evidence that in many cases this is due to the sudden loss of government funding. In fact, research has shown that public money is a less stable source of funding than other types (donated or earned).[6]

BARGAINING POWER OF SELLERS AND BUYERS

As you saw earlier, for-profits face the threat of high bargaining power from those that sell them resources or those who buy their products. The same is true for social enterprises and other nonprofits. Social entrepreneurs, especially in major urban centers, can be the victims of unfavorable market conditions.

- *Labor.* Social ventures frequently have to compete with commercial enterprises and governments for high-quality professional services. The market for executives can be particularly inhospitable for nonprofit organizations, which face revenues that make it hard to pay "market rates" for the best talent. One study from 2004 showed that, among Southern California nonprofits with revenues in the $5 million to $9 million range, the average chief executive compensation was $124,000, compared with $200,000 for top executives at for-profits of the same size.[7] Even worse, public policy and public opinion often make it hard for nonprofits to compete even when they *do* have the revenues. There are many cases in which nonprofits paying markets rates to executives have resulted in scandals. For example, in 2005, the *Baltimore Sun* featured an exposé on Maryland's nonprofit executive compensation, entitled, "Paychecks Raise Eyebrows."[8] The story noted that several nonprofit executives earned more than $1 million per year. These executives were nonprofit hospital administrators by and large, however; and nonprofit hospitals compete in a labor market directly with for-profits.

- *Capital.* Social enterprises require physical, human, and financial capital, just like for-profits. Especially in the financial case, they are frequently at the mercy of financial markets that make loans on the basis of *risk*, not *need* or *social value*. As a result, social entrepreneurs often have little leverage over the price of financing, especially if they are engaged in an endeavor that has little precedent or promise of financial return.

- *Land.* Many cities are exceptionally expensive. Many times, social enterprises compete with for-profits and individuals for operating space such as offices. Landlords face a tremendous opportunity cost if they rent to non-profits at low prices, and the result is that many do not. Not only can this inhibit the entry of social enterprises into the market in cities, but it is also

---

The High Cost of City Life

Social enterprises operating in urban centers can provide services to a greater number of people with less effort than their rural counterparts because of the greater population density. However, there are clear disadvantages as well. For those that work in major cities such as New York or Los Angeles, operating expenses—such as office space—can be astronomical. And it is not always the case that the landlords charging high rents are profit-maximizing commercial organizations. The conflict between the Bowery Residence Committee (BRC) and CBGB, a legendary New York punk music club, is a case in point.[9]

BRC is a neighborhood committee in New York City that provides services for the homeless, mentally ill, and those suffering from substance addictions, offering 23 programs focusing on self-help and personal responsibility. The BRC owns several properties in New York. To finance its operations, BRC leases several of its buildings to various businesses, one of which is CBGB, which has been a New York music institution since 1973. In 2005, however, a dispute between BRC and CBGB broke out over back rent: CBGB was paying $20,000 per month, but was behind $91,000 (an amount that CBGB claimed it was not aware of because it had not been informed of a lease increase).

While that issue went to court, the problems were compounded when BRC decided to double CBGB's rent because of escalating real estate prices citywide. Despite significant support from musicians and others, CBGB concluded it could not afford this amount, and the club was forced to shut down.

---

a major threat to viability if there is the prospect that rents will increase after a venture commences.

- *Products.* For social ventures that acquire revenues from fees and other sorts of earned revenues, the market power of buyers can pose a threat. For example, many health ventures rely on compensation they receive from governments and insurance companies. If these "customers" exert market power to drive down their own costs, it can dramatically affect the bottom line of the social enterprises.

SOCIAL ENTERPRISE GROWTH STRATEGIES

After assessing the threats to social value creation and launching the enterprise, the enterprise grows, ideally according to the trajectory in the organization's business plan. No venture starts out at its maximum size or scale; it takes time and resources to get there. That's why understanding growth is so important in the process of social entrepreneurship.

There are two basic kinds of growth for a social venture: product growth and market growth.

- *Product growth.* This refers to an expansion of product offerings—an enterprise increasing the scope of its activities. A good example of this is the highly entrepreneurial literacy organization ProLiteracy Worldwide. ProLiteracy was formed following the merger of Laubach Literacy International and Literacy Volunteers of America in 2002.[10] It has excelled at its "bread and butter" product of adult literacy, serving about 350,000 adults each year around the world. It has continually grown through the addition of new programs as well, however. These include Women in Literacy International, to meet the particular needs of women, as well as New Readers Press, which has provided original teaching materials for literacy training programs.

- *Market growth.* This kind of growth relies on the core service of the venture but seeks new consumers. An example of this growth pattern is FirstBook, a venture that, from its founding in 1992, has had a single, simple mission: to provide children from low-income families new books.[11] The organization's growth has focused on innovative strategies to find more and more young children who could benefit from the program. To date, by expanding both the communities they operate in and how they reach out to children, First-Book has distributed nearly 40 million books in more than 1,300 communities around the United States. The organization has also developed partnerships with for-profit businesses, governments, and other nonprofits to reach as many children as possible.

Product and market growth can be combined in four ways (see Table 9-1): existing products in existing markets; existing products in new markets; new products in existing markets; and new products in new markets. None of these strategies is mutually exclusive; on the contrary, they are highly complementary.

- *Existing products/existing markets.* This is classic market penetration. For example, Volunteers in Medicine is a social enterprise that has mobilized retired medical professionals (doctors, nurses, dentists, and so forth) to provide medical services to individuals who have no other access to health care. After starting out in one area of Hilton Head, South Carolina, VIM grew with the aim to provide its services to every person living or working in its region.[12]
- *Existing products/new markets.* This is product expansion. VIM used this growth strategy as well. After successfully covering Hilton Head, VIM established the Volunteers in Medicine Institute to "spread the gospel" of volunteer-based medical clinics around the country and world, while helping other clinics overcome the significant challenges they face.
- *New products/existing markets.* This is a product-development strategy. Take the case of College Summit. In 1994, J.B. Schramm was the director of

TABLE 9-1 Social Enterprise Growth Strategies		
	Existing Markets	*New Markets*
Existing products	Market penetration	Market expansion
New products	Product development	Product diversification

an existing teen center in the basement of a low-income housing center in Washington, D.C. Schramm saw that colleges were looking for low-income students, but that many of the teens in his center were not going to college. He launched College Summit to provide college counseling to low-income students and advice to schools to boost college enrollment.[13]

- *New products/new markets.* This is product diversification. College Summit presents an example of this strategy as well. In addition to advising teens about college, the organization grew to advise colleges on reaching low-income teens, as well as train teachers and school counselors on how best to direct low-income youths.

Another increasingly common growth strategy comes from mergers: the joining of two or more social enterprises. For example, America's Second Harvest (ASH) was a food service provider that from its founding in 1979 sought to serve as a clearinghouse for large donations from corporations to food banks around the country, distributing in its first year 2.5 million pounds of food to 13 different food banks.[14] In the 1980s, with food banks established in most cities, expansion of their network slowed down, and the organization looked for another means of growth. In 2000, already the second largest hunger relief operation in the United States, ASH merged with Foodchain, the nation's largest, not only to enhance its food distribution system but also to assume a greater role in food "rescue." Today, America's Second Harvest—The Nation's Food Bank Network operates a system of more than 200 member food banks and distributes over 2 billion pounds of donated food and groceries annually.

Merging doesn't always occur as seamlessly as in the case of ASH. There are many cases of failed mergers, and one research study has sought to diagnose the conditions under which a merger is more or less likely to succeed.[15] The conclusion of this research is that successful social venture mergers answer affirmatively to all or most of the following questions.

1. Are internal perceptions favorable for partnering? When people inside the merging partner organizations are against merging, a merger is usually unsuccessful.
2. Is there a "dominant player" in the merger? One enterprise usually has to lead the partnership.
3. Is there a perception of high stakes in the merger? It is rare that ventures merge when there is little at stake.
4. Is there a catalyst leader? An individual must be the champion of a merger for it to be successful.
5. Is there a group of merger supporters besides the leader? The champion must be able to establish a hard core of influential supporters, such as donors and board members.
6. Is there an extended period of discussion? Mergers don't occur overnight. It is important that there be sufficient time to discuss the partnership. Interestingly, however, *too much* time can also harm the chances of a successful merger.

7. Is there congruence of missions? Two social enterprises cannot become one if the missions are dramatically at variance.

8. Is there opportunity to build trust and interpersonal connections? It is important not to underestimate the role of personal relationships between people in each enterprise.

MYTHS ABOUT GROWTH

One significant impediment to social enterprise growth is a belief in two common myths:[16]

1. *Myth 1. A social venture will not grow quickly unless it is in a high-growth sector.* The highest growth social sector is nonprofit health care, which has more than doubled in revenues over the past two decades and shows no signs of slowing even slightly. Other sectors, such as the arts and culture, are growing much more slowly. Therefore, a health organization must tend to grow much faster than an arts organization. This is not true; on the contrary, fast growth usually depends much more on local demand, proper management, and adequate funding, than it does on trends in the overall sector.

2. *Myth 2. Rapid growth requires a venture being the first of its kind.* This is much truer in the for-profit world than it is in the social sector, where social problems and unmet needs may or may not require a totally new kind of service to meet them, and competition between social enterprises might not exist because of a complete lack of profit opportunities. For example, a foster care agency can be created where there is need and grow very quickly without being either a new service of its kind or any major concern about being undercut by competitive companies.

THE CHALLENGES OF GROWTH AND CHANGE

Many social enterprises have grown very quickly over the past few decades. Figure 9-2 shows the inflation-adjusted revenue growth in several social sectors from 1977–97.

Growth necessarily involves the change of an enterprise, and this can be difficult to manage. In the for-profit world, volumes have been written about the challenges of change. Less is known about the special problems of change in the case of social enterprises, however.

Social enterprise expert Betty Henderson Wingfield has identified six key problem areas in social enterprise change. These are the challenges that social entrepreneurs should anticipate in the growth process:[17]

1. *The stimulus for change is usually different for social entrepreneurs than it is for others in their organizations.* As we have seen, social entrepreneurs are highly opportunity-oriented. Change is an affirmative phenomenon. In contrast, nonentrepreneurs, including many staff and board members of non-profit organizations, tend to see change as necessary only in times of crisis.

FIGURE 9-2 The Growth of Various Social Sectors, 1977–1997

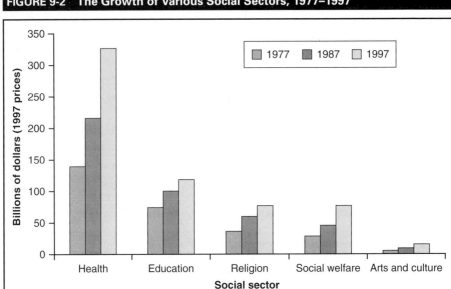

Source: Independent Sector.[18]

The result of this difference is that a social entrepreneur can have a hard time convincing others involved in an enterprise that change is useful or beneficial.

2. *The people involved in social enterprises are frequently resistant to market-based changes.* One of the most common innovations that social entrepreneurs have made over the past decade is the injection of market-oriented approaches in the nonprofit world. As we have seen, for example, fee-based income is a more and more common support strategy in social enterprises. However, some social entrepreneurs find a "culture" in the nonprofit world that is resistant to market-based innovations, believing that they degrade the difference between noncommercial and commercial organizations.

3. *The board is legally at the head of a nonprofit enterprise and can inhibit risk-taking and change.* In commercial enterprises, entrepreneurs have far more flexibility and latitude than they do in social enterprises because of the latter's nonprofit form, which legally vests authority in the board of directors. Boards can be (but are not always) far more risk averse than the social entrepreneur, making it hard to innovate.

4. *The community often feels like a stakeholder in a social enterprise and can affect change.* There is an old axiom that failure is a cost of doing business in the commercial world; in government, it is called "waste, fraud, and abuse." Why? Because the public has little tolerance for failed ventures using tax money. To a certain extent, social entrepreneurs face the same problem in the nonprofit sector because communities often feel invested in all sorts of nonprofit activities.

5. *Demonstrating the results from change in a social enterprise can be especially difficult.* We have already devoted an entire chapter to accountability, outcomes, and effectiveness—and the difficulty in measuring each concept.

6. *Human resource changes can be hard because of the culture of many social enterprises.* Successful ventures must be nimble, and this means being able to make changes in human resources when warranted. Nothing signals a sclerotic, nonentrepreneurial organization more clearly than inefficient workers or workers mismatched with their jobs. The culture of nonprofits—that it is "kinder" than the for-profit world—frequently makes human resource changes very tricky.

INTRAPRENEURSHIP AND ENTREPRENEURIAL INTENSITY

Not all social entrepreneurship involves developing new organizations, and a key concept for social venture growth and development is how established ventures can continue to behave entrepreneurially. In fact, it is quite crucial that they do so. We refer to this as *social intrapreneurship,* where "intra" refers to the fact that the behavior occurs within the established venture.

Authors Kuratko and Hodgetts provide a set of rules for encouraging an intrapreneurial environment. The rules are as appropriate for social enterprises as they are for for-profits.[19]

1. *Encourage action.* Of course, no social enterprise advances from activity that has no purpose, but a culture in which doing is encouraged tends to be most intrapreneurial.

2. *Informal meetings are better than formal meetings.* Formal meetings can stifle the spirit of spontaneity and innovativeness.

3. *Understand failure as a part of the learning process.* Risk is part of entrepreneurship, as is managing it properly. Just as a risk-adverse organization is nonentrepreneurial, so is a risk-adverse workforce nonintrapreneurial.

4. *Be persistent in implementing ideas.* Personnel experience disincentives to innovate when ideas are not implemented.

5. *Make innovation a goal in and of itself.* This is counterintuitive because it sounds counter to the overarching mission of a social enterprise. However, it is important for cultural reasons, and culture is a means to the mission's ends.

6. *Make informal communication in the workplace easier.* Innovation is difficult when people are isolated and do not share ideas. The physical and virtual workspace can be designed to make communication easier.

7. *Encourage the development of new ideas unrelated to current projects.* This is often called "bootlegging," in which people use company and personal time to develop new concepts. Encouraging this serves the goal of innovation for its own sake.

8. *Assign people to think about future issues.* Current problems are not always the most fertile ground for innovative thinking.

9. *Encourage people to find ways around bureaucratic procedures.* Innovation occurs not just in the quantity and quality of services but in procedures. Encouraging people to circumvent red tape creates incentives to innovate.

10. *Reward innovative people.* The reward structure is an important signal of an enterprise's culture. It is the difference between saying innovation is important and demonstrating it.

This list suggests that intrapreneurship relies on both organizational and personal qualities, as depicted in the model in Figure 9-3. The social entrepreneur creates an organization with incentives to bring in, keep, cultivate, and reward innovative people. An event generally triggers the process of intrapreneurship and the willingness and ability of personnel to behave intrapreneurially. The receptive enterprise takes the resulting ideas, depending on the availability of necessary resources and the ability to overcome obstacles, and—depending on the availability of resources and the quality of the ideas—implements the ideas.

Innovation inside a social enterprise does not have to be radical or dramatically organization-altering. On the contrary, it can be incremental. Furthermore, it doesn't have to be sudden and unusual; it can be constant. Intrapreneurship, and social entrepreneurship more generally, are a matter of degree. Entrepreneurship scholar Michael Morris explains the degrees and dimensions of entrepreneurship

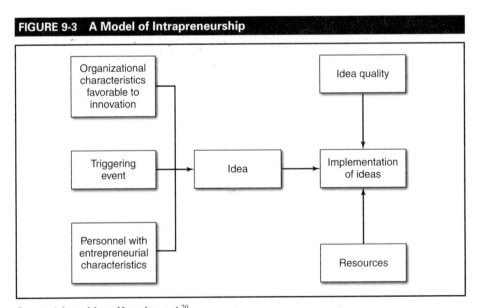

FIGURE 9-3 A Model of Intrapreneurship

Source: Adapted from Hornsby, et al.[20]

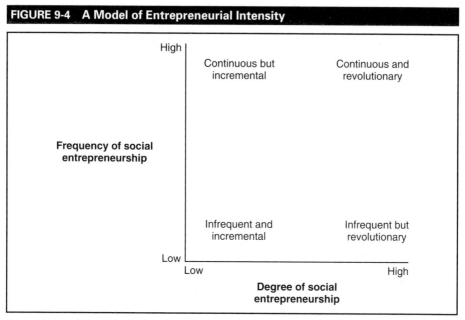

FIGURE 9-4   A Model of Entrepreneurial Intensity

Source: Adapted from Morris (1998).

under the concept of "entrepreneurial intensity," which we can adapt to describe the variations of social intrapreneurship and social entrepreneurship.[21]

- *Degree of social entrepreneurship.* An innovation can be revolutionary or incremental. For example, a nonprofit that suddenly turns away from high levels of government funding in favor of private philanthropy is making revolutionary change, one that seeks to find small ways to serve its donors innovates incrementally.

- *Frequency of social entrepreneurship.* Social innovation can be continuous or periodic. For example, some social ventures make one splash, whereas others seek to innovate constantly.

These two dimensions make possible a two-by-two classification of social intrapreneurship (see Figure 9-4): organizations that innovate infrequently and incrementally; those that innovate incrementally but continuously; organizations in which innovation is infrequent but revolutionary; and those that that undertake revolutionary innovations frequently. Following are some examples of the combinations representing positive intrapreneurship levels:

- *Continuous but incremental.* Rosie's House in Phoenix, Arizona, is the first program in the United States that offers full service musical education aimed at lower-income youth. Since its founding in 1996, Rosie's House has been tuition free, seeking to provide direction, stability, and tools for success to youth through music. Initially a refuge for homeless children, Rosie's

House has grown nearly continuously to serve in excess of 350 students today, constantly innovating in its program offerings.[22]

- *Infrequent but revolutionary.* The Mexican Institute of Greater Houston, Inc., helps to address one of the key issues facing many Mexican immigrants to the United States today: lack of basic computer literacy. With more than half of Latino students dropping out before they finish high school, programs such as the Mexican Institute's are intended to prepare new immigrants for a workforce that requires computer skills in virtually all good jobs. In its first two years, 800 participants graduated from the Institute's classes, and there is a significant waiting list to enroll. The Institute's core innovation is what they have stuck with since their establishment in 1991.[23]

- *Continuous and revolutionary.* Shreveport-Bossier Community Renewal is, and has been practically since its inception in 1994, nationally regarded as one of the most successful organizations devoted to community renewal. Seeking to "restore the foundation of safe and caring communities," SBCR has adopted several unique strategies that are highly innovative and have represented continuous change. First, the Renewal Team was developed to head up traditional renewal urban efforts in conjunction with businesses, churches, civic groups, and governments. Second, the Haven House program offers residents in affected communities the opportunity to interact with their neighbors through socializing (e.g., organizing block parties) and service (mowing each others' lawns). Third, Community Renewal has developed Friendship Houses, which function as community centers for after-school programs, places for continued education, and social centers.[24]

GROWTH AND RISK

When growing, should a social entrepreneur seek to develop an environment in which intrapreneurship is frequent and revolutionary? Or is a more stable service environment better—perhaps one of the intermediate cases (frequent but incremental, or infrequent but revolutionary)? There is reason not to seek the most entrepreneurially intense option reflexively, and this has to do with *risk*. Social entrepreneurs are generally more comfortable with risk than nonentrepreneurs, we know, but this is not the same thing as saying social entrepreneurs should not try to avoid it in many situations.

One the one hand, a nonintrapreneurial environment is the riskiest one of all because it often means stagnation, making it difficult or impossible to adapt to changing conditions. This exposes enterprises to risks in funding, and social entrepreneurs generally understand this intuitively. Frequent, revolutionary change is also risky, however. There are risks that innovations and changes will destabilize an organization or that they will not be accepted by the public. For example, frequent revolutionary change might mean adding fee-based income opportunities at a rapid rate in the growth phase, which requires capital investment and the attention of staff. It is easy to imagine cases in which this strategy does not bear

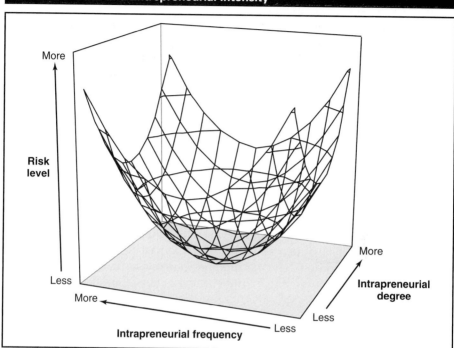

FIGURE 9-5   Risk and Entrepreneurial Intensity

fruit but distracts from core operations. The risk-intrapreneurship tradeoff is depicted graphically in Figure 9-5.

When we speak of risk for a social enterprise, what exactly are we talking about? Generally, discussions of this topic revolve around catastrophic failure — bankruptcy. But risk can be more subtle as well. Social entrepreneurs face the risk of meeting their missions inadequately, or of doing so on a different time frame than what is planned. Clearly, not all risk is created equal.

The degree and frequency of intrapreneurship are not the only institutional forces in the growth phase that affect risk, of course. There are several other variables that are directly related to organizational risk that social entrepreneurs have to consider.[25]

1. *Leadership.* The founder of a social enterprise is a major risk factor because management and leadership make the decisions that can increase or decrease risk. In addition, the board of a nonprofit can encourage or stifle innovation and can help an organization avoid unreasonable risks.

2. *Staff and volunteers.* Staff and volunteers are responsible for much of the risk an enterprise faces. After all, when we encourage an intrapreneurial environment, we must empower people throughout the organization to innovate. Furthermore, a noninnovative staff can drive the venture into the high-risk category described earlier.

3. *Funding.* The most obvious area of risk surrounds the ability to execute mission because of funds. Funding risk has several sources:

   a. *Financial footing.* A tenuous current funding position nearly always drives up the risk of failure. Of course, a key element of social entrepreneurship is striving to achieve without having all resources currently in hand, so this is not necessarily a bad thing.

   b. *Likelihood of future funding.* A fair assessment of future funding is almost synonymous with an assessment of funding risk.

   c. *Diversification.* This is a key concept in all discussions of financial risk management. Ventures that are not diversified in their funding can be exposed to much more risk than those that rely on multiple funding sources. Recall from an earlier chapter that statistically, the riskiest funding portfolio is one that relies exclusively or heavily on government funding. This is not necessarily to assert that ventures with nondiversified funding cannot grow to be very large. In fact, a recent research article in the *Stanford Social Innovation Review* states that, ". . . most of the organizations that have gotten really big over the past three decades did so by concentrating on one type of funding source, not by diversifying across several sources of funding."[26] But risk mitigation is not the same thing as growing to be very large.

4. *Quality of the enterprise concept.* A solid idea makes for a better social opportunity, meaning higher demand for a social enterprise's services—and thus, lower risk.

5. *Marketplace volatility.* Some social ventures face significant marketplace risk because demand or other conditions are inherently unstable. For example, arts and culture organizations often claim they are "pro-cyclical," in that the demand for their services waxes and wanes greatly with changes in the economy (because people patronize the arts with their disposable income). In contrast, social welfare services to aid the elderly—while risky for other reasons on this list—don't tend to see a lot of sudden demand changes.

We saw in the first chapter of this book that risk is inherent in all entrepreneurial endeavors, and that entrepreneurs—including social entrepreneurs—tend to have a relatively high tolerance for risk. This is not to say, however, that social entrepreneurs are risk seekers per se. There is a major difference between a person with tolerance for calculated risk and the ability to manage it and someone who is simply a *gambler.* Risk in and of itself is not a reward for entrepreneurs.

How can social entrepreneurs mitigate and manage risk? The following is a list of risk management strategies that social enterprises can use and learn from:[27]

- *Get outside help from experts, and build networks with other social enterprises.* One of the greatest threats to the viability of social enterprises comes when they are insulated from outside advice, experience, and expertise. There is a tendency for many entrepreneurs to go it alone or to hunker down when times get tough, but these are mistakes. There are many experts in all areas of nonprofit activity, many of whom are happy to provide help pro bono. Further, social enterprises can share experiences that can help ventures avoid each other's mistakes and profit from each other's successes.

- *Gather and use data.* One of the reasons venture philanthropists, foundations, and responsible governments increasingly require evidence of accountability from grantees is because they want evidence about risk. Our criteria for performance and success—the metrics we have defined to measure effectiveness—also provide data to assess risk. A traditional risk measure in financial management is the variance in returns to investments. For example, a stock is "risky" if its returns change a lot from year to year. Social entrepreneurs should use their effectiveness data in the same way: more rises and falls over time means more risk.

- *Model the future realistically and continuously, update strategy regularly, and make contingency plans explicit.* Nothing exacerbates a risky environment more than having no idea what the future holds because preparations cannot be made to deal with contingencies in market shifts, demographic changes, and alterations of the public policy environment. Imagining the future regularly with information that is current can alter growth trajectories in ways that avoid needless errors and provide the opportunity to create appropriate contingencies.

- *Spread risk through a diversified base of support.* Earlier, we learned that funding diversification is not necessarily the path to becoming huge, but it is important for managing risk rationally. This means that a venture's growth path needs to update possible funding sources continuously and exploit new opportunities as they arise. It is a risky strategy to key in to one funder (for example, the government) and ignore alternative sources of support.

- *Make commitments in stages.* When creating a social venture business plan, the social entrepreneur necessarily describes the organization's activities and commitments into the future. However, this does not preclude making "branching" commitments, in which the services provided depend on circumstances and support. In other words, the business plan can describe the growth in services following several possible paths and proceeding at different possible speeds, depending on resource acquisition. All competent venture philanthropists understand that this is sensible.

- *Address organizational weaknesses proactively.* In every social enterprise, weaknesses invisible at the outset present themselves during the process of growth. For example, an organization can find that its Board is inadequately committed to the venture's expansion, or that resources are more expensive than planned. Or staff attrition might be higher than envisioned. Identifying and addressing weaknesses continuously and proactively can help to neutralize them as a source of risk to the enterprise.

- *Avoid all-or-nothing gambits.* There is a very real tendency among social entrepreneurs to define success in a "binary" way: all or nothing. Enterprises shoot for full funding or extremely ambitious services goals and define anything less as failure. This thinking is consistent with the idea of explosive rewards but is not conducive to good risk management. A better approach is to set ambitious long-term goals but also workable medium-term goals that are updated according to the data and circumstances.

THE END OF THE SOCIAL ENTREPRENEURSHIP PROCESS

The last stage of the social entrepreneurship process is goal attainment. In the world of commercial entrepreneurship, this is known as "harvesting the future": taking a company public, selling it to another company, liquidating assets, or passing the venture on to one's heirs. The process of entrepreneurship is inherently goal-oriented, and scholars stress the importance of an "end-point" to focus an entrepreneur's efforts. Social enterprises obviously harvest the future in different ways than for-profits: there is no "ownership" of most social ventures—nonprofit ones in particular—so taking them public or passing them on one's heirs are not possible as strategies. Furthermore, the optimal scenario for some social ventures cannot involve ever being "finished." For example, a symphony orchestra that serves a city will never finish with the "need" for classical music, and liquidating the orchestra's assets would inevitably be seen as failure, not success—certainly it would not be a social entrepreneur's goal. As such, the first chapter of this book laid out three kinds of social enterprise goals worth striving for:

1. *Attainment of a stable and adequate service equilibrium to meet the mission.* A social entrepreneur may envision goal attainment in terms of a certain level of services. Perhaps we seek to provide services to anyone in our city who needs and wants them. Perhaps we seek to inform every person in our county about a certain issue. Perhaps we seek to keep a park perpetually safe and clean. These are goals that involve a stable, adequate service level.

2. *Integration into another social venture.* Another strategy is to join with another institution. A social venture might seek to become part of another social endeavor, as in the case of nonprofit mergers discussed earlier. Some nonprofits aim to create social benefit that is so obvious that their activities are taken up—and they are taken over—by the state. Indeed, there is an important parallel here with the for-profit sector. Commercial entrepreneurs occasionally seek to grow to the point that they will be bought by larger competitors.

3. *Winning and moving on.* In some cases, a social venture seeks to solve a discrete problem; for example, wiping out a disease, or getting a particular piece of legislation passed. True goal attainment goes beyond just meeting such an objective, however, because we have to indicate what we plan to do after "winning." There are two main possibilities.

   a. *Redefinition to meet a new social mission.* A social venture can move on to focus on a new, related challenge. For example, the American Lung Association was enormously successful in helping to make tuberculosis an uncommon disease in the United States. When this objective was met, it

> ## We Won. Now What?
>
> The March of Dimes was originally founded in 1938 as the National Foundation for Infantile Paralysis. It had an ambitious mission, as laid out by President Franklin D. Roosevelt: To "Lead, direct, and unify the fight on every phase" of infantile paralysis, better known as *polio*. The organization sought to raise funds to both research the disease and provide care for those who suffered from it. After the first radio appeal asked everyone to contribute a dime, the name *March of Dimes* stuck.[28]
>
> For the next 17 years, the March of Dimes focused its efforts on polio, funding research into developing vaccines for the disease. By 1955, Dr. Jonas Salk—whose research was partly funded by the March of Dimes—announced that he had found a safe and effective polio vaccine following a nationwide trial that included nearly 2 million schoolchildren in the United States, making it the largest peacetime mobilization of volunteers in history. In combination with another vaccine that was developed and partially funded by the March of Dimes, the World Health Organization was able to declare in 2005 the complete eradication of polio.
>
> The March of Dimes had launched the first wide-scale biomedical initiative led by a charitable organization. However, with the successful development of the vaccine, it faced an organizational dilemma: The *raison d'etre* of the organization itself had disappeared, as cases quickly dropped by nearly 90 percent (no indigenous polio case has been reported in the United States since 1991).
>
> The March of Dimes could take itself out of business, releasing its philanthropic and human assets to other good social ventures. Instead, however, it elected to refocus itself on the broader challenge of infant health. Today, the organization works to fight such threats as premature birth, birth defects, and low birth weight.

    moved on to other important respiratory health goals: asthma, smoking, and air quality.[29]

  b. Shutting down. It rarely occurs to social entrepreneurs that the goal might be to put themselves out of business. Yet when a social objective is met, it is sometimes most appropriate to release the assets—human, physical, philanthropic—to other good causes, led by other social entrepreneurs.

Goal attainment is the planned happy ending to a social enterprise. But of course, there is always the risk of failure as well. In fact, nonprofit and voluntary enterprises disappear at relatively high rates quickly after they are born, as Table 9.2 shows.[30] For example, among all of the environmental nonprofits in the United States that incorporated between 1992 and 1996, fewer than half were still in existence by the end of 1996. The rate was similar for religious nonprofits,[31] and somewhat lower (but still significant) in other areas. Some of these disappearances were no doubt voluntary—for example, there are advocacy organizations that form solely to deal with a particular piece of legislation and cease to exist thereafter—but many were not. It is not implausible to imagine that smaller and purely volunteer enterprises had disappearance rates that were even higher than those given here.

TABLE 9-2 Rate of Organizational Disappearance within First Four Years of Operation in Seven Nonprofit Subsectors, 1992–1996	
Nonprofit Subsector	*Percentage*
Health	27%
International	28%
Human Services	29%
Education	36%
Arts and Culture	38%
Religion	49%
Environmental	51%

Source: Based on "Dimensions of Nonprofit Entrepreneurship," Joseph J. Cordes, C. Eugene Steuerle, and Eric C. Twombly (2001).

Our natural tendency when considering a social venture failure is regret, and our instinct is to help it to survive. You have probably received at least one fundraising letter in the past year asking you to help support a social enterprise in danger of closing for lack of funds. In many cases, these appeals are important, and the threatened failure truly would be regrettable. But we should not assume that a social venture failure is any more inevitably bad than a for-profit failure. When a local restaurant or car dealer threatens to close, we rarely take up a collection to keep it open; the reason is that we understand market signals and the free enterprise system, and know that failure of one commercial enterprise generally creates an opportunity for another. Commercial entrepreneurs themselves—those who are successful—often have a few failures under their belts. Social entrepreneurs have no moral immunity against failure.

Summary

- Before launching a venture, a social entrepreneur assesses the likelihood of a high social return. Four factors impact the likelihood of this return: substitutes for service, socioeconomic and demographic changes, public policy shifts, and the bargaining power of sellers and buyers.
- There are two basic kinds of growth for a social venture: product growth (an expansion of product offerings), and market growth (an expansion of the consumer base). These growth strategies can be combined or used individually. Another growth option is through mergers between two or more social enterprises.
- Typical growth problem areas in social enterprise change include differing perceptions between the social entrepreneur and others within an organization, resistance to market-based changes, a risk-averse board, pressures from the community, trouble demonstrating the results from change, and resistance to human resource changes.

- Social entrepreneurship does not stop after the inception of a venture. Entrepreneurship within established ventures is called social intrapreneurship. Social ventures that continue to behave entrepreneurially can do so in either degree, frequency, or both.
- Risk in the process of growth can come from several sources: leadership, staff and volunteers, funding, quality of the enterprise concept, and marketplace volatility.
- The goals of a social enterprise can involve the attainment of a stable and adequate service equilibrium to meet the mission; the integration into another social venture; or winning and moving on. The process of social entrepreneurship can also end in failure and does so with significant frequency.

Key Terms

- substitutes
- ease of entry
- market power of buyers
- market power of sellers

- competitive pressure
- product growth
- market growth
- social intrapreneurship

- degree of social entrepreneurship
- frequency of social entrepreneurship

End-of-Chapter Questions and Cases

HEALTHY KIDS INC.

You are the founder of a social enterprise called Healthy Kids Inc., which specializes in improving nutrition and reducing child obesity by educating parents in how to feed their children in a healthy way. After a slow but steady start, a major foundation has approached you and asked you to write a grant for major funding that would quadruple your operations within the space of one year. The grant would continue for two years and then be phased out over the next three, during which time you would be expected to replace the foundation's funding with outside donations, grants, fees, and government support. As part of the grant process, the foundation has asked that you assess the risk of your operation.

1. Write a short memo that discusses risk in the following categories.
   a. Leadership
   b. Staff and volunteers
   c. Sustainability of the enterprise concept
   d. Marketplace volatility
2. What are the risks involved in simply accepting such a large increase in funding represented by this grant, especially since the support is temporary?

MANCHESTER BIDWELL CORPORATION

After 40 years of success, social entrepreneur Bill Strickland has seen his organizations take shape, grow and develop, and eventually merge into an enterprise known as the Manchester Bidwell Corporation.

In 1968, Bill Strickland established the Manchester Craftsmen's Guild. As an organization located in one of Pittsburgh's most economically and socially deprived neighborhoods, it provided inner-city youth with informal ceramics classes and a small exhibit space. Growing up in this neighborhood, Strickland knew first-hand the challenges that faced the young people there. Having overcome these challenges through art and jazz, Strickland wanted to give back to his community, hoping that he could provide similar opportunities that he had received.[32]

Strickland became known for his successes, and in 1972, he was invited to assume the leadership of the Bidwell Training Center, which provided vocational education to displaced workers in the same community. As soon as he took the lead, the program began to grow, expanding out of the classroom and partnering with corporations to offer job-specific training programs and externships for anyone who desired a more satisfying and rewarding career.

With the growing demands of both the Manchester Craftsmen's Guild and the Bidwell Training Center, Strickland launched a capital campaign and raised $6.5 million by 1986 to build a new 62,000 sq. ft. arts and career training center. In addition to expanding its career training, it began to offer additional classes, including gourmet food preparation; chemical, office, and medical technologies; and a selection of educational arts programs.

In 1999, Strickland wanted to formalize the partnership and joint planning between the two nonprofit organizations, and thus he led the establishment of the Manchester Bidwell Corporation. This merger between the Manchester Craftsmen's Guild and the Bidwell Training Center helped the organizational stability of both organizations and created a model for a successful community education center.

Bill Strickland's organizations have proven their success by serving more than 2,500 youth per year and impacting communities throughout the country.[33] Since 1968, Strickland has touched the lives of more than 70,000 individuals.[34] This model of success is now in great demand and is being replicated throughout the United States. With the support of The National Center for Arts & Technology, similar programs have been created in San Francisco, Cincinnati, and Grand Rapids, Michigan, with the plans for several more centers to be created by 2009.[35]

1. As the Manchester Bidwell Corporation grows and looks for new locations throughout the country, what factors should it consider to ensure the success? Be specific by using your current home city to evaluate how a new community center might or might not succeed.

2. What kind of growth strategies (product growth, market growth, or both) did Bill Strickland use for his organizations?

3. What factors do you think led to the success of the merger between the Manchester Craftsmen's Guild and the Bidwell Training Center?

End Notes

1. See www.bronxprep.org/about.html. Information on Bronx Prep is courtesy of the Manhattan Institute's Social Entrepreneurship Awards program.
2. Porter, Michael (1980). *Competitive Strategy: Techniques for Analyzing Industries and Competitors.* New York: Free Press.
3. Kiefer, Francine. (April 24, 2002) "For Shaken Institutions, A Demand for Account-ability." *Christian Science Monitor,* A1. See also ARC Annual Reports, which include some specific information on donations through 2005. www.redcross.org/pubs/.
4. See www.theyworkforyou.com/lords/?id=2006-02-10b.973.0&s=speaker%3A13452.
5. Council on Foundations. www.foundationsonthehill.org/.
6. Arthur C. Brooks (December 28, 2006). "Charity for Charities." *Wall Street Journal,* A14.
7. Manzo, Peter (Winter 2004). "The Real Salary Scandal." *Stanford Social Innovation Review.*
8. Smith Hopkins, Jamie (May 15, 2005). "Paychecks Raise Eyebrows." *The Baltimore Sun.*
9. Jedruczek, Cathy (June 17-23, 2006). "CBGB Feeling Punk'd, as Nonprofit Stops Lease Talks." *Downtown Express* 18(4).
10. ProLiteracy Web site. www.literacyvolunteers.org/.
11. First Book Web site. www.firstbook.org/site/c.lwKYJ8NVJvF/b.674337/k.F229/Our_Story.htm.
12. See www.vimclinic.org/.
13. See www.collegesummit.org/about/.
14. See www.secondharvest.org/about_us/.
15. Pietroburgo, Julie, and Stephen Wernet (2007). *Making the Deal: The Art of Association Mergers.* Chicago: William E. Smith Institute for Association Research.
16. Barringer and Ireland (2006) cover similar growth myths in the case of for-profit ventures. Barringer, Bruce R., and R. Duane Ireland (2006). *Entrepreneurship: Successfully Launching New Ventures.* Upper Saddle River, NJ: Prentice-Hall.
17. Wingfield, Betty Henderson (2002). "Managing Organizational Change." In Dees, J., Gregory, Jed Emerson, and Peter Economy (Eds.). *Strategic Tool for Social Entrepreneurs.* New York: Wiley, pp. 267–290.
18. Independent Sector (2002). *Giving and Volunteering in the United States 2001.* Washington, D.C.: Independent Sector.
19. Kuratko, Donald F. and Richard M. Hodgetts (2001). *Entrepreneurship: A Contemporary Approach.* Fort Worth: Harcourt, p. 58.
20. Hornsby, Jeffrey S., Douglas W. Naffziger, Donald F. Kuratko, and Ray V. Montagno (1993). "An Interactive Model of the Corporate Entrepreneurship Process." *Entrepreneurship Theory and Practice* 24(2): 9–24.
21. Morris, Michael H. (1998). *Entrepreneurial Intensity: Sustainable Advantages for Individuals, Organizations, and Societies.* Westport, CT: Quorum Books.
22. See www.rosieshouse.org/.
23. "Mexican Institute Teaches PC to Immigrants." Houston Chronicle. August 26, 2004.
24. See www.sbcr.us/about.cfm.
25. Emerson, Jed (2001). "Understanding Risk, the Social Entrepreneur, and Risk Management." In Dees, J. Gregory, Jed Emerson, and Peter Economy (Eds.). *Enterprising Nonprofits: A Toolkit for Social Entrepreneurs.* New York: Wiley, pp. 125–160.

26. Foster, William, and Gail Fine (Spring 2007). "How Nonprofits Get Really Big." *Stanford Social Innovation Review*.
27. Author Jed Emerson (2001) has listed many similar techniques.
28. See www.marchofdimes.com/aboutus/789_821.asp; President Roosevelt's speech creating the organization can be found online at http://ccat.sas.upenn.edu/goldenage/wonder/Archive/FDRspeech/fdr_NFIP.htm.
29. See www.lungusa.org/site/pp.asp?c=dvLUK9O0E&b=22555.
30. Cordes, Joseph J., C. Eugene Steuerle, and Eric C. Twombly (2001). "Dimensions of Nonprofit Entrepreneurship." Manuscript.
31. This refers to primarily religious social service providers and not houses of worship, which are not required to incorporate.
32. www.manchesterbidwell.org
33. See www.skollfoundation.org/grantees/2007.asp
34. "Manchester Craftsmen's Guild is Western Pa.'s New Champion in Action." Citizens Bank Press Release. April 18, 2007.
35. www.skollfoundation.org/grantees/2007.asp

GLOSSARY

Abstract appeals—Fundraising appeals that focus on particular cases or specific issues.

Accountability—The implicit or explicit social responsibility an enterprise assumes in accepting support to attempt to carry out its mission.

Adaptation—Using existing resources in a reconfigured/new way to reestablish programs or meet new needs.

Administrative costs—Money spent either directly on the enterprise's programs or on running the enterprise itself.

Brainstorming—A process for quick idea generation among a group of people.

Business model—A blueprint for how an organization intends to create value and how the mission will be put into action.

Business plan—The primary mechanism a social entrepreneur uses to represent the enterprise to the outside world. The business plan is completed before the launch of the enterprise.

Business plan pitfalls—The most common pitfalls in commercial business plans, which include failing to communicate realistic goals, failing to anticipate problems, lack of evident dedication to the venture, lack of experience, lack of demand, and failure to demonstrate a market niche.

Capabilities-Resource Model—A four-step process for fulfilling the needed capabilities by defining the capabilities an organization needs, who will provide the capabilities, how those capabilities will be met, and where the resources will come from.

Classical price discrimination—A policy of charging prices that varies by client characteristics (age, race, income, etc.).

Competitive pressure—The degree of rivalry in an industry.

Concentric circles recruitment—A volunteer recruitment strategy in which current volunteers recruit future volunteers.

Concrete appeals—Fundraising appeals that draw attention to something specific.

Core donors—Donors who have given at least three years in a row and are responsible for most of an enterprise's donated revenues.

Core mission—The mission statement, which is a brief summary of the organization's activities, definition of value, goals and measures of success, and an idea of how the enterprise is innovative or adaptive.

Creativity—The generation of ideas that improve the effectiveness of a system.

Crowding out—The principle that, as government subsidies to nonprofits increase, the perceived need of the recipient organizations declines in the eyes of potential donors.

Degree of social entrepreneurship—A measurement of innovation, from incremental to revolutionary.

Direct government subsidy—Government revenues passed directly to a social enterprise.

Double bottom line—A problem faced by social enterprises in that they must make ends meet economically while also seeking to maximize their social impact as defined in the mission.

Ease of entry—The level of difficulty to enter an industry.

Effectiveness—An organization that attains desirable outcomes and impacts in an appropriate way is an "effective" organization. This is often measured and used by donors, clients, and the public.

Enterprise concept—The identification of new markets, products, or constituents to be served.

Enterprise growth—Rate of growth of a social enterprise.

Entrepreneurship—Managerial skill and the willingness to take risks for a venture, involving opportunity recognition, innovation, and a quest for results. Alternatively, the process of pursuing opportunities without limitation by resources currently in hand.

Equity balance—Total assets minus liabilities divided by total annual revenues.

Evaluation—A technique used to guarantee accountability where enterprises evaluate their activities in systematic studies of the quality, success, or worthiness of a program.

Fee income—Income from endeavors directly or indirectly related to a social enterprise's mission.

Focus groups—A small number of individuals that might have a relationship to the potential enterprise who can react to ideas and generate new ideas from the perspective of the stakeholder.

Frequency of social entrepreneurship—A measurement of innovation, from periodic to continuous.

Fundraising—Efforts to stimulate the donated revenues.

Indirect government subsidy—Government revenues foregone on tax-deductible contributions to a social enterprise.

Innovation—Developing a completely new idea.

Intertemporal price discrimination—A policy of charging prices according to time or day.

Joint-issue promotion—A source of financial support in which a social venture and a for-profit join forces to combat a single issue, such as working together to distribute products or information.

"Keep" fundraising strategy—The strategy to maintain current donors.

Lapsed donors—Donors who have given in the past but not over the past year.

Licensing—A source of financial support in which a nonprofit sells the use of its name and/or logo for a fee or a percentage of the sales.

"Lift" fundraising strategy—The strategy to increase the amount of current giving.

Marginal income tax rate—The tax rate on the last dollar of income earned.

Market growth—The expansion of the customer base.

Market power of buyers—The ability that the consumer of a product or service has to set prices, which depends on the number of buyers or the level of competition between sellers.

Market power of sellers—The ability that the seller of a product or service has to set prices, which depends on the number of sellers or the level of competition between buyers.

Maslow's Pyramid—A tool to measure the hierarchy of needs governing human behavior.

Membership income—A source of financial support, usually in exchange for benefits exclusively or primarily to members themselves.

Mission adherence—The degree to which an enterprise maximizes social output (according to mission) while earning enough revenues to cover expenses.

New donors—Donors who have given for the first time.

Operating margin—The money an enterprise has to save or invest as insurance against future uncertainty. It is measured as a percentage of total revenue.

Opportunity cost—The value created if a social entrepreneur's time were truly put to best use.

Opportunity recognition—The point at which an idea becomes the core of a social value creation.

Outcomes and impacts—What social enterprises must measure to demonstrate accountability.

Partnership network—The conglomeration of partnerships that the social entrepreneur will need.

Potential donors—People who have not donated to an enterprise but have been identified as possible donors.

Product growth—The expansion of product offerings.

Profit maximization—A strategy to maximize net revenues.

Promotional appeals—Fundraising appeals that proactively ask people to do something.

Refutational appeals—Fundraising appeals that are designed to counter implicit barriers.

Resource plan—A map of how entrepreneurs will meet the capabilities they need using the resources that are, or potentially will be, available to them.

Return on Investment (ROI)—A measurement of revenues net of total expenditures as a percentage of net assets.

Revenue concentration—The number of revenue sources supporting an enterprise.

Service interface—A description of how the organization connects with its beneficiaries, including clientele as well as anybody who receives positive nonfinancial benefits from their collaboration with the enterprise.

Signal Detection Theory—The relationship between perception and reality when it comes to opportunity, recognizing that people sometimes see opportunities that are not there or fail to see those that are present.

Social enterprise—A socially entrepreneurial endeavor—also called a "social venture."

Social enterprise mission—A statement that clearly identifies the social enterprise's concept, how it is entrepreneurial, why it is important, and how to measure success.

Social entrepreneur—An individual—typically marked by innovativeness, achievement orientation, independence, sense of control over own destiny, low risk aversion, tolerance for ambiguity and community and social awareness—who adopts a mission to create and sustain social value and recognizes and pursues new opportunities to serve that mission.

Social entrepreneurship—Entrepreneurship motivated primarily by social benefit to address social problems or needs that are unmet by government and the private sector in a way that is generally congruent with market forces.

Social intrapreneurship—Entrepreneurial activity occurring within established ventures.

Social Return on Investment (SROI)—An effort to quantify the economic and socioeconomic impacts of social enterprises by breaking the benefits of a social venture into enterprise value (financial return on investment) and social purpose value (costs and savings from serving social mission).

Social value—The impact of an organization on society by fulfilling an unmet social need.

Strategic resources—An enterprise's unique competencies and strategic assets.

Substitutes—Products or services that can replace another in the eyes of consumers.

Target market—A key part of any business plan is to examine the industry and the enterprise's target market, with the expected position of the enterprise in the market.

Targeted recruitment—A volunteer recruitment strategy that focuses on a smaller number of individuals who have specific skills needed for the organization's operations.

Transition donors—Donors who have given two years in a row.

Venture capital—Funds provided by outside investors for financing of entrepreneurial, for-profit businesses.

Venture philanthropist—A donor who is comfortable with relatively high risk but expects high social returns.

Venture philanthropy—Philanthropic funding for social enterprises, usually associated with new wealth accruing to commercial entrepreneurs who have experienced high returns in their businesses and are comfortable with relatively high risk.

Voluntary price discrimination—A policy of charging a low price but augmenting with voluntary donations elicited at the time of sale

Warm body recruitment—A volunteer recruitment strategy that focuses on developing a large volunteer force without much regard for specific skills.

"Win" fundraising strategy—The strategy to gain new donors or regain lapsed donors.

NAME INDEX

SUBJECT INDEX